Table of Contents

LETTERS

ON THE

ORGANIZATION

AND

EARLY HISTORY

OF THE

Methodist Episcopal

Church,

BY

REV. ALEXANDER M'CAINE,

AUTHOR OF "HISTORY AND MYSTERY OF THE
METHODIST EPISCOPACY," AND "DEFENCE OF THE
TRUTH."

Charleston, AR:
COBB PUBLISHING
2017

Letters on the Organization and Early History of the Methodist Episcopal Church (Corrected Edition, 2017) is available in .pdf format **free of charge** at our website:
www.TheCobbSix.com/Jimmie-Beller-Memorial-eLibrary/

Published in the United States of America by:
Cobb Publishing
704 E. Main St.
Charleston, AR 72837
CobbPublishing@gmail.com
www.CobbPublishing.com

ISBN: 979-8-3303-2328-9

PREFACE.

THE following letters were published in the *BOSTON OLIVE BRANCH*, in numbers, weekly; and have been widely circulated through the United States and British North American Provinces. But their great importance has made it desirable that they should be put in a form in which they can be preserved. These letters give the best history of the peculiar organization of the Methodist Episcopal Church now extant, or that can ever be published. Those old ministers, who possess many of the facts given in this book, have their reasons for keeping them from the public, as the character of the first bishops of that church are painfully implicated in these letters. Certain ecclesiastical frauds were practiced in the church in order to impose upon it a sort of Episcopacy in the revered name of JOHN WESLEY, the founder of Methodism. Painful as are these truths, the author of these letters fully proves them. Methodists of the present and future generations should be informed in matters connected with the origin and present organization of their church; the historian and the general reader, also call for the truth — the whole undisguised truth. In these pages, the unvarnished tale of all the facts connected with the origin of Methodist Episcopacy is given. The letters are from the graphic pen of the reverend and venerable ALEXANDER M'CAINE, a man who has been almost three score years a minister, either in the elder or younger branch of the Methodist Church. He who flattereth with his lips is our enemy. Mr. M'CAINE is not guilty of glossing over the faults of the bishops and their agents in the management of the Methodist Episcopal Church. He faithfully tells the most unpalatable truths, and fails not to make such inferences from his facts as the case may require, though they in some instances bear with terrible weight on the character of the actors in those scenes.

Such as the work is, we have felt it to be our duty to Methodists, and the world, to give it to mankind; having full permission of the author to give it a more extended circulation than that which it had in the *BOSTON OLIVE BRANCH*. In that, we printed an edition of more than twenty thousand, which have been sought after, and read perhaps more earnestly than anything else appearing in its columns. With these remarks, we submit the work to the reader, in the form of letters as received from the venerable author, and published as above described.

Thos. F. Norris.
BOSTON, October, 1850.
METHODIST EPISCOPAL CHURCH.

Publisher's Note:

In preparing the *corrected* version (2017) of this work for the press, the following changes have been made:

1. The font type and size has been changed, along with the margins, which results in page numbering which is different from the original.
2. Any obvious typographical errors have been corrected.
3. Quotations from writings, including letters, have been set apart to help the reader discern that it is a quotation.
4. In a few instances, words have been inserted in brackets [] to help make the sentence make sense.
5. The original volume contained a significant amount of variation in the spelling of certain people's names. We have taken the liberty of choosing one spelling and making it uniform.
6. Bible references have been updated to match modern usage. For example, "Romans xiv. 10" is "Romans 14:10"

Otherwise, this book is exactly as the original.

Bradley S. Cobb
Publisher, 2017.

NUMBER I.

The liberal principles by which your paper has been character-ized ever since its establishment, to the present period, and the im-partiality and boldness with which those principles have been ad-vocated and maintained, have induced the writer to select it as the channel through which he thought he might hope to place before the tens of thousands who read its columns, some remarks on the proceedings of the General conference of the Methodist Episcopal Church of 1844 in the case of Bishop Andrew. His attention has been called to this subject, though several years have elapsed since those proceedings took place, by reading in the secular papers of the day, that the "Methodist Episcopal Church, South," has insti-tuted, or is about to institute, legal proceedings against the "Methodist Episcopal Church, North," to recover what she thinks is her proportion of the funds of the "Book Concern," inasmuch as the "Methodist Episcopal Church, South" was, up to the General Conference of 1844, a part of the Methodist Episcopal Church, and when the two branches were united and constituted but one body or church, the Church South contributed by her labors to the estab-lishment of the "Book Concern," and aided by her contributions to swell the amount of its funds as well as that part of the church which is now called the Church North. Avoiding all minuteness of detail as being altogether unnecessary, this is a plain and unvar-nished statement of the cause of the lawsuit as the writer has been able to collect the particulars from published documents.

Although the question cannot now be asked, has the Methodist Episcopal Church been divided? this fact being known in every part of the United States, if not in every part of the civilized world, it may be asked, as it has been asked already by some, had the General Conference of '44 any right, power, or authority to divide the church into two parts, "the church, north" and "the church, south," each part being independent of the other, and if so whence did it derive this authority?

That the General Conference of '44, the members of which were the representatives of their respective annual conferences, had no authority to divide the church is manifest from this fact, that there is not in the constitution of the church any provision made to divide it under any circumstances whatever; nor is there in the book of discipline a chapter, section, paragraph, sentence, line, or word giving authority to the General Conference or any other body to do such a suicidal deed. To suppose that the book of discipline contained such provision or gave such authority, is to suppose that it contained the most monstrous absurdities by making provision to destroy itself.

Again, whoever is acquainted with the history of the Methodist Episcopal Church from its organization in 1784 to the General Conference of 1844, a period of 60 years, knows that at different times and in various quarters, loud complaints were uttered against the powers of the bishops, and many efforts were made to check or abridge those powers by some modification of the government of the church. And how were those complaints answered? Quite in a summary way. One general sentence of condemnation was passed upon their authors, by all in the itinerant ranks from the bishop to the mere licentiate; and history justifies the assertion, that it mattered not with those gentlemen what was the necessity or reasonableness of the change proposed, what were the sacrifices the complainants had made for the sake of the church, or how long they had labored, or with what success, to promote Methodism, if ever they made the least complaint against episcopal powers, or intimated a wish to abridge episcopal prerogatives, they were all included in one sentence of condemnation, and were all branded with the same opprobrious mark — *enemies of the church,* who wanted to destroy the *unity* of the church by destroying its episcopacy. Union, then, was the watchword of Methodism. This was the Shibboleth by the proper pronunciation of which its friends were to be known. This was the talisman that was to preserve the church from all malignant influences, and it was relied on by the friends of the hierarchy as possessing a potency every way sufficient to silence every argument advanced against episcopal powers, and as being perfectly adequate to put down every effort that was made to circumscribe or abridge episcopal prerogatives. Nor was it merely to repel alleged attacks on episcopacy that such an emphasis and stress was put on the term. It was capable of being applied, and was applied, to other purposes also.

When the Methodist societies were to be supplied with an ordained ministry, it was represented that it would be best for all the societies to be united together, and formed into a "separate and independent church under a MODERATE EPISCOPACY," and every step that was subsequently taken by Dr. Coke or Mr. Asbury "to strengthen the episcopacy," was represented as being taken to preserve the *union*. Was it deemed necessary to establish the bishops in their newly acquired powers more firmly than they were? the "Notes on the discipline" were written. Did symptoms of opposition begin to show themselves at an early day, to the exercise of the enormous powers of the bishops? The causes and cure of heart and church divisions was published. Did any enquire why the office of "Presiding Elder" was created? — why the bishop was to have a "council?" — or why a "General Conference" was to be held? the same answer was given to all those enquiries that was given by Mr. Asbury to Mr. O'Kelly when he asked "what will be the business of the council, what powers shall it be invested with, and what benefits may we expect to receive from it?" Mr. Asbury's reply was, "there must be something to preserve the union." It is plain then, that the settled policy of the church was to be united, and many a travelling preacher made it the theme of his rejoicing, as well as Dr. Caper's of the General Conference of '44. "I thank God," said the Dr. "for this unity; a unity which stands not in the episcopacy only, but pervades the entire of our ecclesiastical constitution. We have not one episcopacy only, but one ministry, one doctrine, one discipline — every usage and every principle one for the North and the South." And yet this union which had subsisted so long — which had been the policy of the church to preserve unimpared — and which had been the boast of travelling preachers in private circles and in their public ministrations, has been disrupted and the church divided by the General Conference of '44; and that which had been charged against those who aimed only at the abridgment of the power of the bishops, namely: that they were enemies of the church, and wanted to destroy its unity, has been done by the travelling preachers themselves, and because of *episcopacy.* Well may we exclaim in the language of St. Paul, "O, the depth of the riches both of the wisdom and knowledge of God, how unsearchable are his judgments, and his ways past finding out."

If the General Conference derived no authority for their proceedings from the constitution or the book of discipline, and if their conduct was adverse to the policy by which the church had always been governed, did they derive any authority from the Scriptures to make the division? And here it may be necessary for me to say, that I do not purpose to canvass the general question — has a church of Christ authority from the Scriptures to divide itself into two or more parts, and if so, what are the circumstances which will justify the act? My remarks shall be confined to the subject which I have undertaken to discuss, which is this — had the General Conference of '44 any authority to divide the *Methodist Episcopal Church?* This body of Christians I have always recognized as a Church of Christ, according to the definition which she herself has given in one of "her Articles of Religion." "The visible church of Christ is a congregation of faithful men, in which the pure word of God is preached, and the sacrament duly administered, according to Christ's ordinances in all those things that of necessity are required to the same." — Art. XIII. And I learn from the New Testament, that whether this "congregation" consisted of many or few members — whether it embraced all the Christians in a province, Gal. 1:2, Rev. 1:4, or in a city, Acts 15:4, 22, or in a private house, Philemon 2, it was called "the church of God" as, "The Church of God which is at Corinth" — 1 Cor. 1:2; "The body of Christ" of which "Christ is the Head." Col. 1:18. The question now comes up and looks me full in the face — had the General Conference of '44 any authority to divide "the body of Christ" — this "church of God which He hath purchased with His own blood." — Acts 20:28? As for my part I can find none. Whether the members of the General Conference did, or did not rely on the Scriptures to justify their conduct, I know not, as not one of them quoted a passage from the Bible in support of the division, or the measures which led to it. The reported and published debates now lie before me, and in them there is not a word of reference to the Scriptures, or a quotation from the Scriptures to sustain their conduct, no more than if this great company of divines had never heard of such a book, or if they despised its authority and held it in contempt. Ah! gentlemen, gentlemen, this is not the way "to spread scriptural ho liness through these lands."

But if they made no quotations from the Scriptures, the speakers who advocated the passage of the resolution requiring bishop Andrew to "desist from the exercise of his office so long as this impediment (his connection with slavery) remains," stoutly argued that the bishop was only an officer of the General Conference, and that they had power to displace or depose him as they had power to displace or remove an editor, a book agent, or any other officer appointed by a General Conference. But in arguing after this manner, it strikes me they were representing the ordination service as nothing but a mere farce — the man who professed to be "moved by the Holy Ghost to take on him the office and work of a bishop," a down right liar — and the Methodist Episcopal Church itself nothing more than a mere voluntary association of individuals, bound together by no stronger ties than those which bind the Temperance Societies, or the Independent Order of Odd Fellows. Now I cannot suppose that the speakers wished to be so understood, but such are the conclusions to which their arguments conduct my mind. For in their zeal to depose a man who, as far as it appears from the debates before us, was of irreproachable morals, was sound in the faith, and was faithful in the discharge of all his official duties, they not only advanced the most palpable absurdities, but they render the Methodist Episcopal Church the scorn of the politician and the profane. Nor is this all. They have disparaged their own book of discipline. They have shaken public confidence in the religious vows and protestations of those who profess themselves moved by the Holy Ghost to save at the altar. They have reduced the Methodist Episcopal Church from being a Church of Christ to the condition of a mere human and voluntary association, and they have involved themselves in a lawsuit, and brought on themselves troubles of which we can see no end.

Nor does it appear that the division was made on purely Christian principles, or from the causes which have sometimes divided the members of the same church. It has often occurred that a church had become so numerous that the members of it could not all meet together at the same place, or in the same house for the purpose of religious worship, and the exercise of church discipline. In such a case they have agreed to a separation for their mutual convenience, but they have separated in love, the minister of one of these divisions recognizing the minister of the other division as the servant of Christ and as a fellow laborer with himself in the vineyard of the Lord. These ministers have had access to each others' pulpits, and they have labored together to promote the cause of their common Savior. But is this the case in the instance before us? The whole community, North and South, know it is not. Methodist preachers of the North would not set a foot into the pulpits of Methodist preachers in the South, and these again would not be allowed to preach in the pulpits of Methodist meeting houses in the North. And is this what Methodism has come to? Is this a practical exhibition of the doctrine of SANCTIFICATION which Methodist preachers have preached so long? Is this the result of the labors, of the sufferings, of the sacrifices of those who have died for Methodism? O, gentlemen, for God's sake, think of what injury you have done vital Christianity by your contentions and strifes; and think what you will farther do it, and do to yourselves, by entering the arena of a Court house like gladiators, contending for dollars and cents.

NUMBER II.

In my former communication I alluded to the lawsuit which the "Methodist Episcopal Church" South has commenced, or is about to commence against "the Methodist Episcopal Church" North, for what she conceives to be her proportion of the funds of the "Book Concern." Now as the "Book Concern" is a subject with which few of your readers are acquainted, it may not be an unacceptable service to place before them such information as I have been able to collect from the published records of the church, or as I have picked up from other sources. But at the outset, it may be proper to state, that but very little has been published respecting the "Concern," and consequently, but very little is known about the manner in which it has been conducted. It has always been managed by the travelling preachers for the purpose of assisting those preachers who might be found deficient in their quarterage at their respective annual conferences. The local preachers, or laymen, had no means of knowing how the "Concern" was managed, as they never occupied a seat or place in the General Conference. All that was required of these brethren was to buy the books that were published at the "book room," whether their prices were more or less than books of the same size and binding were sold for at the regular book store. Beyond this, neither local preachers nor laymen were thought to have any right to trouble themselves with the "book room."

But in the prosecution of this lawsuit, do you not think that the curtain of secrecy will be lifted, that the manner in which the business has been conducted will be thoroughly investigated, and the conduct of the agents will be rigidly scrutinized? It seems to me that these things will certainly be done: if not, I am at a loss to conceive how it can be determined what is the proportion to which the "Church South" is entitled, if entitled to anything at all. And by this investigation, if ever it should be printed, the members of the church north and south will have an opportunity of judging for themselves of the fitness or unfitness, the faithfulness or unfaithfulness of those who have had the management of this mammoth "Concern."

When, or by whom, the "book concern" of the "Methodist Episcopal Church" was commenced, I have no recorded information; but I have always understood it was begun in a very small way, by the Rev. John Dickins. The first notice I find of it is in the printed minutes for 1789, when Philip Cox is entered "Book Steward," and John Dickins "Book Steward" also. This entry is not so definite as that of the following year, when Philip Cox is entered on the minutes "Travelling Book Steward," and John Dickins "Superintendent of the printing and book business." From 1789 to 1798, the year in which Mr. Dickins died, he superintended the "Concern," during which time there were several preachers travelling through the connexion, selling books. In the minutes for 1797, I find the following question and answer.

> Ques. 14. What regulations have been made in respect to the printing business, and the publication of books?
>
> Ans. The Philadelphia Conference in whom the management of these affairs was invested by the General

Conference, and who have not time, during their annual sittings, to complete the business, have, by the advice and consent of Bishop Asbury, unanimously appointed the following persons to be a standing committee, viz:

Ezekiel Cooper, Chairman.
Thomas Ware,
John McClaskey,
Christopher Spry, Presiding Elders.
William McLenahan,
Richard Swain,
Solomon Sharp,
Charles Cavender, Elders

The above committee are to meet at Philadelphia on the 2nd of January, 1798, and once a quarter afterwards, or oftener, if necessary, to consider and determine what manuscripts, books, or pamphlets shall be printed. Four of the said committee, when met as above, shall proceed to business, provided that the chairman and one of the presiding elders be present. And the general book steward shall lay before the committee all manuscripts, books, and pamphlets which are designed for publication, except such as the General Conference has authorized him to publish.

From this period until 1804, the book business was continued in Philadelphia, under the management of Ezekiel Cooper, when it was removed by a vote of the General Conference of 1804 to New York, where it was carried on under the control of the same gentleman, aided by Rev. John Wilson as "assistant editor and general book steward."

When the business was removed to New York, Mr. Cooper was allowed $600 a year: and although he was "principal editor," and was receiving the above salary from the book room for his services, he took charge of the society in Brooklyn, Long Island, and insisted upon receiving from that society the disciplinary allowance of a travelling preacher. Such was the statement made to the writer by those who paid the money. Be it, however, as it may, his name stands on the minutes of 1805 and 1806, as being stationed in Brooklyn. In 1808, Mr. Cooper's constitutional term of service expired, and the General Conference of that year, being so well pleased with the manner in which he managed the "Concern," voted him a *bonus* of $1000, so said the reports of the day.

In 1808, John Wilson, who had acted as Mr. Cooper's "assistant," was appointed by the General Conference "principal editor and book steward," having Daniel Hitt for his "assistant;" but Mr.

Wilson died in 1810. In the minutes of that year, the following notice of his death is published:

> "In 1804, the General Conference chose and appointed him to aid in the management of the book concern, for which he was well qualified. By the General Conference of 1808, he was appointed first in charge in that concern, in which he continued with honor and dignity to himself, and usefulness to thousands till the day of his death. In penmanship, for perspicuity and swiftness, in correctness of accounts, and accuracy of calculation in business, he could be exceeded but by few."

After the death of Mr. Wilson, the management of the concern devolved on Mr. Hitt, until the General Conference of 1812, when that body appointed him "principal," and Thomas Ware his "assistant." Mr. Hitt continued in office until 1816, when Joshua Soule was appointed in his place, and Thomas Mason "assistant," in the place of Thomas Ware. The next year Mr. Hitt was a Presiding Elder in the Philadelphia Conference; and in 1818, his name stands associated with that of Abraham Paul, a printer in New York, and a lay member of the Methodist society in that city, printing *on their own account*, a quarto edition of Clarke's Commentary, a volume of which now lies before me. Whether Mr. Hitt's name stands on the minutes of Conference for 1818, I know not, nor have I any means at hand of ascertaining whether it does or not. But one thing I do know, that Joshua Soule, at the General Conference of 1820, made on the floor of Conference some astounding disclosures respecting his predecessor in office. Mr. Soule went out of office in 1820, by being elected to the episcopacy, though he was not ordained until 1824. He was succeeded by Nathan Bangs, and Thomas Mason was continued "assistant;" but Thomas was guilty of some *faux paux* for which he was turned out of office, and, I believe, out of society before the succeeding General Conference. After Dr. Bangs went out, John Emory and Beverly Waugh were appointed, but who was first, or who was last, I do not recollect, nor is it any matter.

I have thus brought down the history of the "Book Concern," to a period when it had become so unwieldly, that it could not well be carried on at one place. A branch of it was therefore established about this time at Cincinnati, Ohio, for the convenience of the societies west of the mountains; but who have been agents there, or in New York, or how the "Concern" has been managed, I have given myself no trouble to find out.

Well, what is the present amount of the funds of the "Book Concern," for which this battle-royal of a lawsuit is to take place? From a secular paper which now lies before me, I make the following extract: "The net capital of the branch of the Methodist Book Concern in Cincinnati city is $182,685, the profits of the past year being about $6,500. The net capital of the parent concern at New York is $634,813.42, and the net profits of the past year amount to $32,883." Adding "the net capital of the branch," and "the net capital of the parent" institution together, we have an aggregate of $817,498: and the "net profits" added together amount to $39,383. Now this capital will appear to a man who does not stop to *think* or make any calculation on the subject, as being an enormous sum, and the "profits" as being very great, though the profits on the "parent" capital is only a little over 5 percent, and the profits on the capital of the "branch," a fraction over 3 percent. The capital, it is true, is large for a knot of itinerant Methodist preachers to possess, who have always represented *wealth* as being a hindrance to vital godliness, and who have exclaimed, though it seems not with so much truth as St. Peter did — "Silver and gold we have none." But great as the capital is, if we consider the facilities the Methodist Episcopal Church has for scattering through the land, by her thousands of travelling preachers, the books which are printed at her book room, and the length of time (about 60 years) the establishment has been in operation, it ought to have been more and would have been more than it is, had the "Concern" been skillfully and faithfully conducted.

The first notice we have of the "Book Concern" is found in the minutes of Conference for 1789, though it is probable it was in operation a few years before that time. From 1789 to 1848 is 59 years: but to accommodate my calculations to the following extract which I take from a paper published in Providence, R.I., I will say the "Concern" has been in operation *just half a century.* Take notice, I do not say what amount of capital was employed in 1789, whether it was $1000, or whether it was more or less: but assuming that sum as the starting point, the question which I wish some of your readers to solve is this: — What will $1000 amount to in fifty years at 6 percent, compound interest? The sum must be great as the following calculations will prove. The Journal says:

> "Every one becomes surprised in examining the Annuity Tables in familiar use in the offices of Life Insurance Companies, at the astonishing aggregate amount of the daily expenditures of small sums when compounded with interest, and finally summed up at the termination of a long life, as exhibited in the following table." (The table I omit for want of room.) "By reference to the preceding table it appears, that if a laboring man or mechanic unnecessarily expends only 2 3/4 cents per day, from the time he becomes of age to the time he attains the age of threescore and ten years, the aggregate with interest amounts to $2,900: and a daily expenditure of 27 1/2 cents amounts to the important sum of $29,000. A six-cent piece saved daily, would prove a fund of nearly $7,000, sufficient to purchase a fine farm. And the man in trade, who can lay by about one dollar per day, will find himself similarly possessed of *one hundred and sixteen thousand dollars* at the end of fifty years." Now if 110 cents (the sum in the table) will amount in fifty years to $116,000, ought not $1000 at the same rate of interest and for the same time, amount to more than $817,498? If it be said it ought not, those who have managed the business can tell the reason why."

The reader need not be reminded, that in placing these views before him, I have assumed 6 percent as the rate of interest — 50 years as the extent of time — and $1000 as the amount of capital at the beginning. But if the capital in 1789 was $2000 or more, if the calculation was made for 60 years instead of 50 — and if the "net profits" were 10, 15, or 20 percent instead of 6, the amount of the funds at present would be proportionally greater than what it is. In fine, if the "book room" has not been able to earn more than 6 percent and her necessary expenses for 50 years, she had better wind up the "Concern," shut up shop, purchase stocks with her funds, or divide them amicably and justly between the "church north" and the "church south." For every merchant knows, that 6 percent on his capital will not remunerate him for his anxieties, his labors and his risks in trade.

NUMBER III.

Assuming it to be a fact, that the "funds" of the "Concern" ought now to be much more than what they are, it may very naturally be inquired, How can the deficiency be accounted for? In reply to this question, the writer will say, he does not know how the business of the "Concern" has been managed, or how its funds have been applied. He can therefore only advert to such things as have been published, as having contributed to this deficiency, and every man will then be able to form his own opinion whether these are adequate causes or not.

The first cause that has been assigned is — the losses the "book room" has sustained by bad debts. That some bad debts have been contracted, no one can doubt who reflects on the amount of business which has been done by the "Concern;" indeed it would be marvellous if the "book room," which has been sending out books to every part of the United States for 50 years, had not made some bad debts in all that time. But to balance this consideration, it ought to be borne in mind, that the "book room" as a mercantile or trading establishment, differs from every other trading establishment in the United States, and has facilities for collecting its dues which no other establishment has. 1. The "book concern" is the property of the travelling preachers, and of the travelling preachers alone. All the real estate, all the presses, all the stock in trade, all

14

the debts due it, and all the cash in hand, belong exclusively to travelling preachers. Whether lay trustees hold this property in trust for the preachers or not, alters not the case: the "Concern" is theirs. It was instituted for the benefit of travelling preachers. It has been under the control of travelling preachers, and travelling preachers have always been its agents. The General Conference, which is composed exclusively of travelling preachers, have, from time to time, made laws for its government, and have prescribed the terms on which books could be obtained from the "book-room." 2. The men who have dealt with the "Concern" have not been men of the world, so called, but were travelling preachers, members of the General Conference, or were represented in that body; and of course, as travelling preachers, had a direct and personal interest in the safe management and prosperity of the establishment. 3. Those preachers who received books from the book room to sell, and did not, or would not settle with the agent at their respective conferences, were liable to be impeached before their Conference. Indeed, it was the duty of the agent to impeach them, if there appeared to be any delinquency or dishonesty in their conduct. From this it is plain, the "book-room" had a double chance of recovering its dues from delinquent preachers: *first*, these preachers could be tried in an ecclesiastical court, and if found guilty of dishonesty, they were expelled the church; and *secondly*, when expelled, they could be sued before the civil tribunals for the amount of their debts. Now as long as the writer has known the Methodist Episcopal Church, he has never known or heard that any travelling preacher was expelled [from] the church on account of dishonest dealings with the "book-room." This speaks well for the travelling preachers, and shows that they have neither withheld any of the proceeds of the books they sold, nor applied any of the profits of the "Concern" to their own use, and as a sequence, the "Concern" has sustained no very great losses by bad debts. Or if, on the other hand, preachers have withheld those proceeds, or have applied them to their own use, such conduct has been passed over as a venial offence by travelling preachers themselves. And here Mr. Editor, I cannot refrain from making one remark, which is this: — if any travelling preacher has applied to his own use the money which he received for books sold belonging to the "Concern," he has been retained in the travelling connexion, notwithstanding such conduct; whilst many a local preacher, and many a lay member have been expelled [from] the church solely because they advocated a change in the government of the church, by a representation from the ranks of the laity, in the General Conference. Reform, then, was the unpardonable sin.

The sums that have been paid to agents as *bonuses* is another cause of the deficiency. Mr. Cooper, it is said, received one of $1000. Mr. Emory received another of $1000. And other Agents may have received the like sum, for what the writer knows. It would be strange, as the precedent had been set, if each agent did not receive his share as well as the others. And against this distribution of its favors, there could be no solid objection preferred. The "Concern" belonged to the General Conference, and the General Conference had a right to vote what sum they pleased to deserving agents, and who were more worthy of their munificence than these faithful men?

Incompetency was another cause. If the agent, in settling with the preachers at an Annual Conference, should settle with some one [on] loose pieces of paper, and if these pieces of paper should get lost before his return to New York, or if the settlement should be made with a pencil, and the pencil marks should be obliterated by rubbing, such an agent would not be deemed competent to manage such a great money concern as is that of the "book room" of the Methodist Episcopal Church. And yet, some such statement as this was made when it was asserted on the floor of the General Conference 1820, that the books of the agent would not balance by $40,000.

Startling as this announcement was at the time it was made, there has been one of more astounding character published in the newspapers some two or three years ago, of a travelling preacher who had been book agent for several years, dying worth $150,000 or $200,000. This was a very surprising announcement to the writer, because he had known the gentleman referred to upwards of 40 years; and so different was the statement from the opinion he had formed of his circumstances, that the report would not have been believed, had not the same papers affirmed, that his will, disposing of this amount of money, had been proved in the courts of law in the State in which he died. Now this preacher entered the travelling connexion in the early days of Methodism, when the salary of a single preacher was only 64 dollars a year, and he entered it, like many others, a poor young man; and yet, when he died he was worth $150,000 or $200,000, a sum nearly one fourth of the present amount of the funds of the "book room." The writer has not heard that the gentleman was ever married, or that he was engaged in mercantile business. How different was then the principle by which he was governed through life, from that by which the Rev. John Wesley was governed! The aim of the one was to accumulate and hoard up wealth; that of the other to lay out all he could save, in works of charity and mercy. The one died worth an immense fortune; the other died not worth ten pounds; and although there was such an unmistakable difference in their spirit, their principle, their life, their end, the one has frequently used for special purposes, Mr. Wesley's dying words — "The best of all is, God is with us."

"O how mysterious are the ways of Providence," is an exclamation that has frequently been uttered, and may be uttered with as much propriety with reference to this lawsuit, as to any affair that has ever fallen under the notice of the writer. On no other grounds can recourse to law be accounted for, as both parties are men who profess to be "the divinely authorized expounders of God's word, and administrators of moral discipline," — men who declare their sole business is "to spread scriptural holiness through these lands," and who profess to enjoy a greater measure of grace than others, pressing sanctification on the members of the church with all its blessedness and fruits. That ministers (for remember this suit is all the work of ministers) should scramble, and quarrel, and go to law about the "funds" of the "book concern," when Christian going to law with Christian is strictly forbidden in the Scriptures, is passing strange. "Dare any of you, having a matter against another, go to law before the unjust and not before the saints." 1 Cor. 6:1. How can these men as Methodists stand up in the pulpit before the community, and preach obedience to law, when they themselves are violating one of the "General Rules" of their church, which forbids "fighting, quarreling, brawling, brother going to law with brother," and for the infraction of which many a lay member has been ex-

pelled [from] the connexion? It would seem that the heathen sentiment is to be fulfilled in these Christian ministers — "Whom the
gods are determined to destroy, they first make mad?" Providence
no doubt will overrule the frenzy of their cupidity to the good of
their church, and will make this lawsuit the means of bringing to
light things that otherwise never would be known.

In view of the good that is likely to result from this lawsuit, no
regrets shall be uttered that it has been commenced, nor censures
pronounced against those who unjustly retain the portion of their
funds, to which the church south is unquestionably entitled. Should
it be asked what possible good can grow out of it, the answer is at
hand.

1. Travelling preachers themselves may be benefited. They
have so long been in the habit of conducting their business *secretly*
among themselves, in their annual conferences to the exclusion of
the laity, that it would be no wonder if they were proud and imperi-
ous. What was the world to them? They were an isolated body,
governed by laws made by themselves — for themselves alone
— and answerable to no other tribunal. They did not look beyond
the precincts of their own fraternity for censure or applause. They
never supposed that the Hon. Daniel Webster, or the Hon. William
Meredith, or any other person would investigate "the book concern," or anything else with which *they* had to do. As travelling
preachers, they were the lords of the property, and nobody had any
right to meddle with their affairs. This lawsuit, however, will teach
them a different lesson, and it is hoped, will greatly improve their
spirit, and mend their manners. 2. The church may be benefited.
How? By opening the eyes of the members to the evils of great
wealth, it may have a tendency to bring back Methodism to its
primitive state. He must be ignorant of *the* Methodism which flour-
ished 40 or 50 years ago, if he thinks *the* Methodism of the present
day is like that; or if he supposes the present race of travelling
preachers is to be compared to those who travelled then, either in
the sacrifices they make to go into the work — in the amount of
their labors — in their heavenly mindedness — in their zeal —
or in the success which attends their ministry. Then it was difficult
to obtain preachers for places — now it is difficult to find places
for preachers. Then plain, honest and holy men "preached golden

sermons in wooden pulpits" and in log cabins — now travelling preachers whittle away in splendid buildings with a wooden saw, and do nothing. Then you could not find a D.D. from Maine to Georgia, and yet it was no uncommon thing to see one or more converted at almost every meeting — now the D.D's are as plenty as blackberries, and yet you never hear of a soul converted at their meetings. Then travelling preachers lived from hand to mouth, and if they got "food and raiment" they were content — now many of them luxuriate in fat pastures — pile up treasure upon treasure, till it becomes a curse, and then they go to law and quarrel about the spoils. When the members stay their hand the plague will stop: for primitive Methodism does not grow in a *rich* soil.

3. The State may be benefited. How? By being divorced from the Church. That there is, or ever has been such a union between the Methodist Episcopal Church and the State, founded on the Constitution of the United States, or on any other specific legal enactment, by which a preference is secured to her above other churches, is neither asserted nor believed. But the writer has been acquainted with the church long enough to know, and has been sufficiently intimate with many travelling preachers who have contributed to shape her policy to say, that exertions have been made from time to time, to obtain an ascendency over other religious denominations in directing the affairs of the nation. Of late years, this has been particularly the case. The extension and growing popularity of Methodism, and the rapid increase of her members, have been felt by travelling preachers, and have inspired them with a hope that ultimately they will succeed in their designs. Nor are others insensible of the great influence of Methodism through her travelling preachers, and hence the court that has been paid to these gentlemen by the politicians of the day. Contemplating the results of the proceedings of the General Conference of 1844, isolated and alone, it matters not whether they acted formally or informally — with law or without it, in dividing the church, as it would be a matter of very little consequence to consider whether the injury done to my wheat field was done by my neighbors cattle going into it through the gate, or by breaking down the fence — the injury was done, the crop was destroyed. But viewing the subject in another point of light, the proceedings of that General Conference are the

more censurable because they acted not only without authority, but contrary to law. They forgot, or rejected the authority of Him who said — "My kingdom is not of this world," and as an ecclesiastical body went out of their province to act on a subject which is purely *civil*. They have condemned without proof what the Constitution of the United States has recognized, and what the decisions of the Supreme Court have declared cannot be disturbed. They have united in their decisions what belongs to the State as belonging to the Church, and by dividing the latter have paved the way for a division of the former. But already has the Church North received an unmistakable rebuke for their conduct, by the declension of that Church in four or five years of tens of thousands of her quandam members. This law suit, it is believed, will be a farther means of opening the people's eyes to the lordly assumptions of Methodist Episcopal travelling preachers, and will farther convince them, that these preachers "were not born ready booted and spurred to ride the citizens of the United States legitimately, by the grace of God."

NUMBER IV.

Was it not a fortunate circumstance for the members of the church, and for the people of the United States, that the General Conference of 1844 determined to publish an account of their proceedings? Were it not for this determination, few, besides the citizens of New York who had an opportunity of being present at the sittings of the Conference, could be enlightened by their discussions. But by adopting the resolution to employ a stenographer to take down the speeches of the several speakers, and to send them out through the length and breadth of the land, they not only wisely departed from the usage of all preceding General Conferences, but happily put it in the power of those at a distance, whether in the church, or out of it, to become as fully and as accurately acquainted with what was said and done by the General Conference, as if they had been in the galleries all the time. A pamphlet containing "a report of debates in Conference" now lies before me, and from it, I have derived all the information that an attentive perusal can impart.

To one disposed to enter into a critical examination of the sen-

timents, the language, the arguments, and the proceedings of the
General Conference, a finer field could not be presented. This the
writer will not attempt; for that would protract his remarks to an
undue length. All that he intends is to place before the reader, who
may not have had an opportunity of seeing the "report," or of
knowing what were the proceedings of the General Conference, the
principal matters under their consideration; and that, not so much
in his own words as in the language of the speakers who bore a
conspicuous part in the debates. And here it may be proper for him
to say, although those proceedings grew but of domestic slavery,
he will not attempt to discuss the merits or demerits of this subject
in these papers. He will not even enquire whether slavery is, in itself, a moral evil or not; or whether it is a sin under all circumstances or only under certain circumstances, as some have affirmed; and if the latter, what those abating circumstances are.

The principal thing which occupied the time and attention of
the General Conference was the case of Bishop Andrew, who, it
was said, "was connected with slavery;" and how to dispose of him
as a Bishop, perplexed the Conference very much. They, at last,
"Resolved, That it is the sense of this General Conference, that he
desist from the exercise of this office, so long as this impediment
remains." But in carrying out this resolution, there was a difficulty
which grew out of the ambiguity of the phrase, "the sense of this
General Conference," many affirming it was only *advisory*, whilst
others insisted it was *judicial* and *mandatory*. Of those who put the
former construction on the words was Dr. Durbin, who seems to
have been a leading member of the majority — he says: "And what
does the resolution propose? Expulsion? No, sir. Deposition? No.
If I am pressed to a decision of this case in its present form, I shall
vote for that substitute, and so will many others: but if after we
have voted for it, any man should come and tell us personally, that
we have voted to *depose* Bishop Andrew we should consider it a
personal — shall I say — insult, sir." The minority consisting of 60
members of Conference viewed, and reasoned on, the resolution
very differently. They say in their protest, "No idea of request, advice, or recommendation, is conveyed by the language of the pre-
amble or resolution; and the recent avowal of an intention to advise
is, in the judgment of the undersigned, disowned by the very terms

in which it is said, the *advice* was given. The whole argument of the majority during a debate of 12 days, turned upon the right of the Conference to displace Bishop Andrew, without resort to trial. No one questioned the legal right of the Conference to advise; and if this only was intended, why the protracted debate on the subject?

> "But further, a resolution, respectfully and affectionately requesting the Bishop to resign, had been laid aside, to entertain the substitute under notice; a motion too, to declare the resolution advisory was promptly rejected by the majority; and in view of all the facts, and the entire proceedings of the majority in the case, the undersigned have been compelled to consider the resolutions as a mandatory judgment to the effect that Bishop Andrew desist from the exercise of his episcopal functions. If the majority have been misunderstood, the language of their own resolution, and the position they occupied in the debate, have led to the misconception; and truth and honor, not less than a most unfortunate use of language, require that they explain themselves."

How Dr. Durbin and those associated with him, considered the remarks — whether as an "insult," or not — they have not told us. If they thought they were no less an "insult," because they were addressed to the majority, than if they had been addressed to each individual "personally," the lessons they had learnt from their Divine Master, no doubt, taught them to bear this "insult," as well as every other indignity, with Christian meekness, and great command of temper. But in the judgment of those who are not attached to either party, these remarks do the doctor and his friends a greater injury than if they had been offered with an intention to "insult" them. For they fasten on them, by a variety of facts, and by a train of reasoning, a *charge* from which there appears to be no possible way to escape. Had the object of the resolution been misunderstood by the minority, or had they attached to the phrase, "the sense of this General Conference," a meaning which the majority did not intend it should bear, how easy was it for those who advocated the passage of the resolution to change its phraseology, and divest it of all ambiguity by the substitution of other terms, which would unequivocally fix their meaning. This "Truth and Honor" obliged them to do. But instead of doing it, they disingenuously retain the controverted expressions — press them to the performance of a double duty — and after they have, by their aid, accomplished the deed of infamy and disgrace, as it respects Bishop Andrew, they mildly say, they did not mean to depose him. "The action of the General Conference was neither judicial, nor punitive. It neither achieves, nor intends a deposition, nor so much as a legal suspension. Bishop Andrew is still a bishop: and should he, against the expressed sense of the General Conference, proceed in the discharge of his functions, his official acts would be valid. J.P. Durbin, Chairman, George Peck, Charles Elliott."

Here let us pause for a moment, and look at this extraordinary announcement, signed by three doctors of divinity, and which by vote, was placed on the journal of the Conference. As there is no argument offered to sustain what is set forth in the statement, it was intended it should be received on the mere ipse dixit principle of the gentlemen whose names are affixed to it. But if the naked fact of its having emanated from the pen of the committee, was sufficient authority for the General Conference to adopt it, is it not requiring too much of those who are not members of the church to receive implicitly what it says, or give credit to all its assertions merely because it bears the names of these three reverend gentlemen? It occurs to us, notwithstanding the weight of those names, the people will inquire, if "the action of the General Conference was neither judicial nor punitive" — if "it neither achieved nor intended, a deposition, nor so much as a legal suspension," what did it intend, what did it achieve? Surely the Conference did not intend to exalt Bishop Andrew higher than he was before. They did not intend to confer on him any powers incidental to episcopacy which he did not possess. They did not intend him any honor which he did not already enjoy. According to our apprehension it was not the intention of the Conference that Bishop Andrew should, in any shape or way, be benefited by the passage of the resolution; and we are assured, that it was not the intention of conference, that he should be injured by it. What, then, was "the sense of the General Conference?" The conclusion is, their "sense" was no "sense," or in other words, was *non* sense; or this announcement declares what is not true.

Again: These gentlemen say, "Bishop Andrew is still a bishop, should he, against the expressed sense of the General Conference, proceed in the discharge of his functions, his official acts would be valid." So then, "Bishop Andrew is still a bishop." He was not, therefore, disqualified by the passage of the resolution, nor was it intended he should be disqualified by it, to "proceed in the discharge of his functions." Now if these gentlemen did not mean that Bishop Andrew had a right to preside in *every* conference of the Union, notwithstanding the passage of the resolution, they said what was not only idle, and not to the purpose, but they conveyed an idea that it was not true. The question now is — would Bishop Andrew be allowed to preside in a New England Conference? would he be permitted to "proceed in the discharge of his functions in that body?" and would "his official acts" be deemed "valid?" If it is said, *he would not*, this response is a flat contradiction of the assertion of these gentlemen: if it is said, *he would*, then it will follow, that the circumstance of being connected with domestic slavery is no disqualification for the discharge of "the official acts" of a Methodist bishop.

The case of Bishop Andrew greatly embarrassed the General Conference. The majority did not want him to continue in office, and he would not resign. They could not try and expel him according to their Discipline, otherwise they would have done it. They therefore placed him in a position that they thought would effectually serve their purpose, but it was such a position as neither the friends nor enemies of Methodist Episcopacy had ever placed a Methodist bishop in before: they said he was only an officer of the General Conference, and therefore they could displace him with, or without, cause. Be that as it may, one thing has been demonstrated by their proceedings, which is this — The General Conference was not agreed what is the true character of a Methodist bishop, nor does the church know, to the present time, what is the nature of Methodist Episcopacy.

Rev. Alfred Griffith.

"A bishop among us is only an officer of the General

Conference, created for specific purposes, and for no other than the purposes specified." Page 82 of the "Report."

"We have the signature of every one of our bishops to a document presented at this conference since our commencement; which says that they regard not themselves as a distinct order separate and apart from presbyters or elders in the church of God by virtue of their ordination, but that they are officers in the strict and proper sense of the term." Page 84.

REV. MR. DRAKE.

"While I hold the Methodist doctrine that the episcopacy is not distinctly an order above elders, yet I have never learned that the office of an editor is of the same character." Page 106.

REV. I. T. PECK.

"Has any man living such a constitutional right to be elected to the episcopal office, or remain in it after he is elected? You might as well talk of a constitutional right to be an editor or a book agent, or any other General Conference officer." Page 116.

REV. DR. G. F. PEARCE.

"He observed he was exceedingly startled at the proposition of Bro. Peck, that a bishop had no constitutional right to be a bishop. Hq had always understood that when a man is legitimately appointed to office, he has a constitutional right to that office for the whole term — that he cannot be ejected unless he has been in fault." Page 121.

REV. DR. BANGS.

"There is a marked difference between an elder, and a deacon, and a bishop. The office and work of a bishop are of a general character, not confined to any particular place; and when he disqualifies himself from exercising his office for the good of the whole church, he disqualifies himself from holding that office." Page 98. Again the Doctor says, "A bishop was a bishop, and not an agent of the General Conference." Page 127.

REV. MR. HAMLINE.

"In clerical orders every man on this floor is his (the bishop's) equal." Page 129. Again Mr. H. says, "I argued that bishops may be displaced at the discretion of the conference." Page 145.

REV. J. A. COLLINS.

"If there were no specific law, the conference had power to remove the officer it makes. (The speaker here read extracts from Bishop Hedding on Methodist Discipline, pp. 8, 10, and 12, and also from Emory's Defense of Methodism, pp. 110, 132, confirmatory of the views to which he had adverted.) These authorities, he said settled that point. According to them, a bishop was but an officer of that General Conference." Page 147.

BISHOP SOULE.

"If the Superintendents are only to be regarded as the officers of the General Conference of the Methodist Episcopal Church, and consequently as officers of the Methodist Episcopal Church liable to be deposed at will by a simple majority of this body without a form of trial, no obligation existing growing out of the constitution and laws of the church, even to assign cause wherefore. I say if this doctrine be a correct one, I have heard for the first time, either on the floor of this conference, in an annual conference, or through the whole of the private membership of the church, this doctrine advanced: this is the first time I have ever heard it." Page 169.

REV. DR. DURBIN.

"It has been maintained here, sir, that the General

Conference has no power to remove a bishop, or to suspend the exercise of his functions, unless by impeachment and trial, in regular form, for some offence regularly charged. If this be true, sir, I have greatly misunderstood the nature of our episcopacy." Page 174.

Rev. Dr. Capers.

"It has been urged that a bishop is only an officer of the General Conference, and that his election and not his consecration gives him his authorship as a bishop. If a bishop is no more than an officer of the General Conference, wherefore is he consecrated? A bishop an officer of the General Conference only! And is it in such a capacity that he ordains and stations the preachers of the annual conferences? An officer of the General Conference only! Then were it both untrue and blasphemous to invest him with the office, with those holy words of the consecration service: 'Receive the Holy Ghost for the office and work of a bishop in the church of God, now committed to thee by the imposition of our hands, in the name of the Father, and of the Son, and of the Holy Ghost.'" Page 181.

O episcopacy, episcopacy, poor Methodist Episcopacy, how art thou fallen! thou, who wast raised to *a third order* in the ministry, distinct from and superior to presbyters, art now no more than an officer of the General Conference! A word in your ear for your comfort. Pope Pius IX. was driven out of Rome by *his own children*, therefore submit to your fate without repining.

NUMBER V.

Many of your readers, no doubt, would think the writer very remiss, if, in taking a view of the proceedings of the General Conference of '44, he allowed the doctrine that was advanced by the majority of that body, with reference to "the nature and true character of Methodist Episcopacy," to pass without note or comment. So novel and so surprising to him was the statement when he first read it, that a Methodist bishop is nothing more than a mere officer of the General Conference, who may be removed from his episcopal office without impeachment and trial, by a vote of the majority, that he thought there must be a mistake somewhere, in the reporter, or in himself. But he soon found there was no mistake at all, and that this was the point of light in which a Methodist bishop was viewed, and in no other. Deeming it absolutely necessary in presenting this doctrine to the public, to establish the fact, that it was the doctrine of the majority of the General Conference, and not a construction of his own, he gave, in his last letter, several extracts from the speeches of speakers, for and against it, so that no one can now say what was often said respecting others, he has misrepresented the speakers and has grossly slandered this holy body of men.

1. But was the doctrine advanced by the majority, a new doctrine? It was. So said Bishop Soule, and surely he had an opportunity to know. "But brethren will permit me to say, strange as it may seem, although I have had the honor and the privilege to be a member of the General Conference of the Methodist Episcopal Church ever since its present organization, though I was honored with a seat in the convention of ministers which organized it, in this respect I have heard for the first time, either on the floor of this conference, in annual conference, or through the whole of the private membership of the church, this doctrine advanced; this is the first time I ever heard it." Page 169.

2. It is confidently believed that there cannot be found any ecclesiastical writer, of any age, or of any nation, who has represented a bishop in the church of God as being on a level with a layman, and who might be removed from the office he filled by a simple vote of the body whose officer he was. If there be such an ecclesiastical writer let his name be given. Certainly this is not the opinion of Episcopalians; for into whatever number of classes they may be divided, they all hold the office of a bishop in higher estimation than a Methodist bishop was esteemed by the majority of the conference; whether they believed the episcopal form of church government is of *human expediency* or of *divine appointment*. Such a sentiment as a parity of bishops with book agents, secretaries, door keepers, or dog whippers of conference never entered into the mind of anyone, in the church or out of the church, learned

or unlearned, Episcopalian, Presbyterian, or independent, before it was conceived in the cranium of those astute doctors who composed the majority of the General Conference.

3. It was just sixty years from the time the church was organized to the General Conference of 1844. Now it is reasonable to suppose, that if the present doctrine was the doctrine of the church, it would have been advanced by somebody or other in all that time. But although the church had been organized 60 years, and in those 60 years hundreds of annual conferences, and fourteen or fifteen General Conferences had been held, in no conference, annual or general, was this doctrine ever advanced; nor was it ever heard to proceed from the lips of a travelling preacher until it was broached in the case of Bishop Andrew.

4. Many have written against the present form of government of the Methodist Episcopal Church, and several of her preachers have undertaken to "advocate" and defend her episcopacy. But not a writer in the church or out of it, either in attacking or defending Methodist Episcopacy, ever represented a Methodist bishop as an officer of the General Conference, who might be deposed without cause by that body. True, the Rev. Dr. Durbin made an effort to prove that a Methodist bishop is such an officer, and that he may be so displaced; but it will be shown hereafter he was mistaken. The point in controversy between those writers for and against Methodist Episcopacy was — whether a Methodist bishop was a *third order* of ministers, distinct from presbyters and above them, or whether he was only of the order of presbyters. Though the doctrine advanced by the majority of the General Conference was entirely a new doctrine, there must have been some reason for broaching it for the first time in the case of Bishop Andrew; and hard as the declaration may bear on the parties concerned, it forces itself with irresistible conviction on the mind of the writer, that it was a resort to stratagem with a view of disposing of Bishop Andrew, which they found they could not do by fair and honorable means. By the discipline he was *beyond* their reach; they therefore "*lassoed*" him, and brought him within their power, that thereby they might have less difficulty in immolating their victim with certainty and despatch. And it seems this was the view Bishop Andrew himself took of their conduct. He said on the floor of Confer-

ence — "that when he arrived at Baltimore he heard a rumor of the *intention* of the conference, and when he arrived at New York he learned that the *edict* was confirmed — that he must resign or be deposed." Page 146.

It is possible that here some obedient son of Methodism, who knows little or nothing of the government of the church, or of the manner in which things are done by the travelling preachers in conference, may throw down the Olive Branch and exclaim as he does it — Shocking! this is the most foul-mouthed piece of slander that has ever been uttered against a body of men so pure and so holy as the travelling preachers are. What! say that these men would resort to trick and stratagem to effect what could not be accomplished fairly and honorably by the discipline? Impossible! But friend, whoever you are, let the writer assure you, that although you do not know him, and perhaps never will, he writes under a conviction that he will have to answer to a higher tribunal than your judgment for what he now places on record. He says it is not impossible, nor improbable that such things should be determined on in *caucus* and carried out in open conference. He himself has known such things done in years gone by; and hundreds, and perhaps thousands, who will read these lines can attest, that *very unfair*, and *very dishonorable* means have been used to expel from the bosom of the church, men whose only crime was a wish to perpetuate her institutions by abridging the exorbitant and overgrown powers of travelling preachers. But their testimony may pass with you for nothing. Well, then, can you not, or will you not believe what travelling preachers themselves say of the discipline of the church? Whether the church *North*, or the church *South* is meant, it matters not — they are both alike — as much alike as two eggs from the same hen. The discipline of these churches not only countenances but justifies a line of conduct in travelling preachers which has been pronounced not only improper but *infamous*. Hear what the Rev. Mr. Hamline, now a bishop in the Methodist Episcopal Church, said, on the floor of the General Conference respecting this discipline in the presence of 180 travelling preachers.

"There ought to be two questions before us. 1st. Has the General Conference constitutional authority to pass this resolution? 2nd. Is it proper or fitting that we should do it? ... I argue this authority in the General Conference, first, *from the genius of our polity on points which the most nearly resemble this."* After enumerating several "church officers subordinate and superior," who are liable to be effected by the discipline, the speaker proceeds: — "In all these instances the manner of removing from office is peculiar. 1st. It is *summary*, without accusation, trial, or formal sentence. It is a ministerial, rather than a judicial act." That is, as there is no specific directions given how the thing must be done, it is left entirely with the minister to do it. It matters not, therefore, *how* it is done, so that it is done *effectually* and *"summarily;"* the end will always sanctify the deed.

2nd. "It is for no crime, and generally for no misdemeanor, but for being unacceptable." This is equal to to the blue-laws of New England, if it does not exceed them. No marvel that the people are unwilling to believe such things as are here asserted of the genius of the polity "of the Methodist Episcopal Church."

3rd. Most of these removals from office are by a sole agent, namely, by a bishop or preacher, whose will is omnipotent in the premises.

4th. The removing officer is not legally obliged to assign any cause for deposing. If he do so, it is through courtesy and not as of right. "What right have they to ask questions about 'cause,' who think themselves so highly honored as to be ridden by men who are born into the world ready booted and spurred, to ride the multitude legitimately by the grace of God?"

5th. The deposed officer has no appeal. "If indiscreetly or unnecessarily removed, he must submit; for there is no tribunal authorized to cure the error, or to rectify the wrong. But we believe that there are good and sufficient reasons for granting this high power of removal to those who exercise it." And it may be added, who are paid handsomely for exercising it. "It promotes religion." What religion? of the crescent or the cross? of Christ or Mahommet? No matter, it is useless to stand upon trifles. "It promotes religion." It does surely. It is submission or decapitation, it is acquiescence or the bow string. "It binds the church in a strong and almost indissoluble unity." What a pity it was not "strong" enough to prevent the *division* which took place at that very conference, and which that very speaker voted should then take place. Thousands and tens of thousands might have been saved to the Methodist Episcopal Church, which are now lost to her forever. "It quickens the communication of healing influences to the infected and feeble parts of the body ecclesiastical," that is Methodistical. And is the Methodist body "infected and enfeebled?" It seems so, or the speaker would not say so. Truth will sometimes slip out when one does not intend it. "In a word, it is a system of surpassing energy." True: Mr. Hamline, true to a letter; for there never was anything possessed of more "surpassing energy," under heaven. Its stroke is *almost* as quick and as destructive as the thunderbolt. "By it, executive power is sent in its most efficient form, and without loss of time" (so quick is the movement that you cannot see the hand that strikes the blow) "from its highest sources or remotest fountains, through the preachers and the class leaders to the humblest member of the church. The system is worthy of all eulogy." Of the eulogy of all Turks and tyrants, for none but such characters would praise such a system.

"A prince whose character is thus marked by every act which may define a tyrant, is unfit to be the ruler of a free people." — Declaration of Independence of the United States. People of New England, descendants of the Pilgrim Fathers, are you willing to be governed in church matters by such principles as have been presented above by Bishop Hamline in his epitome of the genius of the polity "of the Methodist Episcopal Church?" If you are, permit me to request you to have that epitome printed in your school books, that all your children may become acquainted in early life with a "system that is worthy of all eulogy." If you are, when you assemble hereafter on the fourth of July to celebrate the birthday of American freedom, see that this epitome be read instead of the Declaration of Independence. But if you think the principles embodied in the Declaration of Independence are more worthy your regard, your adoption, and your practice, than the principles embodied in the epitome presented by Bishop Hamline, discard the epitome — give its principles to the moles and the bats, lest unhappily by submitting to them in church matters, they may insidiously insinuate themselves into the affairs of the State, and ultimately undermine those institutions for which your fathers poured out their blood like water.

NUMBER VI.

I am in a sad predicament. What shall I do? I promised in my last letter to prove that Dr. Durbin was in error with respect to the views he entertained, and in the representations he made in the General Conference respecting "the true and original character of Methodist Episcopacy;" and now in redeeming my promise, I find myself in a position antagonistic to the doctor. This is a sad predicament indeed, enough to make the stoutest heart, who was not fortified with truth, to tremble. For you know the doctor is a *great man;* if not in his own opinion, at least in the opinion of the majority of the General Conference, who placed him at the head of the committee to draw up a response to the protest of the minority.

Would the reader inquire where this gentleman was born, or how he was brought up? we cannot inform him. It is probable that someone of the Western States has had the honor of giving him to the world; for, he says of himself, the reverend and venerable James B. Finley "called him John from his boy-hood," and Mr. Finley we know is a Western man. We have had the pleasure of hearing the doctor preach once, but that was before he got a handle to his name. He is now dubbed a Doctor of Divinity, and from this circumstance 'tis fair to infer he is a *great preacher*. He is a *great debater*, acquainted with all the rules of the art, as we learn from his speeches in the General Conference. They give proof that he knows when to wheedle and when to scowl — when to parry and when to thrust, and

"E'en though vanquished, he can argue still."

He is a *great scholar*, for he was President of a college near Carlisle, Pa., and none but a *great scholar* would be placed at the head of a college. He is a *great traveller*, for he has been *almost* everywhere — through Palestine — in Egypt — on the track of the Israelites through the wilderness of Arabia, &c., &c., &c. No wonder the windows of the college were all in a blaze of light and glory when this great traveller returned in safety from foreign lands to preside over the destinies of this seat of learning. But with all his greatness, is it not a mortification to reflect that he is not exempt from the effects of the fall? "Now Naaman was a great man and honorable — but he was a leper." Dr. Durbin is a great man, but he has given us proof that he is sensitive and testy, and will consider a thing an "insult" when none may be intended. This is a poor specimen of his improvement in Christian knowledge, "*Learn* of me, for I am *meek* and *lowly*, &c." Such, however, is the man who defends the doctrine we have undertaken to oppose, and although at first sight the odds are greatly against us, we think we stand on even ground with the doctor in one respect, and certainly we have the advantage of him in another. We think we are the doctor's equal — pardon us doctor we do not mean to "insult" you — we only mean to say, that notwithstanding all the adventitious circumstances with which you are surrounded, TRUTH will not fly from us merely because we have not risen to the proud distinction of being a *great preacher* — a *great debater* — a *great scholar* — or a *great traveller*. We are simple enough to believe, that if we sincerely court her, she will not shun our embraces because we have not seen Jerusalem — have not stood where the Saviour may have stood at Nazareth — have not bathed in the sea of Sodom, or Dead Sea — or have not climbed up the rocky sides of Mount Sinai. All these things are things to be talked about, or to be inserted in magazines and books of travels; but a man whose name is not connected with any of them may know "the true and original character of Methodist Episcopacy" as well as Dr. Durbin. In this respect then, we are his equal — in another we have the advantage of him. We are older than he is, and have a personal knowledge of things connected with Methodist Episcopacy that took place, if we are not mistaken, before he or his "beloved Emory" were born.

We will now place before the reader the subject in controversy in the General Conference, that he may judge for himself who was right, and who was wrong. Dr. Durbin says —

> "It has been maintained here, sir, that the General Conference has no power to remove a bishop, or suspend the exercise of his functions, unless by impeachment and trial in regular form, for some offence regularly charged. If this be true, sir, I have greatly misunderstood the nature of our episcopacy. From whence is its power derived? Do we place it upon the ground of

divine right? Surely not, sir. You do not plead any such doctrine. Whence then is it derived? Solely, sir, from the suffrages of the General Conference. There, and there only is the source of episcopal power in our church." Report of Debates. Page 174.

We might have abridged this quotation, but we preferred giving it entire, that we might not be charged with unfairness, had we abridged it. And short as it is, it contains two capital mistakes. — 1st. It disclaims "divine right" as "the ground of our episcopacy," and 2nd, it asserts the power of Methodist Episcopacy "is derived *solely* from the suffrages of the General Conference and from no other source." Had the Dr. reversed his positions, he would have been much nearer the truth than what he was. Had he said "the ground of its power is divine right," he would have hit the nail upon the head. But that would not have answered his purpose to depose Bishop Andrew. Such an avowal would have blasted his own prospects forever. We shall consider "divine right" as the ground of episcopal power first, and then we shall turn to the authorities produced by the doctor to maintain *his* position.

"From whence is the power of our episcopacy derived? Do we place it upon the ground of divine right? Surely not, sir. You do not plead any such doctrine." And here, at the very outset of our remarks, we are constrained to ask, how could Dr. Durbin make this sweeping disclaimer in so confident a manner? Did he never read that such a claim had been set up not only for Methodist Episcopacy, but for the travelling preachers themselves, "to maintain the moral discipline of the church in expelling reformers?" If he did not, it is a proof that his knowledge of her affairs, and of "the ground of the power" of her officers superior and subordinate, is very scanty and much more limited than we thought it was. If he did read of these claims, and in view of this fact, uttered the words that are reported as his — then we say, he said that which is not true. Now we will take occasion to say here once for all, that we do not like to contradict Dr. D. or any minister of the gospel, and place them in such a position that everyone who reads our pieces will see that they have placed their hand and seal to things that are not true: but we have seen so much of this kind of work in years long past, that we shall expose these matters as we go along. The disclaimer is not true; for Methodist Episcopacy has been placed on the ground of "divine right" by some of the "standard" writers of the church.

Our first witness is Bishop Asbury himself. He says —

> "Wednesday, May 22, 1805. We came away to the widow Sherwood's where I preached. I had a little time to read. In this State the subjects of *succession* and *re-baptizing* are much agitated. I will tell the world what I rest my authority upon. 1. Divine authority. 2. Seniority in America. 3. The election of the General Conference. 4. My ordination by Thomas Coke, William Philip Otterbine, German Presbyterian Minister, Richard Whatcoat and Thomas Veasy. 5. Because the signs of an apostle have been seen in me." Asbury's Journal, Vol. III. Page 168.

This mantle of "divine authority," when it fell from our Elijah, was taken up and worn by his successor Elisha. And we defy Dr. D. to say when or where the claim of "divine authority" was ever revoked.

A second witness is the Rev. Dr. Nathan Bangs. He says in his Vindication of Methodist Episcopacy —

> "The government of the church is somewhat different from civil society, because *those min*isters whom God selects to be the shepherds of His flock, and the guardians of His people, possess the right of governing themselves in religious matters, and all those committed to their care."

This is going a step beyond Mr. Asbury. He plead "divine authority" for his being a bishop. Dr. Bangs pleads "divine right" for the travelling preachers to ride and "govern" the people who put themselves under "their care." For this vindication of Methodist Episcopacy, and the "divine right" of travelling preachers to govern themselves, and those who put themselves under "their care," Dr. Bangs received one hundred dollars.

A third witness is the General Conference which met at Pittsburgh in 1828. The testimony of this witness differs somewhat from the testimony of Mr. Asbury and Dr. Bangs. Their testimony was the testimony of individuals, yet of individuals who had a good right to know of what they spake, and whereof they affirmed — *this* is the joint testimony of upwards of a hundred ministers of the Church, gravely pronounced after some consideration. The circumstances which gave birth to this document were as follows. The General Conference was petitioned by a number of Reformers who had been expelled [from] the church in Baltimore (unjustly and contrary to discipline they thought) to be reinstated in their offices and standing in the church. But the General Conference not only rejected the prayer of the petitioners, except on terms which they considered too humiliating and unjust, but they availed themselves of an opportunity that might never occur again, of declaring the full measure of their ministerial character. They accordingly announced themselves — *"the divinely instituted ministry"* — *"the divinely authorized expounders"* — on whom *"the great Head of the Church himself has imposed the duty of preaching the gospel, of administering its ordinances, and of maintaining its moral discipline among those over whom the Holy Ghost has made them overseers."*

Now two of the bishops (Hedding and Soule) who presided at the Pittsburg Conference in 1828, when this claim of "divine right" was so pompously asserted in favor of the travelling preachers, were present in the General Conference of New York in 1844 and heard Dr. Durbin so eloquently and emphatically utter his disclaimer, and yet they did not correct the speaker. Perhaps they had forgotten the claim. Perhaps they thought to interrupt him would be wrong. Perhaps they may think we are mistaken now. Well, if we were as well acquainted with Dr. D. as the Rev. Wm. Finley was, we might say to him "John, I want you to explain these things for me." Although this is a liberty we dare not take with such a *great man,* the doctor may *feel* it his duty to explain these matters some day or other *if he can.* If he cannot, perhaps he may apologize for his silence — he considers the production of such a pen as mine, beneath his notice. Pursue what course you will doctor; you will never be able to *explain away* "divine authority," for "our episco- cy" and the claim of "divine right" for the travelling preachers, or make the extracts given above tally with your unqualified disclaimer. *Apropos!* Can Dr. Durbin tell us what hand his "beloved Emory" had in drawing up the paper from which the above extracts are taken? Some say it was out and out his own. It is a certain fact he was there and voted for its passage. Pray, Dr. Durbin did you?

Let us now turn to the authorities which the doctor relies on to maintain his position. They are 1st. The minutes of conference of 1785. 2nd. The Notes to the Discipline. 3rd. A pamphlet said to be written by the Rev. John Dickins, sanctioned by the General Conference of 1792, and approved by Bishop Asbury. 4th. Bishop Emory's writings, "who gives the sanction of his own authority to the aforesaid pamphlet, by quoting and using it in the twelfth section of the Defense of our Fathers."

This, it will be allowed, is a formidable array of witnesses, sufficient in any court of justice to prove any point, if they all pulled together and affirmed the same thing. But unfortunately for the doctor's cause, they don't furnish a particle of testimony to sustain his point. He carries us back to a period perhaps before he was born, but we can travel as far back as 1785 and further still. He has presented names that are long since gone into another world, and has referred to others with whom we were intimately acquainted in early life. By this reference he has imposed on us a task to give a history of the transactions with which their names were connected, and this he may call raking up the ashes of the dead. But this slang will not do now, although it has been made to serve a purpose on former occasions. We shall therefore approach the subject respectfully, and carefully examine what they have to say: believing it would puzzle the doctor himself to write a *history* of either Church or State without mentioning the names of those who bore a part in the transactions of which he treats.

NUMBER VII.

"The sources of the noblest rivers," says the historian Macaulay, "which spread fertility over continents, and bear richly laden fleets to the sea, are to be sought in wild and barren mountain tracts, incorrectly laid down in maps, and rarely explored by travelers." To such a tract, the history of "our episcopacy" may not unaptly be compared. And as Dr. Durbin has run back to the Minutes of Conference of 1785 to sustain his position, we will go back a little further than that, even to the first appearance of Methodism in this Western World, and will present an account of some of the most prominent things connected with Methodism before the organization of the church. We clip from a secular paper of the day, the following account of the commencement of Methodism in America.

A book on "Church Architecture" recently published in London, contains the following interesting notice of the first Methodist meeting house in America:

"The first Methodist meeting house in America was a log hut: but subsequently through the interest of Captain Webb, a piece of ground was procured upon Golden Hill, *a rising ground near the borders of New York, now named John street*. Materials were purchased and contracts entered into, in the names of those individuals who joined Capt. Webb in the undertaking. The building was 60 feet long by 42 wide. It was opened on the 30th October, 1768, by Mr. Embury, who being by trade a carpenter, had himself constructed the pulpit, from which he preached. It had an area in front of about 30 feet square, separated from the street by a wooden fence. There were three square headed windows surmounted by a circular one near the roof, below which was an arched door, and subsequently side entrances by steps to the galleries. In order to reach the galleries when first erected, it was necessary to mount by a ladder, and then to sit upon platforms; and for a long time benches only with backs were provided below. Such was the construction of the first Methodist Chapel in the Western World."

In reading this description of "the first Methodist Chapel" in America, the mind is carried back to contemplate the congregation that worshipped in it — the services that were performed — and the character of the preachers who officiated there. And we cannot believe that in a building which "for a long time had benches only with backs provided below," the congregation was either very large — very rich — very proud — or very showy. And as for the preachers, although Captain Webb, as a British officer, may have preached in his regimentals, a red coat on his back and an epaulet on his shoulder, he was neither stiff nor starched as many a Methodist preacher of our own times is. There was no strutting, self-conceited fop, dressed like a dancing master, dangling his cane as he walked to the house of God, to set his foot in that pulpit. There was no supercilious coxcomb to flounce and flutter, like a play actor before a starring audience. There was no Doctor of Divinity with "a wig full of learning," to talk to a listening congregation about things he did not understand, or if he did understand them, were not calculated to make his hearers wise unto salvation. There was no vindictive Laud with a heart full of bitterness and wrath against his brethren, to ascend that pulpit and announce, Methodist preachers are "*the* divinely instituted ministry" — "*the* divinely authorized expounders," &c. No! all these improvements in Methodism were reserved for future times. The preachers and people in those days acted under a conviction "Thou God seest me;" and when they assembled to worship, "they worshipped him in spirit and in truth." Methodism being introduced into America by local preachers, it was not long before Mr. Wesley sent over two travelling preachers, Richard Boardman and Joseph Pitmore, who landed in New York in 1769. In the latter end of 1771, Francis Asbury and Richard Wright came over: and in 1773, Thomas Rankin and George Shadford. Thomas Rankin was to act as Mr. Wesley's assistant. The first Conference that was ever held in America, was held in Philadelphia in June, 1773, by these six Englishmen, with four native American preachers, who were lately admitted to travel. In this Conference there was neither a local preacher nor layman, a member or representative. We beg the reader to bear this fact in mind, that six out of the number who composed this conference were Englishmen, inimical to the principles of civil liberty which were at that time greatly agitated, and strongly prejudiced in favor of that ecclesiastical hierarchy, the Church of England, of which they were at home members. This fact shaped the course of preachers and people on this side the Atlantic, and gave birth to that form of government with which the Methodist societies in America are saddled at this day.

When these preachers came to America, they every where represented themselves connected with the Church of England, and under the favor of some of the ministers of that church, found an easy access to the hearts of many God-fearing persons in it. This enabled them to form societies in many places. The pious clergy of that church, such as Messrs. Magaw, Jarrett, McRoberts and others, were so far from opposing them, that they greatly promoted Methodism; not supposing that these preachers would injure the church of which they were ministers. It is hard to tell now, what would have been the case, had all the minsters of that church supported such unblemished characters as the above named gentlemen. But this unhappily was not the fact. Many of them led profligate and wicked lives, which so disgusted the pious members of the Methodist societies, that they refused to receive the ordinances from them. This was a sore grievance for them; for notwithstanding they knew, that baptism and the Lord's supper were Christian ordinances, they could not receive them from the hands of wicked ministers; and in this distress they applied to their own ministers for relief. The preachers in Virginia, in a Conference held at Fluvanna in May, 1779, took the matter into consideration, and resolved that the Methodists should have the ordinances, and accordingly ordained several preachers of their own body. Here was a Presbyterian government and a Presbyterian ordination established, which did not accord with Mr. Asbury's high church notions of episcopacy. He accordingly wrote to the Virginia preachers that they should meet him at Manakin town to consider the matter more maturely. In the meantime he assembled a few preachers in Baltimore, and expelled the twenty-seven preachers in Virginia who had taken steps to have the ordinances. Among the expelled, we find the names of James O'Kelly, Edward Drumgold, Francis Poythress, Henry Willis, Richard Ivey, John Major, and John Dickins. Let us establish these statements by the records of the Conference held by Mr. Ashbury and his few preachers.

"Ques. Shall we continue in close connection with
the church, and press our people to a close communion

41

with her? Ans. Yes.

Ques. Does this whole conference disapprove the step our brethren have taken in Virginia? Ans. Yes.

Ques. Do we look upon them no longer as Methodists in connection with Mr. Wesley and us, till they come back? Ans. Agreed.

Ques. Shall brother Asbury, Garrettson, and Walters attend the Virginian conference, and inform them of our proceedings in this, and receive their answer? Ans. Yes.

Ques. What must be the conditions of our union with our Virginian brethren? Ans. To suspend all their administrations for one year, and all meet together in Baltimore."

The Methodists to a man were astounded at the dogma which that poor, old, blind apostate uttered, after he had deserted the reformers and volunteered to serve "our episcopacy" as prosecuting attorney, *viz:* "a man may be a good Christian and not be a good Methodist." But was he not right after all? He well understood "the *true* and *original* character of Methodist Episcopacy," and knew, that with propriety and truth it could be contrasted with Christianity. And shocking as the above assertion was at the time, disinterested persons who will now carefully examine this "episcopacy," will be led to the discovery, that it does not contain, or ever did contain one single Christian grace or virtue; but is an embodiment of ambition, power and revenge. These hateful principles are the essence of its nature. This trinity in unity constitutes the very body and soul of its existence; and it matters not whether we contemplate its acts in infancy, in youth, or in manhood, we will find a development of these principles, and of no other. Thus we see, that in its very infancy, even before it had a name, or was christened Methodist, it cut off the heads of twenty-seven preachers at a stroke, although those preachers were in Virginia at the time. And what offence had those preachers committed? They had, in "the exigence of necessity," taken steps to obtain the Christian ordinances, baptism and the Lord's supper, which are of divine appointment; and this conduct standing in the way of *ambition*, they were expelled without impeachment, trial, or offence regularly

charged." The omission of these things, however was a mere trifle
in the opinion of "our episcopacy;" they were first expelled, they
could be tried afterwards. A few years after performing this ex-
ploit, it cut off the head of Rev. John Wesley, the father and
founder of Methodism, and from whom it professed to be de-
scended. But Mr. Wesley never acknowledged the paternity of the
upstart brat, and said, that men might call him "a knave, or a fool,
or a rascal, or a scoundrel, but they should never call him a
bishop." Several years after it had expelled Mr. Wesley, it cut off
the heads of eleven ministers and twenty- two laymen in Baltimore, and all these expulsions having been done in that city, enti-
tles Baltimore to the soubriquet of the SMITHFIELD of Methodism.

The Virginia preachers were restored to their former standing;
and after two years the minute of their expulsion was cancelled.

> "Ques. Shall we erase that question proposed in
> Deer-Creek conference respecting the ordinances?
> Ans. Undoubtedly we must: it can have no place in
> our minutes while we stand to our agreement signed in
> conference, it is there disannulled."
> "The conference acknowledged their obligations to
> Rev. Mr. Garrett, for his kind and friendly services to
> the preachers and people, from our first entrance into
> Virginia, and more particularly for attending our con-
> ference in Sussex, public and private; and advise the
> preachers in the South to consult him and take his ad-
> vice in the absence of brother Asbury."

Mr. Wesley was also restored, after two years, to his former relation with the Methodists: but Dr. Coke said "Mr. Wesley never
could hold up his head after the cruel treatment he received from
the conference; and he believed it hastened the old man's death."

"But you have struck Mr. Wesley's name from your minutes in
1787," said Mr. Hammett. "Yes," said Rev. Thomas Morrell, "and
the reasons were substantial: and *for the same cause* we struck it
on again in 1789."

The expelled ministers and laymen of Baltimore were never restored; and this was the heaviest blow that "our episcopacy" ever
received. For they, with hundreds who were excommunicated in

other places, and with thousands who withdrew from the Church on account of the persecutions of the reformers, took suitable measures to organize a new church, the constitution and government of which are much more after the nature of our republican institutions than the Methodist Episcopal Church.

From these historical facts, we think every disinterested person will perceive, what is the "true and original character of Methodist Episcopacy, even in its embryo state;" and we think that any one who would represent it as meek, as modest, and inoffensive as a miss just entering into her teens, is neither acquainted with its history, nor has he studied its nature, or if he has, he does not consider what he says.

NUMBER VIII.

Having presented in my last letter some instances of the power of life and death exercised by "our episcopacy," before and after it was called by that name, it may be well for us now to turn back and take a view of the political state of the country at the time the Methodist preachers arrived who were sent over by Mr. Wesley, and trace the steps by which Mr. Asbury, one of those preachers, became possessed of such tremendous powers as have been exercised by the bishops of the Methodist Episcopal Church.

He must be profoundly ignorant of the history of the American Colonies, and of the causes which led to the Revolutionary war, who does not know, that at the period of the arrival of those missionaries, the inhabitants of the country were in a state of the greatest excitement bordering on rebellion against the acts of the British Parliament and the government of George the Third. And every year after their arrival, instead of the country becoming more tranquil, the dissatisfaction increased, and things grew worse and worse, until at last the people from Maine to Georgia were engaged in a general war with Great Britain. Now, how did these six missionaries, who were the first preachers Mr. Wesley sent over, conduct themselves in those exciting times? We are under no necessity of drawing on our imagination for an answer to this question, for history furnishes the reply. Mr. Wesley himself was strongly opposed to the proceedings of the Colonists: and that the reader may know what were his sentiments with respect to the claims of the Americans, we will furnish an extract from a communication he sent for publication to Lloyd's Evening Post, Nov. 27, 1775.

> "Now there is no possible way to put out this flame, or hinder its rising higher and higher, but to show, that the Americans are not used either cruelly or unjustly, that they are not injured at all, seeing they are not contending for *liberty;* (this they had even in its full extent, both civil and religious,) neither for any *legal privileges;* for they enjoy all their charters grant. But what they contend for is, the Illegal Privilege of being exempt from parliamentary taxation. A privilege this which no charter ever gave to any American Colony yet; which no charter can give, unless it be confirmed both by King, Lords, and Commons: which in fact, our colonies never had; which they never claimed till the present reign. This being the real state of the question, without any coloring or aggravation, what impartial man can either blame the king or commend the Americans? — With this view, to quench the fire by laying the blame where it was due, the "Calm Address" was written. I am, Sir,
>
> Your humble servant,
John Wesley."

Entertaining these opinions, it cannot be supposed that Mr. Wesley would have sent over missionaries who were in favor of the American cause, even if he had any such preachers in his connection. No, never. The men who were sent over by him were, to a man, of Wesley's sentiments. They knew what his sentiments were. They knew he had written and published them; and they knew they dare not advance any sentiments contrary to his, if they were so inclined. But they were not. They were all men after his own heart in respect to these things; and knowing his opposition to the American cause, they reechoed his sentiments wherever they went. Had they, when they arrived in a country that was agitated from its centre to its utmost boundaries by political matters, confined themselves to their legitimate, calling — had they been content to preach the gospel, and in the discharge of this high and holy calling aimed at the glory of God and the salvation of immortal souls, we cannot suppose they would have met with the opposition they did from the American people. But as Englishmen, they blended politics with their religious services. As subjects of the king of Great Britain, they insulted the Americans, calling them *rebels*, and spoke contemptuously of that cause which the people had sworn to support. They extolled the measures of the British ministry, thereby proving themselves enemies of liberty and advocates of oppression. And what was the result? What every man of common sense might know would be the result — hatred and opposition to them wherever they went: until at last, five out of the six fled for their lives, and the sixth, Mr. Asbury, was obliged to lie concealed in Mr. White's, in the State of Delaware. Nor is there any evidence that Mr.

Asbury, though he remained in the country, was less inimical to the American cause than his brethren and countrymen were who fled for their lives. Nor has it ever fallen within the knowledge of the writer that Mr. Asbury ever became a citizen of the United States of America, or renounced his allegiance to the king of Great Britain to the day of his death.

Nor was it the English preachers only who involved themselves in trouble by their hostility to the cause in which the colonies were engaged. For we learn from the history of those times, that there were many Tories among the native Americans, who were willing to live under British rule, notwithstanding their countrymen were striving to shake off the authority of the British crown. As this class of men had it in their power to do great injury to the cause of the Colonies, it was necessary to watch them closely, and prevent them from doing that injury they were disposed to do. Among the natives who were disaffected to the American cause, we think we have a right to place the name of Freeborn Garrettson, a travelling preacher, because he, like Mr. Asbury, refused to take "the oath of fidelity." He tells us himself, that his friends urged him to take it, assigning as a reason that he might be more useful among the people — *"but it was all to no purpose."* This was enough to awaken suspicion in the public mind against him, and to convince the whigs, that if he ever had been "a professed friend to the American cause," his mind had undergone a change, perhaps through the influence of Mr. Asbury, or of some other of the English preachers. Whether it was owing to his refusal to take "the oath of fidelity," or whether it was owing to an avowed hostility to the cause in which America was engaged, that he was committed to prison, we do not undertake to determine; but so it was, Mr. Garrettson was safely lodged in jail. In his address to the magistrate who committed him, he says — "I beseech you to think seriously of what you have done, and prepare to meet God; be assured I am not ashamed of the cross of Christ; for I consider it an honor to be imprisoned for the gospel of my dear Lord." Is it not strange that Mr Garrettson should consider his being imprisoned, an imprisonment for preaching the gospel of Christ, when it is as clear as a sun beam, that he was imprisoned for being disaffected to the cause of his country? Surely these are very different causes. The one was altogether of a political character; the other was of a purely religious nature. At no period of our life have we heard or read that the Americans have ever warred against religion or religious characters; no, they warred against tyranny and tyrants. The civil authorities had reason to suspect native American preachers, who would not take the oath, as well as foreigners, as being enemies to the American cause, and they treated them accordingly. All therefore that Mr. G. or J.H. or any other preacher suffered, they brought it on themselves by their imprudence and attachment to King George and the British government; and not by preaching the gospel of Christ, or their attachment to Christianity.

In confirmation of our views we will present an extract from the writings of Mr. William Watters, another American preacher of those early times. He says — "Our quarterly meeting was held at Maberry's chapel in August, 1777. We had a very large assembly of people, and many preachers. We were a little interrupted just before our meeting commenced. Several of us being from another State, a magistrate presented to us the oath of allegiance (just published) which required ministers of every denomination belonging to another state, if they refused taking it, to give bond and security to leave the state in a given time, or go to jail. As it respected myself, I had no hesitation in taking it, but the difficulty was, several of my brethren" (mark that) "could not, and my taking it would make them the more suspected, though there was no more to be feared from them than myself. Finding from our conversation the magistrate grew very uneasy, I concluded that if I was to take the oath he would overlook the others present, as the quarterly meeting was called mine. A. Y — n [perhaps Andrew Yeargan,] a Virginian, and myself took the oath, and it was as I expected, he quietly retired. I do not know that I ever before or since the war, travelled with more safety."

We will now notice the steps by which Mr. Asbury rose to power; stating that we are indebted to the ministers of the Annual Conference from 1773 to 1813 for the information we have on the subject, and shall make a remark or two to help the reader, when it is deemed necessary, as we go along.

1773."Ought not the authority of Mr. Wesley and that Conference be extended to the preachers and people in America, as well as in Great Britain and Ireland? Ans. Yes." Note this was the first Conference; and the starting point of Methodist organization was submission to Mr. Wesley's authority.

1774, '75, and '76 — there was no change one way or another.

1777. "Ques. As the present distress is such, are the preachers resolved to take no step to detatch themselves from the work of God for the ensuing year? Ans. We purpose by the grace of God not to take any step that may separate us from the brethren, or from the blessed work in which we are engaged." N.B. Ordination was not yet obtained.

1778. The five British preachers fled to Europe before the sitting of the Conference; and Mr. Asbury found an asylum at Mr.

White's in Delaware. Mr. Asbury's name is not published in the Minutes of this year. Why? because he dare not travel at large.

1779. There were two Conferences this year, and the minutes of each are bound in the volume. One Conference was held in Kent County, state of Delaware, where Mr. Asbury was concealed, the other was held in Fluvanna, Virginia.

> "Ques. Why was the Delaware conference held? Ans. For the convenience of the preachers in the northern stations, that we all might have an opportunity of meeting in conference; *it being unadvisable for brother*

Asbury and brother Ruff and some others" (notice that reader) "to attend in Virginia; it is considered also as preparatory to the conference in Virginia. Our sentiments to be given in by brother Watters." Tories did not think it safe to travel in 1779.

"Ques. Shall we guard against a separation from the Church, directly or indirectly? Ans. By all means."

"Ques. Ought not brother Asbury to act as General Assistant in America?

"Ans. He ought: 1st, on account of his age: 2nd, because originally appointed by Mr. Wesley: 3rd, being joined with Messrs. Rankin and Shadford by express order from Mr. Wesley."

Was not one reason split in two to swell the number? Be it as it may; there is none now greater than Mr. Asbury; he is next to Mr. Wesley himself in power and authority. Only in the throne was Pharaoh greater than Joseph. But how did Mr. Asbury get so near the throne? Not by Mr. Wesley's appointment. Not by an election of the majority of the travelling preachers, but by a few tory preachers, who met in Kent County, state of Delaware, and said, Mr. Asbury *"ought"* to be General Assistant. That is the way business was done, and the platform of Methodist Episcopacy was laid after this fashion.

The same tory conference next year expelled twenty-seven preachers in Virginia, for striving to have the ordinances.

1780.

"Ques. Shall *all the travelling preachers* take a license from every conference, importing that they are assistants or helpers in connection with us? Ans. Yes."

"Ques. Shall brother Asbury sign it in behalf of the Conference? Ans. Yes.

"Ques. Ought it to be strictly enjoined on all our local preachers and exhorters, that no one presume to speak in public without taking a note every quarter (if required,) and be examined by the assistant with respect to his qualification and reception? Ans. Yes." Note, Mr. Asbury is now General Assistant, and is to sign the licences of "all the travelling preachers'" and no local preacher or exhorter is to "*presume*" to open his mouth without Mr. Asbury's consent.

1781. "Ques. Shall any assistant take a local preacher to travel in the circuit, in the vacancy of conference without consulting brother Asbury? Ans. No."

1782. Ques. Do the brethren in Conference unanimously choose brother Asbury to act according to Mr. Wesley's original appointment, and preside over the American conferences, and the whole work? Ans. Yes."

Mr. Norris. — From the bottom of my heart I am glad my sheet is full, and that I can write no more of such stuff. I am sick, literally sick, in contemplating the ambition of an Englishman and an enemy to our country, trying to get into the saddle to ride native Americans — and I am disgusted beyond expression with the meanness of soul of those Americans, for letting him do it.

NUMBER IX.

In tracing the steps by which Mr. Asbury arrived at the power with which he was invested, we proceeded as we would proceed, if we were about to purchase a piece of land. We would examine the titles, beginning with the grant, if that could be obtained, and then look at the conveyances of the different persons through whose hands it had passed, until we arrived at the title of the person from whom we were about to purchase. Proceeding in this way, we soon found that the records of Methodist Episcopacy could not be depended on; for in every instance there were representations made which did not bear the stamp of truth, or the records were altered from what they originally were. We found they were pretty much like the surveyor's land-plots that we have heard of. How is that, say you? We will tell you. There was a surveyor in one of our southern States, who, a few years after the Revolutionary war, conceived the design of making a fortune in a little time, by taking up a large body of worthless, vacant land: and to make up for the badness of the soil, he hit upon an expedient to carry out his purpose. He furnished himself with a sufficient number of twigs or cuttings of walnut, hickory, oak, dogwood and such trees as indicate by

their growth, the richness of the soil where they are found; and being thus furnished he went to the woods and commenced operations. He first stuck down a walnut twig, and made it a *corner*. He
then stretched his chain a few times, stuck down a hickory switch,
and called it a *station*. He then ran a few chains more, stuck down
an oak for another *corner*, and made his dogwood cuttings *witnesses*. having run several thousand acres of land in this way, he
then formed his plots according to his notes — took them to New
York — sold his land at auction — put the proceeds in his pocket,
and went home. But when the purchasers went to look at their land,
they could not find a Walnut, Hickory, Oak, or Dogwood tree on
all that they had purchased. Now what do you call such conduct as
this? We think it would puzzle a Philadelphia lawyer to make it out
anything else than a swindling transaction. As there are some very
striking points of similarity between the land titles of the above
surveyor, and the titles of Methodist Episcopacy, we shall re-sur-
vey "our episcopacy," construct a new plot, establish the true and
original landmarks, and present a map of the whole, compiled from
the most accurate authorities.

In the meantime another aspirant after the honors of the Episcopal office may present himself before the public, and disregard-
ing the truth of history, may undertake to prove that Mr. Wesley
was never opposed to America in her revolutionary struggles, but
that his "Calm Address to the Colonies," was written to excite indignation in the people of England against the British ministry, and
thereby promote the American cause. He may go farther and say
that the six missionaries, while they remained in the country, were
friendly to the cause of the Colonies — that not one of them ever
fled for his life; that Mr. Asbury never lay concealed at Mr.
White's, in Delaware; that there were no tory preachers among the
native Americans; that none of them were sent to jail, and deny
that others dare not travel at large; and that it is a libel on "the fair
and honorable fame" of those holy men to insinuate any of those
things. If such statements should be published it would not surprise
the writer, for assertions equally absurd and *untrue* have been published already.

We are now come to the period when the Rev. Thomas Coke,
LL.D., arrived in the United States, authorized by Mr. Wesley to

confer ordination on the American preachers. The doctor landed in New York, on the 3rd day of November, 1784; and without spending unnecessary time either there, or in Philadelphia, he hastened on to the South to find Mr. Asbury. As Mr. Asbury was undoubtedly the most prominent person of those times, it may not be amiss to present at one view the power he possessed prior to the Conference of 1784 when, it is said, he was "elected" to the office of superintendent or bishop. 1. He was General Assistant, and as such presided in all the conferences. 2. "On hearing every preacher for and against what is in debate, the right of determination shall rest with him." 3. Every travelling preacher shall take a license from conference bearing his signature, and without it no preacher shall travel. ("No negro shall be found without the limits of his master's plantation without a ticket;" so says the law in slave States.) 4. No local preacher or exhorter shall "presume" to speak in public without taking a note every quarter, that he has been examined by Mr. Asbury, which note shall have his signature. 5. The colored people are to be met by the Assistant, or those persons he may appoint in his absence. 6. No preacher shall take a local preacher to travel on the circuit with him without consulting Mr. Asbury. 7. No place from which preaching has been removed shall have it again without his leave. And, 8. He shall see that all the meeting-houses, and every description of property shall be secured according to discipline. These were the powers, as we learn from the minutes of those years, with which Mr. Asbury was invested, before the sitting of the Conference of 1784; nor can we conceive of any which he did not, at that period, enjoy, save the power of ordination. Now we submit it to the reader, was it likely that a man of Mr. Asbury's ambition and love of authority would put all these prerogatives to the hazard of a vote, when he was very certain that nothing could be gained by so doing? We think not. For, 1. He knew that election to office was no part of Mr. Wesley's policy. 2. He knew that Mr. Wesley, by his letter to the American Methodists, had "appointed" him superintendent with Dr. Coke. 3. He knew that the doctor was "commissioned and directed to ordain him." 4. He knew that he and a few tory preachers in Baltimore, in 1780, had excommunicated a very large majority of the travelling preachers a few years before; and how could he tell that those preachers would not now be avenged on him, and withhold their votes from him? However, as it has been affirmed by some, that both he and Dr. Coke were elected by that conference to the Episcopal office; and the Minutes of that conference have been appealed to in proof of this affirmation; and as this averment has been positively denied by others, let us turn to the records and see what they say on the subject.

We have now lying before us three editions of the book of Discipline of the Methodist Episcopal Church. The first was printed in "Elizabeth Town, by Shepard Kollock, in 1788." The second was printed in "New York, by T. Kirk, No. 48 Maiden Lane, for the Methodist Society, and sold by E. Cooper and J. Wilson, at the Book-room, 1804." The third was "published by N. Bangs, and I. Emory, at the Methodist Printing office, New York, 1825." The second and third agree in their statements respecting the induction of the Methodist bishops into office, but both differ very much from the first. But all, first, second, and third, differ from the minutes of conference of 1784, on which Dr. Durbin relied to prove that a Methodist bishop was only an officer of the conference, and could be removed without impeachment or trial.

Let us now examine each of those editions, and then compare what they say with the minutes of 1785. The title page of the first edition runs thus: "A form of Discipline for the Ministers, Preachers, and Members of the Methodist Episcopal Church in America, considered and approved at a Conference held at Baltimore, in the State of Maryland, on Monday the 27th of December, 1784: in which the Reverend Thomas Coke, LL.D., and the Reverend Francis Asbury, presided." And what does this edition of the Discipline say respecting Thomas Coke and Francis Asbury, being elected to the Episcopal office at the Conference of 1784-5? Not one word. Does the reader wish to know what it does say? Here it is:

> "We are thoroughly convinced, that the Church of England, to which we have been united, is deficient in several of the most important parts of Christian discipline; and that (a few ministers and members excepted) it has lost the life and power of religion. We are not ignorant of the spirit and designs it has ever discovered in Europe, of rising to pre-eminence and worldly dignities

by virtue of a national establishment, and by the most servile devotion to the will of temporal governors: and we fear the same spirit will lead the same Church in these United States (though altered in its name) to similar designs and attempts, if the number and strength of its members will ever afford a probability of success; and particularly to obtain a national establishment, which we cordially abhor as the great bane of truth and holiness, and a great impediment to the progress of vital Christianity. For these reasons, we have thought it our duty to form ourselves into an independent Church. And as the most excellent mode of church government, according to our maturest judgment, is that of *a moderate Episcopacy;* and as we are persuaded, that the uninterrupted succession of Bishops from the Apostles, can be proved neither from Scripture nor antiquity; we therefore have constituted ourselves into an Episcopal Church under the direction of Bishops, Elders, Deacons and Preachers, according to the forms of ordination annexed to our prayer-book, and the regulations laid down in this form of discipline."

Now the reader will perceive that there is not one word here about electing Dr. Coke, or Mr. Asbury, to the office of superintendent or bishop. Indeed, so far is it from countenancing an election, that the whole phraseology is adverse to such an idea. It therefore only contradicts Dr. Durbin's interpretations of the minutes of Conference of 1784-5. But it falsifies the statements made in those minutes which say — "and following the counsel of Mr. John Wesley, who recommended the Episcopal mode of church government, we thought it best to become an Episcopal Church," &c. *When, where,* and *to whom,* did Mr. Wesley give this "counsel?" Who ever saw his "recommendation?" No one. Who can believe that he gave either the one or the other, when he says near the close of his letter, — "They are now at full liberty, simply to follow the Scriptures and the primitive church." Never was there a greater fraud, in our opinion, practiced upon a confiding people than is the government of the Methodist Episcopal Church, and these minutes we will mark a "Walnut corner."

We will next see if the second or third edition of the book of Discipline will sustain the assertion, that Dr. Coke and Mr. Asbury were elected by the Conference of 1784-5, to the office of a super-intendent or bishop. They say in Chap. I, Sec. 1, which treats "of the origin of the Methodist Episcopal Church:" — In consequence of this, our venerable friend, who under God, had been the father of the great revival of religion now extending over the earth, by the means of the Methodists, determined to ordain ministers for Amer-ica; and for this purpose, in the year 1784, sent over three regularly ordained clergy; but preferring the Episcopal mode of church gov-ernment to any other, he solemnly set apart, by the imposition of his hands and prayer, one of them, viz: *Thomas Coke*, Doctor of civil Law, late of Jesus College, in the University of Oxford, and a presbyter of the Church of England, for the Episcopal office; and having delivered to him letters of episcopal orders commissioned and directed him to set apart *Francis Asbury*, then general assistant of the Methodist society in America for the same episcopal office, he, the said *Francis Asbury,* being first ordained deacon and elder. In consequence of which, the said *Francis Asbury* was solemnly set apart for the said episcopal office, by prayer and the imposition of the hands of the said Thomas Coke, other regularly ordained ministers assisting in the sacred ceremony. At which time the Gen-eral Conference held at Baltimorc, did unanimously receive the said *Thomas Coke* and *Francis Asbury*, as their bishops, being fully satisfied of the validity of their Episcopal ordination." Well, is there any thing here about electing either Dr. Coke or Mr. As-bury to the office of superintendent or bishop? Not a word. It says — "the Conference did unanimously *receive* them as their bishops, being fully satisfied of their Episcopal ordination." Receiving, then, is one thing, electing is another. The people of a Territory *re-ceive* a governor appointed by the President of the States — the people *elect* their own Governor when they are admitted as a State into the Union. But even if it had been asserted they were elected, we could not credit the statement, because this is a false document fabricated to perpetuate the fraud of Methodist Episcopacy. Let the reader collate what this contains with what is contained in the Dis-cipline of 1788: he has both documents before him in this letter. If the one of 1788 is true, this is false — if this is true, that is false. We believe the record of 1788 is true, for it bears the internal marks of truth. We believe this is false, for it bears *"prima facie"* evidence of its falsity. The former ascribes the adoption of the Episcopal form of government to their *"maturest judgment"* — this ascribes it to Mr. Wesley's *"preference"* for this form of government. The former does not say one word about Mr. Wesley's ordaining Thomas Coke to the Episcopal office — it does not even mention Mr. Wesley's name — this abounds with the most pompous terms — "three regularly ordained clergy" — "setting apart Thomas Coke for the Episcopal office" — "giving him letters of Episcopal orders," &c. The former was written at the time the transactions took place of which it treats — the latter was written several years afterward, when Mr. Wesley was dead and could not contradict its false statements. The Church was organized in 1784. Mr. Wesley died the 2nd of March, 1791, and this record speaks of him as "the *late* Rev. John Wesley." This word *"late"* has proved the falsity of the records. Reader, look in your book of Discipline and you will find what I say is true. I shall therefore stick down a Hickory switch here as a mark of falsehood, and call this the *"Hickory station."*

NUMBER X.

It must be extremely mortifying to the members of the Methodist Episcopal Church, both North and South, to see such grave statements go out to the world as are contained in these letters, that there can be no reliance placed on the records of the Church, as we now have them, in as much as these records have been fabricated to foist Episcopacy on the Methodist societies, or were altered to perpetuate the institution. Some pious souls, who have always thought the founders of the government of the church were so holy and self- sacrificing as to be above the little arts of trickery and deceit, will stand astounded at the revelations which these letters contain; unwilling to believe such heavy charges, and yet unable to disprove them. Some, again, having a direct interest in perpetuating "our episcopacy," as their own support and the support of their families depend on its continuance, (and the whole body of the travelling preachers are of this class,) may feign to treat this subject with indifference — ascribe these statements to unworthy motives on the part of the writer — represent him as aspiring after the Episcopal office himself, and induce the great body of the Methodists to believe, or affect to believe, what these gentlemen say. Whilst others, who stand connected with the society, as the mistletoe does with the oak, and who are strangers to the graces which form the Christian, will get mad, denounce the Olive Branch for giving circulation to those statements, and wish that all the curses which the Church of Rome has pronounced against heretics, may fall on the head of the writer. But one reply will suit all classes of doubters and objectors: gentlemen, subdue your wrath — withhold your maledictions, and confute these charges if you can. If the statements here made are false, their falsity can be proved: if true, why condemn the writer for writing what is true? It was certainly deserving of censure to forge or alter the records; but it remains to be proved that it is wrong to say they have been forged or altered.

Of those records which are false, the minutes of Conference of 1784-5, hold a conspicuous place. They begin thus — "As it was unanimously agreed at this conference that circumstances made it expedient for us to become a separate body under the denomination of the *Methodist Episcopal Church*, it is necessary that we should here assign some reason for so doing.

The following extract of a letter from the Rev. Mr. John Wesley will afford as good an explanation as can be given on this subject." They then insert this "extract," and proceed to say, — "Therefore, at this Conference we formed ourselves into an Independent Church; and followed the counsel of Mr. John Wesley, who recommended the Episcopal mode of church government, we thought it best to become an Episcopal Church, making the Episcopal office elective, and the elected superintendent or bishop, amenable to the body of ministers or preachers."

Before we enter on the proofs of the falsity of these minutes, or institute an enquiry as to the "circumstances which made it expedient" for them "to become a separate body" — "an Independent Church," we will take occasion to say, that the phraseology here used does not invalidate what we have heretofore said about Dr.

Coke and Mr. Asbury not being elected to the office of superintendent or bishop by this Conference. It was declared when the church was organized, "that the uninterrupted succession of Bishops from the Apostles can be proved neither from Scripture nor antiquity," and the Conference, having given up the doctrine of "uninterrupted succession" as untenable, they were obliged to resort to that of election as they had formed themselves into an "Independent Church" — *independent of Mr. Wesley* — but their making "the Episcopal office elective," had regard to those who might subsequently be elevated to that high station, and not to Dr. Coke or Mr. Asbury who had been appointed by Mr. Wesley, and had been inducted into office.

That these minutes are not the true and original minutes of the Conference of 1784-5, I argue, —

1. Because "the volume of Minutes, published by the Rev. John Dickens," being out of print, it was succeeded by the present volume, which contains what purports to be the minutes of the several conferences from 1773 to 1813, inclusive. This volume was prepared by Mr. Asbury, and everything was omitted that it was thought would invalidate the claims of "our episcopacy."

2. The language of these minutes is the language of past time. "It was unanimously agreed" — "circumstances made it expedient for us to become a separate body" — "we formed ourselves into an Episcopal Church," &c.

3. The term *bishop* which occurs in these minutes was never used before 1787, when Mr. Asbury desired the preachers, when they wrote to him, to style him *bishop.* When Mr. Wesley was expelled by the conference of 1787, the next year the minutes read thus, —

> "*Q.* Who are the Bishops of our church for the United States?
>
> *A.* Thomas Coke, Francis Asbury."

Before this they read, — "who are the superintendents?"

4. Because we have the testimony of the Rev. Jesse Lee, that the minutes were altered. "In the course of this year (1787) Mr. Asbury reprinted the General Minutes, but *in a different form from what they were before. ...* This was the first time that our superin-

tendents ever gave themselves the title of bishops in the minutes. They changed the title themselves without the consent of the conference; and at the next Conference they asked the preachers if the word *bishop* might stand in the minutes, seeing that it was a scriptural name, and the meaning of the word *bishop* was the same with that of superintendent. Some of the preachers opposed the alteration, and wished to retain the former title, but a majority of the preachers agreed to let the word bishop remain." Lee's History of Methodism, page 128.

5. There is no document written *before* Mr. Wesley's death which ascribes the Episcopal form of Church government to him, his "*counsel*," advice or "recommendation:" but as soon as ever death had imposed silence on his tongue, and his hand had been rendered incapable of contradicting their statements, then do these reverend bishops ascribe the mode of church government to him, and pass it off on the credulous Methodists under the sanction of Mr. Wesley's name.

6. The Minutes which were taken at the Conference of 1784 — 5, were printed by Charles Cist, of Philadelphia, a copy of them was taken by Dr. Coke to England, and with the Prayer book which had been abridged by Mr. Wesley, were re-printed, not at Mr. Wesley's press, but at that of "Frys & Couchman, Worship street, Upper Moorsfield, 1786." These Minutes, which are the *true and original ones*, consist of seventy-six questions with their answers, occupying thirty-three pages of an *octavo* Prayer book. The minutes which we have in the bound volume consist of seventeen questions with their answers, and occupy seven pages of a *12mo.* We shall notice only one question in the original minutes and its answer.

> "*Q.* 3. As the ecclesiastical as well as civil affairs of the United States have passed through a very considerable change by the revolution, what plan of Church government shall we hereafter pursue?[1]

---

[1] This question will fix the lie forever on the declaration that Mr. Wesley was the author of the Episcopal form of Church government for the Methodist societies in the United States, no matter how modified the language of the statement may be, or by whom made. For if the conference were acting under the di-

A. We will form ourselves into an Episcopal Church, under the direction of superintendents, elders, deacons, and helpers according to the forms of ordination annexed to our Liturgy, and the form of discipline set forth in these minutes."

The reader is now requested to compare this account of the origin of our Episcopal government, with the account published in the book of Discipline, and with that in the volume of Minutes. The difference is so glaring that everyone must see it. In this answer, there is not a word about Mr. Wesley's *"recommending the Episcopal mode of church government"* — nothing about his "preferring" that mode to any other; nothing about his "counsel" to ordain a third order of ministers; nothing about "a separate and independent church." Nothing. These things never had Mr. Wesley's approbation. As soon as Dr. Coke and Mr. Asbury had announced themselves Bishops in the minutes of conference, Mr. Wesley wrote Mr. Asbury the following letter. See Moore's Life of Wesley. Vol. II. p. 285.

"LONDON, Sept. 20th, 1788.

"There is, indeed, a wide difference between the relation wherein you stand to the Americans, and the relation wherein I stand to *all* the Methodists. You are the elder brother of the American Methodists; I am, under God, the father of the whole family. Therefore, I naturally care for you all, in a manner no other person can do. Therefore I, in a measure, provide for you all; for the supplies which Dr. Coke provides for you, he could

---

rection of Mr. Wesley, or in conformity with his instruction and "counsel" in this thing, there could have been no room to ask, "what plan of church government shall we hereafter pursue?" Dr. Durbin knew, in debate, that the minutes of 1784-5 were altered, or he did not. If he did not know they were altered, he is very ignorant of Methodist Episcopacy and the history of the Church. If he did know this to be the fact, and we believe he did, because it was proved in the work to which "the Defense of our Fathers" purported to be a reply, it will follow that the doctor has knowingly appealed to a *forged* document to prove a *false* proposition. Is this the system of ethics, Doctor, that was taught at the College of Carlisle, over which you presided? Ah, doctor, there is nothing like TRUTH to carry a man safe through this world.

not provide, were it not for me; were it not that I not
only permit him to collect, but support him in so doing.

"But in one point, my dear brother, I am afraid both
the Doctor and you differ from me. I study to be *little,*
you study to be *great.* I *creep,* you *strut* along. I found a
school, you a *college.* Nay, and call it after your own
name! O beware! Do not seek to be *something!* Let me
be nothing, and Christ be all in all.

"One instance of this your greatness has given me
great concern. How can you, how dare you suffer yourself to be called a *Bishop!* I shudder, I start at the very
thought. Men may call *me* a *knave,* or a *fool,* a *rascal,* a
scoundrel, and I am content; but they shall never by my
consent, call me a *Bishop!* For my sake, for God's sake,
for Christ's sake, put a full end to this! Let the Presbyterians do what they please, but let the Methodists know
their calling better. Thus my dear Franky, I have told
you all that is in my heart, and let this, when I am no
more seen, bear witness how sincerely, I am your affectionate friend and brother,

"John Wesley."

Respecting this letter which did not see the light for near forty
years after the death of Mr. Wesley, it may be proper to make a
few remarks: 1. Mr. Wesley bequeathed his manuscripts and papers to the following persons, — "I give all my manuscripts to
Thomas Coke, Doctor Whitehead, and Henry Moore, to be burnt or
published as they see good." 2. "Dr. Whitehead was solicited to
write Mr. Wesley's life by the executors, preachers, and others." 3.
"The three persons to whom Mr. Wesley had bequeathed his
manuscripts, of whom Dr. Whitehead was one, deliberately agreed
that the Doctor should have the use of those manuscripts to assist
him in executing the work, and they having been delivered uncon-
ditionally to him for that end, he had a right to the discretional use
of them, notwithstanding that two of those persons afterwards
changed their mind on the subject." 4. This letter does not appear
in Whitehead's life of Wesley, Coke and Moore having changed
their mind with respect to the doctor having a right to the discre-

tional use of Mr. Wesley's papers. 5. Shortly after Mr. Wesley's death, Coke and Moore published a life of Mr. Wesley. It is highly probable this work was written by Dr. Coke, though published under the names of the two gentlemen. Be that as it may, this letter does not appear in that work, for reasons too plain and obvious to be mistaken. 6. Several years after Dr. Coke had sailed to India, and had died on the passage, Mr. Moore published a life of Mr. Wesley in two volumes, *octavo;* and then, for the first time this noted letter was given to the public. This letter alone, we think, is sufficient to settle the matter of Mr. Wesley's recommendation of the Episcopal form of church government with every intelligent and disinterested person; but if it serves to prove his "recommendation," it may be asked why was "our beloved Emory" afraid to publish it in his "Defense of our Fathers"? Seriously, we think as soon as this letter was received, steps ought to have been taken to do Mr. Wesley justice, by stating in the Minutes that he was opposed to the name of Bishop, and to have taken upon themselves all the responsibility of creating an Episcopal form of government. This, however, they had not the magnanimity to do. The above letter was suppressed. Its contents were never suffered to transpire. But Mr. Wesley was made to speak a language he never spoke. His name was used to give a sanction to their measures, which it was thought would disarm resistance, if any were offered; and by this means was an Episcopal form of government established, the name of the Rev. John Wesley being given as a passport to all the ecclesiastical honors it could bestow.

NUMBER XI.

As it has been affirmed in the minutes for 1784-5 that "circumstances made it expedient for us at this conference to become a separate body," the next step in the investigation is to enquire, what were those "circumstances," and from whom did they make it expedient for this conference to separate? To be able to give a true answer to these enquiries it will be proper to consider the state and relation of the Methodist societies in America *before*, and *during* the Revolutionary war.

1st. These societies were connected with Mr. Wesley and the

English Methodists, esteeming themselves and being esteemed, as one family. In proof of this position let us hear what Mr. Wesley says; — "It pleased God, sixty years ago, by me to awaken and join together a little company of people at Oxford, and a few years after, a small company in London, whence they spread throughout the land. Sometime after, I was much importuned to send some of my children to America, to which I cheerfully consented. God prospered their labors: but they and their children still esteemed themselves one family; no otherwise divided than as Methodists on one side of the Thames are divided from the other."

2nd. The societies in America were cared for, and to a very considerable extent provided for, in pecuniary matters, by Mr. Wesley. In a letter to Mr. Asbury, he says: — "There is indeed a wide difference between the relation wherein you stand to the Americans, and the relation wherein I stand to *all* the Methodists. You are the elder brother of the American Methodists; I am, under God, the father of the whole family. Therefore I naturally care for you all, in a manner no other person can do. Therefore I, in a measure, provide for you all: for the supplies which Dr. Coke provides for you, he could not provide, were it not for me; were it not that I not only permit him to collect, but support him in so doing." The condition, therefore, of the American societies up to the close of the Revolutionary war, was a condition of union with, and dependence on, Mr. Wesley; and not with the church of England, only so far as he was connected with that church.

3rd. Mr. Wesley was importuned before the commencement of actual hostilities, but especially during the continuance of the war, to assist the societies in spiritual matters, by taking some steps to procure for them "the sacraments of baptism and the Lord's supper inasmuch as they were obliged to receive those sacraments from the hands of men who, in general, were not thought fit persons to officiate in Divine things, or go without the ordinances. He accordingly made application to the Bishop of London to ordain "one only" for them; but his request being refused, he took measures, after the close of the war, to comply with their solicitations, by ordaining and sending over some of his preachers to administer those sacred ordinances. Hence it is plain that the "circumstances which made it expedient for the conference to become a separate body" did not grow out of the connection of the societies with Mr. Wesley and the English Methodists, nor to any want of care on his part, to provide for their temporal wants, or their spiritual exigencies. If then, they did not grow out of either of these things, did they grow out of their connection with the Church of England? It is from the Church of England, abstractly considered, that the conference deemed it expedient to separate, and the reasons for doing so are set forth in the sermon preached by Dr. Coke on the occasion of Mr. Asbury's ordination to the Episcopal office. He says: "The church of England, of which the society of Methodists, in general, have till lately professed themselves a part, did for many years groan in America under grievances of the heaviest kind. Subjected to a hierarchy, which weighs everything in the scales of politics, its most important interests were repeatedly sacrificed to the supposed advantages of England. The churches were, in general, filled with the parasites and bottle-companions of the rich and the great. The humble and most importunate entreaties of the oppressed flocks, yea the representation of a general assembly itself, (the Assembly of Virginia) were condemned and despised; everything sacred must lie down at the feet of a party, the holiness and happiness of mankind be sacrificed to their views; and the drunkard, the fornicator, and the extortioner, triumphed over bleeding Zion, because they were faithful abettors of the ruling powers. Blessed be God, and praised be his holy name, that the memorable Revolution has struck off those intolerable fetters, and broken the antichristian union which before subsisted between Church and State. And had there been no other advantage arising from that glorious epoch, this itself, I believe, would have made ample compensation for all the calamities of the war. One happy consequence of which was the expulsion of most of those hirelings *who ate the fat and clothed themselves with the wool, but strengthened not the diseased, neither healed that which was sick, neither bound up that which was broken, neither brought again that which was driven away, neither sought that which was lost.*"

On this paragraph let it be remarked, that bad as these ministers were represented to be, Thomas Coke applied to be received into their fellowship!! His letter to Bishop White, to be given hereafter, will prove this fact. But he goes on —

"The Parochial churches in general being hereby vacant, our people were deprived of the sacraments through the greatest part of these States and continue so still. What method can we take at this critical juncture? God has given us sufficient resources in ourselves, and after mature deliberation, we believe we are called to draw them forth.

"But what right have you to ordain? The same right as most of the reformed churches in Christendom. Our ordination, in its lowest view, being equal to any of the Presbyterian, as originating with three presbyters of the church of England."

"It is possible," says Dr. Whitehead in his life of Wesley, "the doctor might believe himself when he wrote this sentence. But is it true, that the presence of three presbyters in a private chamber is the only requisite essentially necessary to give validity to an ordination among the Presbyterians? I apprehend not. Nor do I know any denomination of Dissenters, among whom such a secret ordination would be deemed valid."

Dr. Coke proceeds in his sermon —

"But what right have you to exercise the *Episcopal office?* To me the most manifest and clear, God has been pleased by Mr. Wesley to raise up in America and Europe, a numerous society, well known by the name of Methodists. The whole body have invariably esteemed *this man* as their chief pastor under Christ. He has constantly appointed all their religious officers from the highest to the lowest, by himself or his delegate. And we are fully persuaded there is no church-office which he judges expedient for the welfare of the people entrusted to his charge, but, as *essential* to his station, he has a power to ordain. After long deliberation, he saw it his duty to form his society in America into an independent church;[2] but he loved the most excellent

---

[2] We think we shall be able to prove, from Mr. Wesley himself, that this assertion is absolutely false.

liturgy of the *Church of England*, he loved its rites and ceremonies, and therefore adopted them in most instances for the present case."

Dr. Whitehead remarks on this passage —

"Now, if these words contain anything like an argument, they must mean that the officers whom Mr. Wesley had always appointed, were church officers; and consequently, that his societies were churches. If this be not the meaning, then the words which go before, have no immediate connexion with the conclusion drawn from them. But the minutes of conference, and Mr. Wesley's other writings testify in the most express manner, that the Methodist societies were not churches.

"But there is another view of this argument, which makes it appear still more absurd. Whatever power Mr. Wesley had always exercised over the Methodist societies, it was no proof of his right. Power and right are two things. Power does not imply right; otherwise, the power of speech would imply a right to speak treason: the power of deceiving and robbing would imply a right so to do? Whatever right, therefore, Mr. Wesley might have for making prudential regulations for the societies, it cannot be proved from his power. But Dr. Coke here brings forward Mr. Wesley's power, and his former practice in the exercise of it, as a proof that he has a right to do what he may think expedient for the good of the people. Now if a man in common life were to plead his former practice as a proof that he had a right to do what he might judge expedient in future, and should act on this principle, I suppose he would soon be sent to Bedlam or to Newgate. *Whitehead's Life of Wesley.* Page 262.

We have, in this extract from Dr. Coke's sermon, his reasons for "this conference becoming a separate body," from the church of England. We ask now, is the reader satisfied with these reasons? Is he convinced, plausible as they seem to be, that they contain the truth, the whole truth, and nothing but the truth? If he is, we are not, and dropping Dr. Coke and the part *he* took in the separation for the present, we offer for our dissent the following reasons.

1st. The irregularity or sinfulness of the lives of the clergy of the church of England is made the ground of the separation, but this was *known* and *felt* by the Methodist societies both before and during the war, as well as after the peace. If this then was the true ground, and there is no other assigned, we are at a loss to conceive why the separation did not take place before the conference of '84. If this was the true ground, why did Mr. Asbury expel from the connection the whole body of the Southern preachers, with John Dickens at their head, because they had taken steps in 1779 to become independent of the church of England and her sinful clergy? There is certainly inconsistency if not falsehood here.

2nd. At the period when this separation is said to have taken place, there was no connection between the Methodist societies and the Church of England, only so far as they were connected with Mr. Wesley; nor had there been for upwards of two years. This is the opinion of Mr. Wesley himself. He says — "By a very uncommon train of providences, many of the provinces of North America are totally disjoined from the British empire, and erected into Independent States. The English government has no authority over them either civil or ecclesiastical, any more than over the States of Holland. A civil authority is exercised over them, partly by the Congress, partly by the State Assemblies. But no one either exercises, or claims any ecclesiastical authority at all."

3rd. If it was from the Church of England that "this conference deemed it expedient to separate," on what ground can we account for their formally receiving her prayer-book, using her liturgy, and conforming to her rites and ceremonies?

4th. In a former paper we gave numerous extracts from the minutes of conference from 1773 to 1784, setting forth Mr. Asbury's attachment to the church of England — his determination not to leave her communion — his fixed purpose not to administer the sacraments to any of the societies — and his decided measures to prevent any of the preachers from doing it. But all this time he was not ordained, though he was anxiously waiting for it. Now that he has obtained that which he had long hoped to enjoy, and has been made a bishop, he is resolved to get rid of Mr. Wesley and all connection with him as quick as possible. This is the secret of the whole business. This explains the "circumstances which made it expedient for us at this conference to become a separate body — an independent church" — independent of Mr. Wesley, and his authority: and although Mr. Asbury wished it to take place then, the preachers out of affection for Mr. Wesley, passed the following resolution.

Q. "What can be done in order to the future union of the Methodists?

A. During the life of the Rev. Mr. Wesley, we acknowledge ourselves his sons in the gospel, ready in matters belonging to church government to obey his commands. And we *do engage*, after his death, to do every thing that we judge consistent with the cause of religion in America, and the political interests of these States, to preserve and promote our *union* with the Methodists in Europe."

The steps by which Mr. Asbury arrived at the height of power which he enjoyed, prior to the conference of '84-5, have been pointed out in a preceding letter. It is no wonder then, as he had class leaders, exhorters, local and travelling preachers, nay the whole connexion under his thumb, he was unwiling that Mr. Wesley should share any part of the government of the American Methodist societies: so that Mr. Wesley being out of the way he might sing with Robinson Crusoe the words put in his mouth by Cowper,

> "I am monarch of all I survey,
> My right there is none to dispute,
> From the centre all round to the sea,
> I am lord of the fowl and the brute."

NUMBER XII.

No man who has read the preceding letters with any degree of attention and care, can fail to perceive the opinion the writer entertains respecting the nature and origin of the government of the Methodist Episcopal Church. If, however, he has any doubt on the subject, we will now tell him in language plain and intelligible, and uttered with the utmost sincerity and truth, that we consider it one of the most unjust and oppressive systems of ecclesiastical rule that ever was organized, and that it originated in one of the deepest laid schemes of deception that was ever passed off on a Christian community for the truth. We shall therefore always speak of it as a fraud — as a fraud of the basest character.

We are fully aware that such an averment is calculated to arouse the indignation of those who have been taught to believe, that "the system is worthy of all eulogy," and that it is the pure and legitimate offspring of one of the holiest and best men that ever lived — the Rev. John Wesley. But as we cannot subscribe to these statements, we shall speak of it as a *fraud*, notwithstanding the censure that will most certainly follow, if we fail to establish the correctness of our opinion, in the judgment of an intelligent and impartial public. We will now turn to Dr. Coke and begin with him.

That this gentleman did not stand very high in the estimation of those who had the best opportunity of knowing him in Europe, will appear from the following extracts. Lamenting the loss that Mr. Wesley's connexion sustained by the death of Rev. John Fletcher, Dr. Whitehead says: — "He would, at least, have prevented the influence which a person some years afterwards acquired through the connexion, with talents very inferior to most of the preachers; who has been the chief means of introducing innovations into the original plan of Methodism, which have already produced much mischief, and threaten much more in the issue: and whose rash and inconsistent conduct, on several occasions, has brought the whole body of preachers into disgrace, and embarrassed them with many difficulties." Life of Wesley. Page 219.

Again: "It has already been observed, that a party existed among the preachers, who wished the Methodists to be erected into an independent body, and a total separation to be made from the established church. One of this party was frequently about Mr. Wesley's person; and under various pretences sometimes led him into measures that offended the people and embarrassed his affairs, while the true authority lay concealed, as much as possible, behind the scenes." *Ibid.* page 247.

Once more: "It has already appeared in this history, that Mr.

Wesley claimed the power or right of ordaining to the ministry, but said it was not probable that he should ever exercise it. We have likewise seen, how steadily for a long course of years, he resisted every measure which tended to alter the relative situation of the societies to the established church, and to the various denominations of dissenters to which any of the members might belong. It is not easy to assign a sufficient reason why Mr. Wesley, in the eighty-second year of his age, should depart from a line of conduct he had hitherto so strictly observed; especially if he acted according to his own judgment, and of his free choice. However this may be, a plan was proposed in private, to a few clergymen who attended the conference this year at Leeds, that Mr. Wesley should ordain one or two preachers for the societies in America. But the clergymen opposed it. Mr. Fletcher was consulted by letter; who advised, that a bishop should be prevailed upon if possible to ordain them, and then Mr. Wesley might appoint them to such offices in the societies as he thought proper, and give them letters testimonial of the appointments he had given them. Mr. Wesley well knew, that no bishop would ordain them at his recommendation, and therefore seemed inclined to do it himself. In this purpose, however, he appeared so languid, if not wavering, that Dr. Coke thought it necessary to use some further means to urge him to the performance of it. Accordingly, August 9th, Mr. Wesley being then in Wales, on his way to Bristol, the doctor sent him the following letter:

> "Honored and dear sir, — The more maturely I consider the subject, the more expedient it appears to me, that the power of ordaining others should be received by me from you, by the imposition of your hands; and that you should lay hands on brother Whatcoat, and brother Vasey for the following reasons: 1st. It seems to me the most scriptural way, and most agreeable to the practice of the primitive churches. 2nd. I may want all the influence in America, which you can throw into my scale. Mr. Brackenbury informed me at Leeds, that he saw a letter in London from Mr. Asbury, in which he observed, that he would not receive any person deputed by you with any part of the superinten-

dency of the work invested in him; or words which evidently implied so much. I do not find any, the least degree of prejudice in my mind against Mr. Asbury; on the contrary, a very great love and esteem; and am determined not to stir a finger without his consent, unless mere sheer necessity obliges me; but rather to lie at his feet in all things. But as the journey is long, and you cannot spare me often, and it is well to provide against all events, and an authority formally received from you will (I am conscious of it) be fully admitted by the people, and my exercising the office of ordination without that formal authority may be disputed, if there be any opposition on any other account I could therefore earnestly wish you would exercise that power, in this instance, which I have not the shadow of a doubt but God hath invested you with, for the good of our connexion. I think you have tried me too often to doubt, whether I will in any degree use the power you are pleased to invest me with, farther than I believe absolutely necessary for the prosperity of the work. 3. In respect of my brethren (brother Whatcoat and Vasey) it is very uncertain indeed, whether any of the clergy mentioned by brother Rankin, will stir a step with me in the work, except Mr. Jaritt; and it is by no means certain that even he will choose to join me in ordaining; and propriety and universal practice make it expedient, that I should have two presbyters with me in this work. In short, it appears to me that everything should be prepared, and everything proper be done, that can possibly be done this side of the water. You can do all this in Mr. C___n's house, in your chamber; and afterwards (according to Mr. Fletcher's advice) give us letters testimonial of the different offices with which you have been pleased to invest us. For the purpose of laying hands on brother Whatcoat and Yasey, I can bring Mr. C___ down with me, by which you will have two presbyters with you. In respect to brother Rankin's argument, that you will escape a great deal of odium by omitting this, it is nothing. Either it will be known or not known; if not known, then no odium will arise: but if known, you will be obliged to acknowledge that I acted under your direction, or suffer me to sink under the weight of my enemies, with perhaps your brother at the head of them. I shall entreat you to ponder these things.

Your most dutiful,
T. Coke."

"This letter," says Dr. Whitehead, "affords matter for several observations, both of the serious and comic kind: but I shall not indulge myself on the occasion it so fairly offers. The attentive reader who examines every part of it, will be at no loss to conjecture to whose influence we must impute Mr. Wesley's conduct in the present business. That Mr. Wesley should suffer himself to be influenced, in a matter of the utmost importance both to his own character and to the societies, by a man, of whose judgment in advising, and talents in conducting any affair, he had no very high opinion, is truly astonishing: but so it was! Mr. Wesley came to Bristol, and Sept. 1st, everything being prepared as proposed above, he complied with the doctor's earnest wish, by consecrating him one of the bishops, and Mr. Whatcoat and Vasey presbyters of the new Methodist Episcopal Church in America.

In confirmation of the correctness of Dr. Whitehead's opinion that Mr. Wesley's conduct in the matter of ordination must be attributed to Dr. Coke's influence over Mr. Wesley, it is proper to remark that he (Mr. W.) did not submit the matter of ordaining preachers for America, to the British conference — he never consulted the conference on the business at all. Hear what one of that body says: "Ordination — among Methodists! Amazing indeed! I could not force myself to credit the report which spread here, having not then seen the minutes; but now I can doubt it no longer. And so, we have Methodist parsons of our own! And a new mode of ordination, to be sure — on the Presbyterian plan! In spite of a million of declarations to the contrary! I am fairly confounded. Now the ice is broken, let us conjecture a little the probable issue of this new thing in the earth. You say we must reason and debate the matter. Alas! it is too late. Surely it never began in the midst of a multitude of counsellors; and I greatly fear the Son of Man was not Secretary of State, or not present when the business was brought on and carried, I suppose, with very few dissentient voices. Who could imagine that this important matter would have stole into being, and be obtruded upon the body without their being so much as apprized of it, or consulted on so weighty a point? Who is the father of this monster, so long dreaded by the father of his people, and by most of his sons? Whoever he be, time will prove him a felon to Methodism,[3] and discover his assassinating knife sticking fast in the vitals of its body. This has been my steadfast opinion for years past; and years to come will speak in groans the opprobrious anniversary of our religious madness for gowns and bands." Life of Wesley. Page 257- 8.

> "Another old preacher, writing to his friend, delivers his opinion to the following purpose — I wish they had been asleep when they began this business of ordination: it is neither Episcopal nor Presbyterian, but a mere hodge-podge of inconsistencies."

2. "A plan was proposed in private, to a few clergymen who attended the conference this year at Leeds, that Mr. Wesley should ordain one or two preachers for the societies in America. But the clergymen opposed it. Mr. Fletcher was consulted by letter, who advised, that a bishop should be prevailed upon, if possible to ordain them, and then Mr. Wesley might appoint them to such offices in the societies as he thought proper, and give them letters testimonial of the appointments he had given them." We see from this that the clergymen who were consulted on the subject were opposed to his ordaining any of his preachers, and as for Mr. Fletcher he never advised Mr. Wesley to ordain, but to apply to a bishop to have them ordained. We have seen his name connected with the transaction as approving of Mr. Wesley's conduct, but nothing can be farther from the truth.

3. "Mr. Charles Wesley in his letter to Dr. Chandler, in the beginning of the year 1785 says — I can scarcely yet believe it; that

____

[3] This will be proved hereafter by Dr. Coke himself.

in his eighty-second year, my brother, my old intimate friend and companion, should have assumed the episcopal character; ordained elders, consecrated a bishop, and sent him over to ordain our lay-preachers in America! I was then in Bristol, at his elbow, yet he never gave me the least hint of his intention. How was he surprised into so rash an action? He certainly persuaded himself that it was right.

"Lord Mansfield told me last year, that ordination was separation. This my brother does not, and will not see: or, that he has renounced the principles and practice of his whole life; that he has acted contrary to all his declarations, protestations, and writings; robbed his friends of their boastings; realized the Nag's-head ordination; and left an indelible blot on his name, as long as it shall be remembered."

In a letter to his brother John, he says —

"Near thirty years since then, you have stood against the importunate solicitation of your preachers, who have scarcely at last prevailed. I was your natural ally, and your faithful friend: and while you continued faithful to yourself, we two could chase a thousand. If they had not divided us, they could never overcome you. But when once you began ordaining for America, I knew, and you knew, that your preachers here would never rest, till you ordained them. You told me 'they would separate by and by.' The doctor tells us the same. His Methodist Episcopal church at Baltimore was intended to beget a Methodist Episcopal church here. You know he comes armed with your authority, to make us all Dissenters. One of your sons assured me, that not a preacher in London would refuse orders from the doctor. It is evident, that all seek their own, and prefer their own interest to your honor; which not one of them scruples to sacrifice to his own ambition. Alas what trouble you are preparing for yourself, as well as me, and for your oldest, and truest and best friends! Before you have quite broken down the bridge, stop, and consider! If your sons have no regard for you, have some for yourself. Go to your grave in peace; at least suffer me to go first, before this ruin be under your hand. So much, I think, you owe to my father, to my brother, and to me, as to stay till I am taken away from the evil. I am on the brink of the grave, do not push me in; or embitter my last moments. Let us not leave an indelible blot upon our memory, but let us leave behind us the name and character of honest men." Whitehead's Life of Wesley. Page 565.

NUMBER XIII.

Before we proceed any farther, it is proper to notice the ordination of Dr. Coke, which took place shortly after his letter of August 9th, to Mr. Wesley. The Rev. James Creighton, in a letter addressed to Mr. Samuel Bradburn, printed in London 1793, says — "You take notice of a meeting which Mr. Wesley had with some clergymen at Leeds in August 1784, at which he consulted them concerning the ordination of preachers for America. Mr. Fletcher was present, and I believe Mr. Selton, and two or three others. They did not approve of the scheme; because it seemed inconsistent with Mr. Wesley's former professions respecting the church. Upon this the meeting was abruptly broken up by Mr. Wesley's going out." Is it not strange then, that notwithstanding the opposition of all the clergy to Mr. W's scheme of ordaining any for the American societies, it being "inconsistent with his former professions respecting the church," Dr. C.'s ordination should take place in Mr. Wesley's chamber in Bristol? The only clergymen present with Mr. Wesley were Dr. Coke and Rev. James Creighton. Mr. Wesley ordained Mr. Whatcoat and Mr. Vasey, deacons first, and immediately afterwards, they were ordained elders: and these gentlemen being double ordained in a trice, turn round and assist Mr. Wesley to ordain Dr. Coke a bishop for America! And although the transaction is without a parallel in the history of ordinations, the author of the "Defense of our Fathers," has the impudence to affirm that "Dr. Coke's ordination was performed as ordinations usually are" — and Dr. Durbin has the hardihood to declare, that the author of the above work is a "*standard*" writer! O shame where is thy blush!

But let us hear what the sentiments of others are respecting this ordination. Dr. Whitehead says —

> "In direct opposition to the practice of the primitive church, the ordinations among the Methodists were performed in secret. The people were not assembled: they were not consulted: nor even so much as acquainted that ministers were to be ordained among the Methodists as their proper pastors. The whole was performed by an arbitrary power, in the exercise of which no regard was had to the rights of the people. But Dr. Coke tells us, they have the same qualifications for an Episcopal Church, which the church at Alexandria possessed. "Our bishops," says he, "having been elected, or received, by the suffrage of the old body of our ministers through the continent, assembled in General Conference." There were but two bishops, so called, Dr. Coke and Mr. Asbury, in America. Now these surely were not elected, in any sense whatever, either by the preachers, or people. But, "They were elected or received." When a writer thus links words together of different import, as though the meaning amounted to the same thing, we have just cause to suspect that he intends to deceive us, and lead us into a false notion of the subject he is discussing. It is manifest indeed, from first to last, that this whole affair bears no resemblance to the mode of electing and ordaining ministers in the purer ages of the primitive church." Life of Wesley. Page 264.

The same writer says —

> "Mr. Wesley's episcopal authority, was a mere gratuitous assumption of power to himself, contrary to the usage of every church, ancient or modern, where the order of bishops has been admitted. There is no precedent

either in the New Testament, or in church history, that can justify his proceedings in this affair. And as Mr. Wesley had received no right to exercise episcopal authority, either from any bishops, presbyters, or people, he certainly could not convey any right to others: his ordinations are therefore spurious and of no validity."

"Let us review the arguments on this subject reduced to a few propositions. 1st. Mr. Wesley in ordaining or consecrating Dr. Coke a bishop, acted in direct contradiction to the principle on which he attempts to defend his practice of ordaining at all. 2nd. As Mr. Wesley was never elected or chosen by any church to be a bishop, nor even consecrated to the office, either by bishops or presbyters, he had not the shadow of right to exercise episcopal authority in ordaining others, according to the rules of any church, ancient or modern. 3rd. Had he possessed the proper right to ordain, either as a bishop or presbyter, (though he never did ordain as a presbyter) yet his ordinations being done in secret, were rendered thereby invalid and of no effect, according to the established order of the primitive church, and of all protestant churches. 4th. The consequence from the whole is, that the persons whom Mr. Wesley ordained, have no more right to exercise the ministerial functions than they had before he laid hands upon them." *Ibid.* Page 269.

Heretofore we have said, the government of the Methodist Episcopal Church is a *fraud;* we will now give our reasons for this assertion. But we are not so ignorant of human nature as to suppose any of the travelling preachers will credit what we say; for it is their interest to deny it, and to make this assertion appear a malicious slander if they can. Nor do we believe that many of the members will credit our statements; for they have been so long accustomed to look on the itinerant preachers as an order of men so far above the arts of deception, prevarication, and falsehood, that it would lessen, if it would not destroy the comforts of the religion they profess, were they to contemplate the itinerant preachers in any other light than as little angels. We do not, therefore, address our remarks to the travelling ministers, or to the members of the church; but to ministers and members of other churches, and to high-minded and honorable men who are not members of any religious denomination, not doubting but every lover of truth will concur with us in the view we take of the subject.

The government of the church is a fraud, first, in that it is represented that Mr. Wesley "counselled," and "recommended" the episcopal form of government for the American societies — and secondly, that he ordained Dr. Coke a bishop, and directed him to ordain Mr. Asbury to the same high and holy office for these societies. The fraud then is two-fold — first that Mr. Wesley recommended the episcopal form of government for this "Independent Church" — and second, that he ordained Dr. Coke a bishop for this church. To prove the falsity of these statements, we will begin with their forming themselves into an "Independent Church."

1st. We deny that there is, or ever was, a line written by Mr. Wesley in which the "counsel" or "recommendation" was given to Dr. Coke, Mr. Asbury, or any other person, to form the Methodist societies in America, into "a separate body," or an Episcopal Church. If there be such a document, let it be produced. But we know there is none.

2nd. When the church was organized in 1784-5, the separation was ascribed to other "reasons" than to Mr. Wesley's "recommendation." It is distinctly stated that it was "because the Church of England to which we have been united, is deficient in several of the most important parts of Christian discipline, and that (a few ministers and members excepted) it has lost the life and power of religion. For these reasons, we have thought it our duty to form ourselves into an independent church."

3rd. The minutes of the annual conferences from 1773 to 1784 express the determination of the preachers and people to continue in connexion with Mr. Wesley and the English Methodists. The first question in the minutes of '73, is — "Ought not the authority of Mr. Wesley and the conference to extend to the preachers and people in America, as well as in Great Britain and Ireland? Ans. Yes."

Again, in the conference of 1780 it was asked, "shall we continue in close connexion with the church, and press our people to a closer communion with her? Ans. Yes."

4th. Mr. Asbury, and 12 or 13 preachers at Baltimore in 1780 expelled 27 preachers in Virginia because, in the preceeding year, the Virginia preachers ordained some of their own body, and had commenced administering the sacraments to the societies. This move, it was argued, was a separation from the church. "Ques. What must be the condition of our union with our Virginia brethren? Ans. To suspend all their administrations for one year, and all meet together in Baltimore."

5th. When the preachers in Virginia agreed to suspend the administration of the ordinances, Mr. Wesley was applied to for advice and assistance, and this application he does not fail to set forth as the ground-work of his proceedings, in his letter to Dr. Coke. He says — "Whereas, many of the people in the Southern provinces of North America, who desire to continue under my care, and still adhere to the doctrine and discipline of the Church of England, are greatly distressed for want of ministers to administer the sacraments of baptism and the Lord's supper, according to the usage of the same church; and whereas there does not appear to be any other way of supplying them with ministers, know all men, that I John Wesley &c." Now, how Dr. Coke could, with this letter in his pocket, form the Methodists societies into an "Independent Church," and intimate in his letter to Bishop White, that it was the work of Mr. Wesley in whole or in part, is beyond our comprehension — if he confined himself to the truth. But alas!

The promises and representations adverted to in the above letter from Dr. Coke, were made to Mr. Wesley in good faith, or they were intended to deceive him, and to induce him to grant them ordination. If they were made in sincerity and truth, why did the conference of 1784-5 become a separate body, the very moment they obtained ordination? Perhaps it will be said, as it has been said, " the changes in ecclesiastical and civil affairs produced by the revolution," obliged them to the measure. But this could not be; for those changes were past, and the Independence of the United States acknowledged, before Mr. Wesley ordained preachers for America. Those changes therefore, had no more to do with their becoming "a separate body," than they had to do with the division of the Methodist Episcopal Church, into the Church North, and the Church South, at the General Conference of 1844.

If they were not made in sincerity and truth, is it not obvious that those who made them did so to deceive Mr. Wesley and to induce him to ordain preachers for America, as without ordination they could not get along?

But what object could Dr. Coke have in view by forming the Methodists societies into an "Independent Church?" He wanted to be a bishop; and the present opportunity of rising to that dignified station, he thought was too favorable not to be improved. He had wheedled Mr. Wesley to ordain him and others, to serve the Americans, not so much for their sakes as for his own aggrandizement; and now he is in America, he wheedles the preachers to become an "Independent Church," and to adopt the government of a "*Moderate Episcopacy.*"

That Dr. Coke's object all along was to be a bishop, will be sufficiently proved hereafter. In the meantime it may be remarked, that in England, even under Mr. Wesley's nose, he was anxious that the Methodists should become "a separate body," an "Independent Church;" but in this he was defeated by Mr. Wesley's fixed determination to remain connected with that church as long as he lived. Dr. Whitehead says — "It has already been observed, that a party existed among the preachers, who wished the Methodists to be erected into an independent body, and a total separation to be made from the established church. One of this party was frequently about Mr. Wesley's person; and under various pretences sometimes led him into measures that offended the people, and embarrassed his affairs, while the true author lay concealed, as much as possible, behind the scene." And what means did he use to accomplish his plan? He suppressed the letter given him by Mr. Wesley as the testimonial of the office he was to fill, and the work he was to do: this letter he never suffered to see the light, nor did it, until after his death, when it was published by his executor, Mr. Drew. He destroyed the "little sketch" which Mr. Wesley tells us he drew up for the use of the societies, on the principle, "a dead man tells no tales." He mutilated the letter addressed "to Dr. Coke, Mr. Asbury, and our brethren in North America, dated Bristol, Sept. 10th, 1784," and gave only an "extract" from it. He violated the most sacred injunctions imposed on him by Mr. Wesley. "With respect to the title of bishop, I know that Mr. Wesley enjoined the Doctor and his associates, and *in the most solemn manner*, that it should not be taken. In a letter to Mrs. Gilbert, the widow of the excellent Nathaniel Gilbert, Esq., of Antigua, a copy of which now lies before me, he states this in the strongest manner. In this and in every deviation, I cannot be the apologist of Dr. Coke: and I can state in contradiction to all that Dr. Whitehead and Mr. Hampson have said, that Mr. Wesley never gave his sanction to any of these things; nor was he the author of one line of all that Dr. Coke published in America on this subject. His views on these points were very different from those of his zealous son in the gospel. He knew that a work of God neither needed, nor could be aided, nor could recommend itself to pious minds by such additions." Moore's Life of Wesley, Vol. 2. Pages 279-280.

Whilst these documents shew the manner episcopacy was foisted on the Methodist societies, it is humiliating to write on plate the picture they present — the picture of a man whose name stands on the records of the church, and on the page of history, as the first bishop of the Methodist Episcopal Church. Nor do we know a more exact parallel in the case of anyone, than in the case of Ananias. Acts 5:1-6.

NUMBER XIV.

Taking up the subject with which we closed our last letter, we must say we cannot conceive how any honest man can read the evidences of fraud which these letters contain, and differ from us in the opinion we have expressed respecting the organization of the government of the Methodist Episcopal Church. If there was no design on the part of Dr. Coke to depart from Mr. Wesley's instructions, why did he suppress one document entirely — mutilate a second — and destroy a third? He could not say he was ignorant of Mr. Wesley's designs: for the disposition he made of those documents is proof that he understood them well, and that they were adverse to his ambitious designs and projects. And besides the instructions which those papers contained, we are told by Rev. Henry Moore, Mr. Wesley's biographer, "that the doctor was enjoined *in the most solemn manner* not to take on him the title of bishop." And yet, notwithstanding the pains which Mr. Wesley took to set forth the nature of the office to which the doctor was appointed, and the extent of the authority with which he was invested, the very first thing he did was contrary to Mr. Wesley's instructions, by adopting episcopacy and imposing an Episcopal form of government on the Methodist societies in America, under the sanction of Mr. Wesley's name. That the doctor was bound by every principle of honor, of honesty, and of truth, to conform to Mr. Wesley's directions, in whose name, and by whose authority, he was acting, will be denied by none: nor do we think any disinterested person will be found, who will offer an apology or excuse for the Doctor's violating the sacred vows and promises he made Mr. Wesley when he appointed him to serve the societies in the United States as his representative. With some propriety then may his conduct be compared with that of Ananias, whose history is recorded in the Acts of the apostles.

Were some of the early Christians in distress, and did they stand in need of assistance from the Christians? So were the Methodist societies in America at the close of the Revolutionary War: they were in want of ministers to administer the sacraments of baptism and the Lord's supper, and they applied to Mr. Wesley for assistance. The early Christians "were of one heart and of one soul, neither was there among them any that lacked; for as many as were possessors of lands or houses sold them, and brought the prices of the things that were sold, and laid them down at the apostle's feet." Mr. Wesley assisted the Methodist societies in America with men and money. "Richard Boardman and Joseph Philmore landed in Philadelphia in the latter part of 1769; and brought with them a present of £50 sterling, as a donation to the society of New York, from Mr. Wesley." "When Mr. Asbury offered himself a missionary, some of the preachers objected to him, but as no other could be had, he was accepted. Many of Mr. Asbury's acquaintances *were struck with wonder[4]* when they heard that Mr. Wesley received him. Some whose prospects in life were as gloomy as Mr. Asbury's, wished their situation would allow them to go with him.

---

[4] See Arminian Magazine, vol. i. p. 185.

That his prospects in life were gloomy indeed will appear from this one fact — when he came to Bristol to take shipping for America, *he had not one penny in his pocket*. However, Mr Wesley's friends supplied him with clothes and ten pounds sterling. The expenses of the voyage were no doubt paid out of Mr. Wesley's pocket." "Therefore, I naturally care for you all, in a manner no other person can do. Therefore I, in a measure, provide for you all: for the supplies which Dr. Coke provides for you he could not provide, were it not for me — were it not, that I not only permit him to collect, but support him in so doing."

"But a certain man named Ananias with Sapphira his wife, sold a possession and kept back part of the price, his wife being privy to it, and brought a certain part and laid it at the apostle's feet." Dr. Coke withheld, mutilated, and destroyed documents that were given him by Mr. Wesley, laying only "a part at the feet" of the conference — imposed on the societies an Episcopal form of government — and then said it was done by Mr. Wesley's "counsel," and in compliance with his "recommendation!!" "But Peter said, Ananias, why hath satan filled thine heart to lie to the Holy Ghost? Thou hast not lied unto men, but unto God." This language may be pronounced by some other aspirant as *"too severe"* — too coarse, too vulgar, or not sufficiently refined for modern ears. But as it is the language of inspiration, used to point out a detestable crime, we shall make no apology for applying it to those who originated and would defend this abominable fraud. "And Ananias hearing these words fell down and gave up the ghost." ... "Then fell she down straightway at his feet, and yielded up the ghost: and the young men came in and found her dead, and carrying her forth buried her by her husband." Now is it not a most awful reflection, that the two men who stand out on the pages of Methodist history as the most prominent in originating and defending this ecclesiastical fraud, should both die suddenly and without any apparent cause: and if a coroner's inquest had been held over both, the verdict in each case probably would have been — *came to his death by a visitation of God*. Let sycophants and aspirants beware.

But there is another matter which will prove that the Doctor's proceedings were *unfair*. On the 3rd November, 1784, he landed in New York. "The intelligence of his arrival soon brought to the house the travelling preachers stationed in that city. To him Dr. Coke unfolded the plan which Mr. Wesley had adopted for the regulation and government of *his societies in America.*" Will the reader bear this in mind — "*his societies,*" and yet the first thing that was done, was to form themselves into "a separate body" — an "independent church." But to go on with the extract — "And it was no small consolation to him to learn that the plan met his entire approbation; and so confident was he of Mr. Asbury's concurrence, that he advised him immediately to make it public throughout all the societies, being fully assured that the name of Mr. Wesley would impart a degree of sanction to the measure, which would disarm resistance, even if any were to be apprehended. *But that nothing might be done precipitately, Dr. Coke declined carrying the advice into execution, until he had seen Mr. Asbury, to whom he had a particular message, although they were personally unknown to each other, that they might act in concert, and take no step that should not be the result of calm deliberation* — Drew's Life of Coke, p. 90.[5]

Now there is no evidence in the above extract that Dr. Coke showed Mr. Dickins his "letters of episcopal authority" as they have been called — the "little sketch" which Mr. Wesley says he "drew up," nor indeed any other document; it only says, the Doctor "unfolded his plan." The Doctor next pushed on to Philadelphia, stated his plan to the society there, not however for their approval, for with that they had nothing to do, but as a thing, he said, which he was authorized to carry out, and then hurried to meet Mr. Asbury. "On the 14th" of the same month, he met Mr. Asbury and about fifteen of the preachers at a quarterly meeting held in Barrett's chapel, Kent county, state of Delaware." — Cooper, p. 104. "On leaving the chapel, they repaired together to the house of a hospitable friend." — Drew's Life of Coke, p. 92. And Rev. Jesse Lee, in his history of Methodism, says, p. 98, "The Doctor and Mr. Asbury retired together to consult about the plan." Now, why should these two gentlemen leave the preachers and retire into a secret chamber "to consult about the plan," if they were acting according to the instructions of Mr. Wesley? Their conduct in this

---

[5] The italicizing is mine.

particular may justly be deemed *suspicious,* if it be not emphatically *a deed of darkness;* for here, no doubt, was hatched that form of church government which both of those gentlemen were anxious to see established; and that it might be received the more cordially, it was represented as having originated with Mr. Wesley himself. In confirmation of these views the reader will recollect, that Dr. Whitehead has set forth the efforts that were made by Dr. Coke to induce Mr. Wesley to separate from the Church of England, and for the Methodists to become an independent body. Having, however, failed in his scheme there — ("in Europe, where some steps had been taken, tending to a separation, all is at an end, Mr. Wesley is a determined enemy to it." See the Doctor's letter to Bishop White.) A fine opportunity presents itself on this side the Atlantic to his ambitious and aspiring mind to become a bishop, if he can only manage the documents committed to him by Mr. Wesley. Well, he withholds one — mutilates another — and "burns" a third. The Doctor, in his letter to Bishop White, which shall be given hereafter, says — "You, I believe, are conscious that I was brought up in the Church of England, and have been ordained, a presbyter of that church. For many years I was prejudiced, even to bigotry, in favor of it." Nor was his attachment to episcopacy and the Church of England greater than was Mr. Asbury's.

1. Mr. Asbury was brought up in the Church of England, and was strongly prepossessed in favor of all her forms and *orders.*

2. Mr. Drew, in his account of the schism which took place among the preachers in this country in 1778, respecting the ordinances, says: "Mr. Asbury on hearing their statement and request, found himself in an unpleasant situation. *From principle* he was strongly attached to the episcopacy which had been abolished." [Drew's Life of Coke, p. 60.] And on the next page, he says: "Mr. Asbury, in the mean while, who had not yet shaken off the rusty fetters of *Apostolical succession,* found himself comparatively deserted by those whose respect for him still remained undiminished."

3. Dr. Coke and Moore, in their life of Wesley, express themselves thus: — "Mr. Asbury's attachment to the *Church of England,* was at this time (in 1778) *exceedingly strong.*" p. 350.

4. Mr. Asbury himself, says: — "I read and *transcribed* some

of Potter's church government; and must *prefer* the Episcopal mode of church government to the Presbyterian." Journals, vol. I. p. 285. And on the next page, he says, "I read and *transcribed* some of Potter's church government till ten o'clock." From the circumstance of his transcribing parts of this work "till ten o'clock," it may be inferred, that Arch-bishop Potter was a great favorite with Mr. Asbury; and yet no writer more strenuously defends *apostolical succession* — the *divine right* of the priesthood — and a *third order* of ministers, than does Arch-bishop Potter.

There is another thing that claims particular attention here, as it has been frequently asserted that Mr. Asbury was elected by the Conference of 1784-5, to the office of a bishop. Indeed, it is upon this asserted election that Dr. Durbin built his argument, that a bishop in the Methodist Episcopal Church is nothing more than an officer of the General Conference, and may be removed from office by a vote of the majority without impeachment, or trial. Now, if Mr. Asbury submitted to an election before he would be ordained, was it that the General Conference might thus easily get rid of him hereafter, whenever they chose? Let his views of episcopacy, as given above, answer that question. True it is, Mr. Ezekiel Cooper, in the funeral sermon which he published on the death of Mr. Asbury says, and the same thing may have been said by others for what we know — "that Mr. Asbury would not be ordained unless he was chosen by vote, or the voice of the conference." p. 108. Admitting the truth of this statement for the sake of argument, it does not invalidate what has been said heretofore, denying the election of Dr. Coke and Mr. Asbury, to the office of superintendent, according to the universal meaning of the term to *elect*. Dr. Coke was ordained, consecrated, or invested with authority by Mr. Wesley *before* he left England, and he was never elected to the office of superintendent or bishop, by the Conference of 1784, or by any other: and Mr. Asbury was "appointed" by Mr. Wesley, and his name was inserted in the letter addressed "to Dr. Coke, Mr. Asbury, and our brethren in North America," as *& joint-superintendent* with Dr. Coke, at the very time the Doctor received his "letters of Episcopal authority." Now, will any one tell us why did Mr. Asbury take a stand that would give room to infer there was some *dark design* at the bottom of this movement? Why did he require "a vote" to be taken before he would receive ordination, a thing which he knew the societies wanted, which they had frequently solicited Mr. Wesley to confer, and which he was conscious was the desire of his heart for many years? There must have been some very weighty reason for his objection. What was it? Was it because "being from principle so strongly attached to the episcopacy of the Church of England which had been abolished here, he dreaded to countenance any mode of conduct that might seem to interfere with its formerly acknowledged authority"? True, such a consideration might have operated on the mind of a *high church* man, and lead him to conclude, that an ordination by presbyters could not raise a man to a higher order in the church of Christ than themselves, and that therefore the *episcopal* ordination of Mr. Wesley was insufficient for the purpose. But how a vote of the Conference could remedy this matter, we cannot conceive. Or, was it because Mr. Asbury was so much of a republican, and had for a number of years been so much in the habit of respecting the rights of the members of the church in general, and the rights of the travelling preachers in particular, that he could not allow himself to step into any office to which he was "appointed" by Mr. Wesley, without having first obtained "a vote" of those who were to be under his authority? Let his history from the day he landed on the shores of America to the day of his death, serve as an answer to this question. Or was it because, at every period of his life, he was so averse to be clothed with power and authority, that he thought "a vote" of the conference might happily relieve him from the tremendous responsibilities which attach to the episcopal office, though appointed to that office by Mr. Wesley himself? Nothing of all this. There was but one reason for this unparalleled objection — to be independent of Mr. Wesley, and set his authority at defiance. Or to give the reason in Mr. Asbury's own words; "Mr. Wesley and I are like Caesar and Pompey; he will bear no equal, and I will bear no superior." To men who can justify a violation of sacred and oft repeated promises — who can advocate the most flagrant act of injustice to Mr. Wesley, the father and founder of Methodism; and who can commend the basest ingratitude, we give Mr. Asbury's election to the episcopacy by the Conference of 1784, to make of it all that they possibly can towards their own elevation.

NUMBER XV.

The "plan," by which the Methodist societies in America were to be governed in future, having been settled by Dr. Coke and Mr. Asbury in a private apartment, to which these gentlemen had retired after the public services were over, it was agreed on that a conference of all the preachers in full connection should be called, to meet in the city of Baltimore on the following Christmas, to take the "plan" into consideration. Intelligence of this meeting was accordingly sent off to every part of the work; Mr. Freeborn Garrettson being appointed to go through Maryland and Virginia, to give information to the preachers in the South and in the West.

"On Christmas eve the preachers met in the city of Baltimore, according to previous appointment, to begin their conference, at which nearly sixty were present: but the whole number at that time in the connection on the continent amounted to eighty-one. In this assembly the plans advised by Mr. Wesley, and now committed to their care for execution, were fully unfolded; and, under existing circumstances, their general principles received unanimous approbation. On the 27th of December, Dr. Coke, agreeably to the letter he had received from Mr. Wesley, prior to his departure from Bristol, proceeded to impart to Mr. Asbury that branch of the office to which he was designated." — Drew's Life of Dr. Coke, p. 95.

Let us here make a few remarks on this extract:

1. E. Cooper says: — "The Conference met the 27th of December, 1784, and continued their deliberations and sittings until sometime in January, 1785. — Cooper on Asbury, p. 108.

W. Waters says — "25th December, 1784: We became instead of a religious society, a separate church, under the name of Methodist Episcopal Church." — Memoirs, p. 102.

I. Emory says — "The General Conference of 1784, commenced its session on the 25th of December, and closed on the 1st of January, 1785." — Defense, &c., p. 42. So contradictory are the accounts of some of the "standard" writers on Methodism.

2. The conference met in the church in Light street. Did it hold its session in *secret*, or were the members of society permitted to be present as spectators — for no layman was ever yet allowed to partake in the deliberations, either of an annual, or general confer-

ence? We have never seen any document which would justify us in saying the sittings and deliberations of that conference were conducted with open doors. And here it may not be amiss to call the attention of the reader to the subject of *secrecy*, which has marked the origin and progress of the Methodist Episcopacy; as if it was a thing which could not bear the light. Mr. Charles Wesley complained bitterly of the *secrecy* practiced by his brother John, in the ordination of Dr. Coke. This ceremony took place in a private chamber at Bristol, without Mr. C. Wesley's knowledge, although he "was at his brother's elbow at the time!" And Dr. Coke improving on the manner of his own ordination, "first opened the design of organizing Methodists in America into an independent Episcopal church to Mr. Asbury," and all we know of what Mr. Asbury thought of the communication is what he tells us himself — "If the preachers unanimously choose me, I shall not act in the capacity I have hitherto done by Mr. Wesley's appointment." — Jounals, vol. I. p. 376. This explains the reason why Mr. Asbury so readily concurred in the societies becoming an "independent church;" he had no idea of acting in a subordinate station — "Pompey would bear no superior."

3. Mr. Drew says above — "In this assembly the plans devised by Mr. Wesley, and now committed to their care for execution, were fully developed." We cannot think so. The plans developed at this conference were none of Mr. Wesley's, but originated with Dr. Coke, and had the concurrence of Mr. Asbury. Mr. Drew compiled his "life of Coke" from the doctor's papers, and no doubt believed the statement he has here made. But we know better: for the "*little sketch*" which Mr. Wesley says he "*drew up*" for the societies, was destroyed, and forged minutes were published in the place of the real minutes of conference which were taken at the time.

4. Neither local preachers nor laymen had any voice in the deliberations of this assembly, either personally or by representative. And this is such an incredible thing, that it requires to be repeated over and over again. A strange world this is! That Americans who have endured a seven years war, *fighting for liberty* — who had expended a vast amount of treasure in carrying on the contest, who had shed their blood like water in the struggle with Great Britain,

and who had just thrown off the authority of King George III., should, in some two or three years thereafter, tamely submit to be governed in ecclesiastical matters by a semi-pauper, who, when he came to Bristol a few years before, to take passage to America, *"had not a penny in his pocket."* Can there be found a parallel to this in the history of the world? We think not. And yet it is a positive and undeniable fact, that none but travelling preachers have had any thing to do with the organization of the Methodist Episcopal Church; nor to the present moment have either local preachers or laymen a voice in either an annual or general conference!!! Americans, be consistent. Attend no more mass- meetings to give utterance to your sympathies for the oppressed Hungarians: but as members of the Methodist Episcopal church, *resolve* that you will no longer submit to be governed by rules, in the forming of which you have no voice, personally or by representative; for as the matter stands at present, you are the veriest slave on the face of the earth.

5. Our astonishment at this submission rises when we contemplate the number and qualifications of those who composed this conference. A list of the names of the members now lies before me; but whether it is correct or not, we have no means of ascertaining. Instead, therefore, of transcribing their names, we shall give the number of those who are marked as being present, and the years they were in the travelling connection, when the conference met. Dr. Coke says, "about sixty were present, and most of these were young men." Drew says above — "nearly sixty were present."

Of these, *One* had travelled 10 years — *Three*, 9 years — *Three*, 8 years — *Eight*, 7 years — *Four*, 6 years — *Six*, five years — *Eight*, 4 years — *Thirteen*, 3 years — *Eight*, 2 years — and *Eleven*, 1 year. According to this list we have 65 present,[6] *forty* of whom had travelled under four years!!! So then, about *two-thirds* of this first conference had not the experience of five years travel; and perhaps some of them could not give out a stanza of a hymn in a congregation, without spelling some of the words. And these are the men who laid the foundation of an ecclesiastical es-

---

[6] Besides Coke, Asbury, Whatcoat, and Vasey.

tablishment that has affected the fate of thousands, and may perhaps yet affect the Union of our country. Hurl it, hurl it, to the moles and the bats, and let it sink into the category of things that *were*.

6. The last thing we shall notice in this paragraph, is the ordination of Mr. Asbury. But whether he was ordained deacon, elder, and superintendent in one day, or in three consecutive days, we have no means of determining. The only thing we can say positively is, that he was ordained a superintendent, not *bishop* — because he says himself, "I was ordained a superintendent, as my parchments will prove." Let us suppose that he was ordained a deacon the first day, by which office he was authorized to perform the rights of marriage and baptism in the absence of Dr. Coke, Mr. Whatcoat and Mr. Vasey, and to assist them in the administration of the Lord's supper. He professed himself inwardly moved by the Holy Ghost, to take upon himself this office, and promised due obedience with a glad heart and willing mind to the godly admonitions of these gentlemen. He also promised before high Heaven, that "he would gladly and willingly search for the sick, poor, and impotent, that they may be visited and relieved;" and yet none of these things were ever done. Now we think it is a very solemn thing to make such promises in the name of the Holy Ghost. Pshaw, you fool, says one, all this is only matter of form. Well, the next day he is advanced another step higher, and was ordained an elder. He now shakes off the authority of Mr. Whatcoat and Mr. Vasey, being their equal; but bound himself a second time "to follow the godly admonitions, and submit to the godly judgment of Dr. Coke. Here again there is no duty done, although it is affirmed that the Holy Ghost had moved him to perform the duties of an elder. The third day comes, and Messrs. Whatcoat and Vasey present this godly man to Dr. Coke to be ordained a superintendent. Again he professes to be moved by the Holy Ghost, is ordained a superintendent or bishop, throws off the authority of Dr. Coke, and is advanced to the *ne plus ultra* of his ardent wishes. Respecting the ordination of Dr. Coke, Mr. C. Wesley said:

"So easily are Bishop's made,
By man's or woman's whim;
Wesley his hands on Coke hath laid,

But he laid hands on him."

Respecting Mr. Asbury's ordination, the same writer said:

A Roman emperor 'tis said,
His favorite horse a consul made;
But Coke brings greater things to pass,
He makes a bishop of an ass."

As might be expected on an occasion so important, a consecration sermon was preached by Dr. Coke — the first part of which was the vindication of the conduct of the Methodists in becoming a "separate body" — an "independent church" of an Episcopal character, and of their assuming the right to ordain. Several reasons then advanced, have been given in a former letter, taken from Whitehead's Life of Wesley.

We will now give a letter which Mr. Wesley addressed to the Methodists in America, as publish in the minutes of 1784-5.

"BRISTOL, Sept. 10th, 1784.

"To Dr. Coke, Mr. Asbury, and our Brethren in North America:

"1. By a very uncommon train of providences, many of the provinces of North America are totally disjoined from the British empire, and erected into Independent States. The English government has no authority over them either civil or ecclesiastical, any more than over the States of Holland. A civil authority is exercised over them, partly by the Congress, partly by the State Assemblies. But no one either exercises or claims any ecclesiastical authority at all. In this peculiar situation some thousands of the inhabitants of these States desire my advice; and in compliance with their desire I have drawn up a little sketch.

2. Lord King's account of the primitive church convinced me many years ago, that bishops and presbyters are the same order, and consequently, have the same right to ordain. For many years I have been importuned from time to time, to exercise this right, by ordaining part of our travelling preachers. But I have still refused, not only for peace sake, but because I was determined as little as possible to violate the established order of the national church to which I belonged.

3. But the case is widely different between England and North America. Here, there are bishops who have a legal jurisdiction. In America there are none, and but a few parish ministers. So that for

some hundred miles together there is none either to baptize, or to administer the Lord's supper. Here, therfore, my scruples are at an end: and I conceive myself at full liberty, as I violate no order and invade no man's right, by appointing and sending laborers into the harvest.

4. I have accordingly appointed Dr. Coke and Mr. Francis Asbury joint superintendents,[7] over our brethren in North America. As also, RICHARD WHATCOAT and THOMAS VASEY to act as *elders* among them by baptizing and administering the Lord's supper.

5. If any one will point out a more rational and scriptural way of feeding and guiding those poor sheep in the wilderness, I will gladly embrace it. At present I cannot see any better method than that I have taken.

6. It has indeed been proposed, to desire the English bishops to ordain part of our preachers for America. But to this I object, — 1. I desired the Bishop of London to ordain one only; but I could not prevail. 2. If they consented, we know the slowness of their proceedings; but the matter admits of no delay. 3. If they would ordain them *now*, they would likewise expect to govern them. And how grievously would this entangle us? 4. As our American brethren are now totally disentangled both from the State and from the English hierarchy, we dare not entangle them again, either with the one or the other. They are now at full liberty, simply to follow the Scriptures and the primitive church. And we judge it best that they should stand fast in that liberty, wherewith God has so strangely made them free. JOHN WESLEY."

NUMBER XVI.

As the point at which we have arrived is of great importance in the history of the fraud that has been perpetrated in organizing the Methodist Episcopal Church, it is highly proper that we should place the particulars clearly and distinctly before the reader, although in so doing, we may subject ourselves to the charge of repetition. Our first enquiry, then, relates to the state of the societies when Mr. Wesley was applied to for his advice and assistance.

---

[7] "As the translators of our version of the Bible have used the English word Bishop instead of *Superintendent,* it has been thought by us, that it would appear more scriptural to adopt their term Bishop."

1. The Methodist Societies in America, before and at the close of the revolutionary war, were very much distressed for want of ministers to administer the sacraments, "so that for some hundreds of miles together," says Mr. Wesley, "there is none either to baptize or to administer the Lord's supper." In this state of destitution it certainly was the duty of the societies to take all proper steps to obtain the ordinances; and Mr. Wesley was the person of all others, to whom application should be made. — 1. On account of his age and experience. — 2. On account of his knowledge and piety. — 3. On account of the relation he sustained to the societies, being the father to the whole Methodist family in Europe and America.

2nd. Let us next consider the representations that were made and the promises that were given him, when he was solicited to ordain preachers for America. These we have in the letter of "episcopal authority," as it has been called, which was delivered to Dr. Coke, at the time he was created a superintendent. It says — "Whereas many of the people in the Southern provinces of North America, *who desire to continue under my care*, and still adhere to the doctrines and discipline of the Church of England, are greatly distressed for want of ministers to administer the sacraments of baptism and the Lord's supper, according to the usage of the same church: and whereas there does not appear to be any other way of supplying them with ministers, — Know all men, that I, John Wesley, think myself to be providentially called at this time to set apart some persons for the work of the ministry in America, &c." Language cannot be more plain and explicit than is the language of this letter of authority, delivered to Dr. Coke, viz.: that those who applied to Mr. Wesley for assistance (and perhaps the urgent and repeated applications were made by Mr. Asbury, who stood at the head of the American societies,) assured him in their communications that they *"desired to continue under hie care"* and yet the first thing that Dr. Coke and Mr. Asbury did, when the conference met in Baltimore, was "to form the societies into a separate body" and to become "an independent church." What perfidy!! Now, we ask, where is the difference in *principle* between obtaining goods under fraudulent pretences, and obtaining ordination under such false assurances? In the former case we know what punishment follows such mercantile transactions; we would like to know what punishment should follow such *sacred* duplicity and falsehood? By all honorable men we know such conduct will be considered infamous; and yet there have been found some in the church who would write a "defense" of the parties concerned, and the church in turn has elevated the writer to the highest ecclesiastical distinction for his "masterly performance." The turpitude of the ungateful return made Mr. Wesley, assumes a deeper tinge when we reflect that the document which contains the above assurances was Dr. Coke's letter of ordination, and that this letter was withheld and never suffered to see the light; but instead of the developments it contains, the first section of the first chapter of the book of discipline has been published as a full and true account of the origin of the church.

3rd. "In this peculiar situation," says Mr. Wesley, "some thousands of the inhabitants of these States desire my advice; and in compliance with their desire, I have drawn up a "little sketch." Can the ingenuity of man twist, torture, or make these words bear any other meaning than this plain and obvious one, namely, that Mr. Wesley did "draw up a little sketch" in compliance with the wishes of those who applied to him for advice? Well, where is this "little sketch?" Who ever saw it? What was the nature of its contents? and what has become of it? We said in a former letter that this "little sketch" was destroyed, on the principle that *"dead men tell no tales;"* and we now say we have no doubt, that if it was brought across the Atlantic, one or the other, or both, Dr. Coke and Mr. Asbury, destroyed it, because it stood in the way of their ambitious designs. Had it been in favor of the episcopacy which they were anxious to establish, can any one suppose it would have been destroyed? Never! What an outrage then on the confidence of private friendship, and on official obligation. Mr. Wesley committed this document to the care of Dr. Coke, as one man would deliver an important letter to the care of another, to be delivered to the writer's friend, and Dr. Coke destroyed it! And this the morality of Methodist Episcopacy! If so, it requires the aid of a lawyer to defend it. If this is the way that some gentlemen would dispose of letters committed to their care, we would fear for the safe delivery of one if it covered a ten dollar bill. But apart from the duty of private friendship, there was an official obligation on Dr. Coke to submit this "little sketch" to the preachers in conference. Mr. Wesley gave him a letter of authority for himself; and likewise this "little sketch" containing his advice to the societies. Now we insist on it, Dr. Coke was bound by every principle of truth, of honor, and of official duty, to place this document, which was drawn up for the societies, before the preachers when they met in Baltimore. But instead of that, it was destroyed.

This declaration of Mr. Wesley, that he had "drawn up a little sketch," sadly perplexed "our beloved Emory," when he was writing his "Defense of our Fathers." He did not dare to contradict what Mr. Wesley says, for that would be to give him the lie — though that is a thing he was not backward to do in several places in his work — and to pass it over unnoticed he knew would not do; — he therefore disposed of it in the following manner.

"Dr. Coke's letters of ordination" (here "our beloved" is wrong, there was but *one* letter of ordination) "as a superintendent, were dated Sept. 2, 1784. Mr. Wesley's preface to the first edition of his abridgment of the prayer book was dated Sept. 9, 1784, and his letter "to Dr. Coke, Mr. Asbury, and our brethren in North America," bore date Sept. 10, of the same year. These documents, therefore, so nearly synchronous, are to be regarded, with the prayer book, as parts of one whole; and as constituting together the "little sketch" which Mr. Wesley says he had drawn up in compliance with the desire of some thousands of the inhabitants of these States. — "Defense of our Fathers," p. 37. We have made this extract as a *literary curiosity,* to show the ingenuity of the lawyer, and the inviolable adherence to truth in the Doctor of Divinity. Any man who can swallow this monstrous pill of absurdity may do it. Can Dr. Durbin?

4th. The letter of Sept. 10, 1784, addressed "to Dr. Coke, Mr. Asbury, and our brethren in North America," was *mutilated,* and only an "extract" of it was given in the minutes of 1784-5. The letter is inserted entire in the *British minutes* of 1785, in Whitehead's Life of Wesley, and in Drew's Life of Dr. Coke, and is the same in all. — In the American minutes, the paragraphs are numbered, and the part that was expunged belongs to the *fourth* paragraph. We will now give that paragraph entire, as it stands in the above-named works, which we carefully collated, placing all that was expunged in italics: — 4. "I have accordingly appointed Dr. Coke and Mr. Asbury to be joint superintendents over our brethren in North America: as also Richard Whatcoat and Thomas Vasey to act as Elders among them, by baptizing and administering the Lord's supper. *And I have prepared a Liturgy, little differing from that of the Church of England, (I think the best constituted national church in the world) which I advise all the travelling preachers to use on the Lord's day, in all the congregations, reading the Litany only on Wednesdays and Fridays, and praying extempore on all other days. I also advise the elders to administer the supper of the Lord on the Lord's day.*" It is not necessary for us to enquire *why* was this letter mutilated, and only an "extract" of it given to the societies. Those who mutilated it had some object in view which it is altogether useless for us to conjecture. All we have to do with, is the fact of its being mutilated, and this fact is fully established. Now when we reflect that this letter was mutilated, — Dr. Coke's letter of ordination was kept back and was never suffered to see the light — the "little sketch" was destroyed — and forged minutes were published in the room of the genuine ones — we are constrained to declare we believe such another system of falsehood, deception, and fraud, in the organizing of an ecclesiastical establishment, is not to be found on the face of the earth, no, not even in the church of Rome.

5th. Mr. Wesley says — "Whereas many of the people in the Southern provinces of North America who desire to continue under my care, and still to adhere to the doctrine and discipline of the Church of England, are greatly distressed for want of ministers to administer the sacraments of baptism and the Lord's supper, according to the usage of the same church." From this extract it is plain, that the applicants assured Mr. Wesley, that it was their "*desire to adhere to the doctrines of the Church of England, and to have the sacraments administered according to the usage of the same church.*" Now let it be distinctly noticed, that this proposition came from those on this side of the Atlantic, not from Mr. Wesley — that it originated with them, not with him — and that it was in compliance with their urgent and repeated solicitations he undertook to assist them in their distress. He accordingly prepared a liturgy for them, little differing from that of the Church of England, which he advised the preachers to use, agreeably to the directions given above. In doing this Mr. Wesley could not suppose that these representations and assurances were made to induce him to do a thing, which those who made them might ultimately use to promote their own ambitious designs; nor do we say they were made for such purposes. But we do say, that it is a very extraordinary circumstance, that this prayer book, which was prepared in compliance with the above representations and assurances, should be laid aside almost as soon as ordination was obtained; and although thus rejected, that it should be used as an argument to prove that the government of the Methodist Episcopal Church was instituted in conformity with Mr. Wesley's "counsel" and "recommendation." Nor is this all. This same rejected prayer book has latterly been brought forward to prove that Mr. Wesley designed that the Methodist Episcopal Church should have *three orders* or ministers, (although every one knows that Mr. Wesley believed there were but *two orders*,) and that she has *three orders*, Bishops, Elders, and Deacons, a doctrine which Mr. Wesley did not hold. When a good man is dealing with professors of religion, or who are men of honor and veracity, he is more apt to be off his guard than when he is dealing with men of a different character. If this good man should be overreached in the transaction, how detestable to see those in whom he had confided, and by whom he was deceived, chuckling over the advantage they had gained over their easy and unsuspecting victim. And yet how apt are such to triumph, and turn the advantage against their dupe. Mr. Wesley lived long enough after the occurrences which we are here recording to regret the steps he had taken in the matter of ordination; and although Dr. Coke has been pronounced by Rev. Henry Moore unworthy of credit, we will give part of a sentence in his letter to Bishop White — "*He went farther, I am sure, than he would have gone, if he had foreseen some events which followed.*

And this I am certain of — *that he is now sorry for the separation.*" And the Rev. James Creighton, in reply to Mr. Samuel Bradburn, says — "I must take the liberty positively to contradict you. He did repent of it, (ordination) and with *tears* in his eyes expressed his sorrow both in public and private." Again he says — "He likewise expressed his sorrow respecting this matter at Leeds conference, in 1789, and occasionally afterwards in London, until his death." — p. 18. Poor Mr. Wesley!!

To prove that the prayer book had no connection with the originating of the form of government for the Methodist societies in America, we will give extracts from letters of three gentlemen who were members of the conference of 1784-5.

Extract of a letter dated

> "BRUNSWICK, 26th Sept. 1828.
>
> I do not recollect that there was any proposition for our receiving the prayer book and episcopacy connected. And it is certain the preachers never considered themselves obliged to conform to the prayer book, for they did not make use of it on Wednesdays and Fridays *as recommended.*
>
> Yours very sincerely,
> Edward Dromgoole, Sen."

Extract of a letter from Rev. Thomas Ware, dated

> "SALEM, Dec. 1, 1828.
>
> Dr. Coke was in favor of taking the name of Methodist Episcopal Church; argued the plan of general superintendency was in fact a species of episcopacy, but did not, I think, bring the prayer book into view. THOMAS WARE.

The following is from Rev. Jonathan Forrest:

"As for what Mr. Emory has said in the "Defense of our Fathers" respecting the recommendation of the prayer book abridged by Mr. Wesley, being a recommendation of the Episcopal form of church government for the American Methodist societies, I did not consider it in that light at the conference of 1784. Nor have I considered it in that light at any time since. Nor do I consider it in that light now. Nor do I believe it was so considered by any person in the conference of 1784.

Jonathan Forrest."

NUMBER XVII.

Up to this date, we have sent you sixteen sheets of *"cap"* paper closely written and full to overflowing with matter relating to the state and condition of the early Methodist societies in America; and notwithstanding all that has been said on these subjects, we have not advanced one step beyond the year 1784; the year in which those societies were formed into an *independent Episcopal Church.* This period we will call the first period of American Methodism; and the principal points which properly belong to it, and of which we have treated in the preceding letters, are: — the destitution and distress of the societies, both before and during the revolutionary war, for the want of the sacraments of baptism and the Lord's supper; the means by which Mr. Asbury arrived at the possession of absolute power, by which he, assisted by a few tory preachers, expelled twenty-seven preachers in Virginia, because they had taken measures to have the ordinances; the frequent applications that were made to Mr. Wesley to send over ordained ministers; the promises and assurances that were made him that the societies desired "to continue under his care, and still to adhere to the doctrine and discipline of the Church of England," and to have the sacraments administered "according to the usage of the same church;" the part Dr. Coke took to induce Mr. Wesley to ordain him and others to come to the United States; and the means he, in conjunction with Mr. Asbury, used to fix on the societies an episcopal form of government under the sanction of Mr. Wesley's name, viz: by suppressing the letter of authority given to Dr. Coke, signifying the office to which he was appointed; by destroying the "little sketch," which Mr. Wesley assures us he drew up in compliance with "the desire of some thousands" — by mutilating the circular letter of Sept. 10, 1784, addressed "to Dr. Coke, Mr. Asbury, and our brethren in North America" — and by forging and publishing a document purporting to be the minutes of the conference of 1784, in the place of the true and genuine ones of that year. By these means were the preachers who composed that conference kept in the dark, and in confirmation of this statement we will present an extract of a letter from one who was a member of that body. He says — "I am fully persuaded the preachers in 1784 believed they were acting in accordance with the will of Mr. Wesley, when they adopted the episcopal form, or *the plan of general superintendency.* Dr. Coke was in favor of taking the name of

Methodist Episcopal Church; argued, the plan of general superintendency was in fact a species of episcopacy, but did not, I think, bring the prayer-book into view."

Not only were the preachers who composed that conference deceived by these means, but great pains have been taken from that time to the present, to impress the societies and the public with the belief that all that was done by that conference was done agreeably to the express directions of Mr. Wesley. The bishops, to the present day, have represented and affirmed, that all that was done at the conference of '84 in the way of forming the societies into an Episcopal Church, originated with Mr. Wesley, was "recommended" by him, and when completed had his entire approbation, than which nothing can be farther from the truth. And to give an air of plausibility to this scheme of imposition, two facts have been adduced, and on these facts, twisted and perverted as they have been, do the advocates of the hierarchy rely to sustain their position: *First*, that Mr. Wesley, by setting apart Dr. Coke a superintendent, intended to ordain him a *bishop*, as the Doctor, before the performance of the ceremony, was a presbyter of the Church of England. And *second*, that Mr. Wesley abridged the prayer-book of that church, and sent it over for the use of the societies. Let us examine each of these facts. To determine the weight of the first argument, it is necessary to ascertain in what light did Mr. Wesley consider a bishop at the time he set Dr. Coke apart for the office of a superintendent. Some ecclesiastical writers say, there are *three orders* of ministers in the church of Christ, *bishops*, *presbyters*, and *deacons*, and as this doctrine has been advanced by several writers in the Methodist Episcopal Church with reference to the ministers of their own denomination, the question is, in what light did Mr. Wesley consider a *bishop*, when he set Dr. Coke apart as a superintendent? Dip he consider a bishop a third order of ministers, distinct from, and superior to presbyters? He did not. For he says expressly, "Lord King's account of the primitive church convinced me many years ago, that bishops and presbyters are the same order." He could not, therefore, without the greatest duplicity and falsehood declare, that there were but *two orders*, if by setting Dr. Coke apart as a superintendent, he intended the American societies should have *three*.

But it may be asked, if Mr. Wesley did not intend to raise Dr. Coke to a third order, why did he lay his hand on him when he appointed him a superintendent? To this it may be answered.

1. The distressed situation of the American societies; their being destitute of the sacraments of baptism and the Lord's supper; and their repeated and pressing importunities that he would ordain and send over some of his preachers to administer the sacraments, were the reasons why Mr. Wesley ordained at all. These reasons are set out in the letter of authority which he gave Dr. Coke, and in the one addressed "To Dr. Coke, Mr. Asbury, and our brethren in North America, Sept. 10, 1784." In the former he says — "Whereas many of the people in the Southern Provinces of North America, who desire to continue under my care, and still adhere to the doctrine and discipline of the Church of England, are greatly distressed for the want of ministers to administer the sacraments of baptism and the Lord's supper." And in the latter he says — "In this peculiar situation some thousands of the inhabitants of these States desire my advice, and in compliance with their desire, I have drawn up a little sketch." Again, he says — "For many years I have been importuned from time to time to exercise this right by ordaining part of our travelling preachers. Here therefore my scruples are at an end, and I conceive myself at full liberty, as I violate no order and invade no man's right, by appointing and sending laborers into the harvest."

2nd. Mr. Wesley considered himself, under God, the father of all the Methodists in Europe and America. He considered that he had a right to govern those societies that had been raised by his instrumentality, or had put themselves "under his care." If he was in America he could superintend the societies himself; but as he was not; he considered it his prerogative to transfer the power of governing them to Dr. Coke, or any other person that he might appoint. This transfer of right is called by him an investing of the doctor with "fuller powers."

3. To overcome the opposition which the doctor apprehended he would have to encounter from Mr. Asbury, if he came to this country to superintend the societies without having first received authority so to do from Mr. Wesley, was offered by the doctor as a reason why he should receive this authority in a formal way, from

Mr. Wesley. He says — "The more maturely I consider the sub-ject, the more expedient it appears to me that the power of ordain-ing should be received by me from you, by the imposition of your hands. As the journey is long and you cannot spare me often, it is well to provide *against all events*, and an authority formally re-ceived from you will (I am certain of it) be fully *admitted by the people;* and my exercising the office of ordination without that for-mal authority may be disputed, if there be any opposition on any other account; I could therefore earnestly wish you would exercise that power in this instance. I may want all the influence in America which you can throw into my scale. Mr. Brackenburg informed me at Leeds that he saw a letter in London from Mr. Asbury, in which he observed, that *he would not receive any person deputed by you to take any part of the superintendency of the work invested in him*, or words evidently implying so much."

4. Dr. Coke did not believe that his being invested with author-ity to superintend the Methodists societies in America by the for-mal imposition of Mr. Wesley's hands was intended to raise, or did raise him to any higher rank or order in the ministry, than he was in before that ceremony was performed. For he tells us him self, in a letter he addressed to the General Conference of 1808, — "I am of our late venerable father, Mr. Wesley's opinion, that the order of bishops and presbyters is *one* and the *same*. From all I have ad-vanced, you may easily perceive, my dear brethren, that I do not consider the imposition of hands on the one hand, as essentially necessary for any office in the Church; nor do I, on the other hand, think that the repetition of the imposition of hands for the same of-fice, when important circumstances require it, is at all improper."

5. Nor did Mr. Wesley intend by the ceremony he performed at the time he invested Dr. Coke with authority to superintend the American societies, to raise the doctor to any higher rank or order the ministry than that of presbyter; for he did not believe there was any higher order in the church of Christ, bishop and presbyter be-ing, in his view, *one* and *the same order*. It is clear, then, that the nature and design of this ceremony was well understood by the doctor, and that he was conscious Mr. Wesley did not design by it to make him a bishop, distinct from, and superior to a presbyter. Mr. Wesley held no such doctrine — had no such design. Why

then did the doctor avail himself of every opportunity to represent himself a bishop? If we apply to him the remarks Mr. Wesley makes of himself, respecting the oath he took at his ordination, it will show the turpitude of Dr. Coke's conduct more fully. Mr. Wesley says — "The true sense of the words of on oath, and the mode and extent of its obligation, are not to be determined by him that takes it, but by him who requires it." — Moore's Life of Wesley, vol. I, p. 193. And besides, the doctor was enjoined not to take the title of bishop. Mr. Moore says — "With respect to the title of bishop, I know that Mr. Wesley enjoined the doctor and his associates, and in *the most solemn manner*, that it should not be taken." I contend then that knowing Mr. Wesley's sentiments, the doctor was under the most sacred obligations to regard them. That he was bound by every principle of honor, and of truth, to adhere rigidly to the instructions ho had received. That in departing from them he violated his promise and disobeyed a most solemn injunction: and in so doing he has been a party to one of the greatest frauds that has ever been practiced on any religious denomination.

6. To cast some farther light on this transaction, we will introduce a subject exactly similar, recorded in Acts 13:2-3. "As they ministered to the Lord and fasted, the Holy Ghost said, separate me Barnabas and Saul for the work whereunto I have called them. And when they had fasted and prayed and laid their hands on them, they sent them away." Now the transaction in the Acts so much resembles the one under consideration that no material difference can be perceived between them. The one was intended for a *special purpose;* so was the other. The one was performed "*by the imposition of hands and prayer;*" so was the other. The one was performed "*by ordained ministers;*" so was the other. The one "*was done under the protection of Almighty God;*" so was the other. Before we offer Mr. Wesley's opinion of this transaction, we will present the reader with that of Dr. Macknight. He says — "St. Paul was first made an apostle by Christ, when he appeared to him on the way to Damascus. — Acts 9:15. And three years after that his apostolic commission was received. — Acts 22:20. So that he was first sent forth, neither by the church at Jerusalem, nor by that at Antioch. The Holy Gost, indeed, ordered the prophets at Antioch (Acts 13:21) to separate Paul and Barnabas; but it was unto the work,

whereunto he had called them formerly. This separation was simply a recommending them to the grace of God by prayer. And in fact it is so termed, Acts 14:26." Let us now hear Mr. Wesley.

"But when St. Paul and Barnabas were separated for the work to which they were called, this was *not ordaining* them. St. Paul was ordained long before, and that not of man or by man. It was only *inducting* him to the province for which our Lord had appointed him from the beginning. For this end the prophets and teachers fasted, prayed, and laid their hands upon them; a rite which was used *not in ordination only*, but in blessing, and *on many other occasions* ." — Wesley's Works, vol. x., p. 237.

NUMBER XVIII.

It is said that George III. once visited a teacher of youth, who was celebrated for preparing young men for college, to ascertain by what means he was successful above all others in making his pupils such good scholars. When the king had entered his apartment, and had informed him of the object of his visit, the teacher made him this reply: — "May it please your Majesty, the whole art of teaching consists in two words — simplify and repeat — simplify and repeat. If I am successful above others in preparing young men for the university, as your majesty is pleased to say I am, I attribute all my success to this method of imparting instruction. I practice no other art than to make subjects plain and intelligible by simplifying them, and to repeat my exposition until I have fixed the idea permanently in the mind of my pupil."

Profiting by this reply, we have collected and arranged in the preceding letters, the principal facts that took place from the preaching of the first Methodist preachers in America, until the societies were formed into an Episcopal church; and we have dwelt on these facts with a view of impressing them deeply and permanently on the mind of the reader. The period embracing these facts we have denominated the first period of American Methodism, and dates from 1766 to 1784, when the societies were formed into an "independent Episcopal Church." Looking at the time when this organization took place, we find it was just forty years from the time when Mr. Wesley held his first conference. There is nothing

strange to be sure in this historical fact; but is it not a little remarkable that a second period of American Methodism should consist
of just forty years also. For, commencing at the organization of the
church in 1784, and running on forty years will bring us to the
General Conference of 1824, and the interval between these two
dates we call a second period of American Methodism. It was in
this latter year that those who petitioned the General Conference
for a REPRESENTATION in the law-making department of the
church, received an answer from that body that never will be forgotten — that never ought to be forgotten by American freemen
— *"Pardon us if we know no such rights; if we comprehend no
such privileges."* From the moment that this answer was received,
the petitioners determined to spread before the church and the
world the reasons why they thought the local preachers and the lay
members were entitled to be represented in the General Conference. And here commences a third period in American Methodist
history; for here commenced the publication of the periodical
called the "Mutual Rights" — the formation of Union societies
— then the expulsion of Reformers — and finally, the organization of the Methodist Protestant Church. Having noticed these peri-
ods or divisions, it is worthy of farther remark that just half a period, or twenty years had elapsed when the church was divided in
1844 into the church North and the church South; and by the time
the other half of the cycle shall have come round, Methodist Episcopacy shall be no more. It certainly cannot live much longer. It is
now on its last legs, and is tottering to its fall.

The facts and incidents which we shall notice as belonging to
the second period of American Methodism are — The prayer
book of 1786 — The first section of the first chapter of the book
of discipline — The Notes of the Discipline, on which Dr. Durbin
relied, among other things to prove his position, the nomination of
Richard Whatcoat to be a superintendent — The rejection of Mr.
Wesley's authority, and leaving his name off the American minutes — The contention and struggle between Dr. Coke and Mr.
Asbury for power — The degradation of Dr. Coke, and Mr. Asbury's vindic tive triumph over him — The creation of the Council — Dr. Coke's application to Bishop White to be received into
the fellowship of the Protestant Episcopal church — The seces-

sion occasioned by the withdrawal of James O'Kelley, William McKendree, Rice Haggard, and others from the Methodist Episcopal Church — Dr. Coke's abandoning the American connection, and his application to the Bishop of London, to obtain ordination for some of the Methodist preachers in Great Britain, and failing twice in his application to the church, then turns to the State, and begs the Hon. W. Wilberforce to use his influence with the Prince Regent to appoint him Bishop for India. These are the topics which we mean to discuss as belonging to the second period, to all which we invite the most profound attention of the reader.

I. *Of the Prayer Book of* 1786. Mr. Wesley having been assured by Mr. Asbury and others, that the societies here "desired to continue under his care, and still adhere to the doctrine and discipline of the Church of England, and have the sacraments administered according the usage of the same church," abridged the prayer book of that church for the use of the societies in America, and sent it over by Dr. Coke in 1784. This abridged edition was printed at Mr. Wesley's press; for it must be borne in mind that he had a printing press for his own use, as may be seen by the following extract of his will: — "Feb. 25. 1789. I give my types, printing presses, and every thing pertaining thereto, to Thomas Rankin and George Whitefield in trust, for the use of the conference. — John Wesley." The title page of this abridged edition runs thus: "The Sunday service of the Methodists in *North America*, with other occasional services. London, printed in the year MDCCLXXXIV." This title page is given to be compared with the title page of the prayer book of 1786, which is in the following words: "The Sunday services of the Methodists in the *United States of America*, with other occasional services. Printed by *Frys & Couchman, Worship street, Moorfields*, 1786." Now, although the prayer book of '84 was received by the Conference of that year, and was used for a while by a few of the preachers, it was soon laid aside; so that of the hundreds of thousands who now compose the Methodist Episcopal Church, not one, perhaps in ten thousand ever saw the book, or has heard that such a prayer book was abridged by Mr. Wesley.

But what bearing, says one, has the publication of the prayer book of 1786 on the charge of *fraud,* and how will it contribute to establish the truth of that charge? We answer, it has a very important bearing on the case, as will be shown presently. In a former letter of this series, we related the tricks of a surveyor in one of the Southern States, who, being about to take up some worthless land, with a view of passing it off as being of a superior quality to what it really was, stuck down some twigs of black walnut, hickory, oak, dogwood, &c., intending thereby to represent them as the natural growth of the soil. The sticking of these twigs down was intended to cheat the purchaser. A similar use is made of the prayer book of 1786, to cheat the societies by representing all that was done by the Conference of 1784 as being done in accordance with Mr. Wesley's "counsel" and "recommendation," and when it was done, as meeting with his entire approbation. It was for this purpose, and for this alone, we solemnly believe that the prayer book of 1786 was printed; and the publication of it by Dr. Coke is not a whit behind the artifice and cunning of the Southern surveyor. But let us examine the subject closely.

1. The prayer book of 1784 was abridged by Mr. Wesley, was printed at his press, and was sent over to America with Dr. Coke, for the use of the American Methodists. Now, take notice, that in this prayer book there was not one word from beginning to end, about bishops — about episcopacy — or about an episcopal form of government. The fact is, these terms are not even mentioned in it, much less are the things "recommended." And how things can be "recommended," and those things not be as much mentioned in the recommendation, is what we cannot understand.

2. The prayer-book of 1786 is precisely like that of 1784, except in the following particulars. 1st. It differs from that of '84 in the title page, as may be seen by comparing the title pages as given above. 2nd. It contains one more Article of Religion than is in the prayer of '84. 3rd. It contains the true and genuine minutes of conference of 1784, which consists of 76 questions and their answers, occupying thirty-three pages, and having the following title — "The General Minutes of the Conferences of the Methodist Episcopal Church in America, forming the Constitution of the said Church." 4th. It was printed at the press of *Frys and Couchman, Worship street, Upper Moorefields, London*," and was paid for by Dr. Coke out of his own funds.

3. The conference, at which the church was organized, closed

its sessions on January 1st, 1785. Dr. Coke left Baltimore on the 3rd of the month, and from the 8th to the 19th, he was in Philadelphia, where he had the minutes printed by Charles Cist of that city. On the 2nd of the following June, the Doctor sailed from Baltimore for England, and was present at the British Conference which commenced in London on the 26th of July. All this is plain and circumstantial, and may be gathered from the Doctor's journal. But what does he say about having the prayer book reprinted, with the min utes of the Methodist Episcopal Church in America bound up in it? Not a word. On this subject he is as silent as the grave; and we are left to gather all the certain information we have on the subject, from the prayer-book itself, and not from Doctor Coke's Journal, or from his pen.

4. When Mr. Wesley had the prayer-book printed, he had a sufficient number struck off to serve his societies. The short time that elapsed between the close of the conference, and Dr. Coke's leaving the United States, (just five months,) was not long enough for him to distribute the number he brought over with him; or to ascertain whether more would be wanted soon, or not. And even if he had ascertained that there was not a sufficient supply, the minutes and prayer book were both in this country, and could be reprinted here as well as in England. Had the prayer book and minutes been reprinted here, there would have been a saving of freight, risk, &c., on them, besides having them ready for distribution at a much earlier date than if they were printed in England. If a further supply was necessary, everything was in favor of having them reprinted here; and to men of common sense, the matter will appear unaccountable if there were no particular and private ends to answer, why they were reprinted in London, a few moths after the Doctor's return to England, and not in the United States.

5. But why was the prayer book and minutes reprinted at the press of Frys and Couchman, and not at Mr. Wesley's? Because the proceedings of the conference of 1784, in forming themselves into an "independent church," and assuming the title of the "Methodist Episcopal Church," were displeasing to Mr. Wesley. It must be admitted he saw those minutes, or he did not. If he did not see them, it will follow, that Dr. Coke was conscious of having exceeded Mr. Wesley's instructions, and of having done that which

he was sensible would be displeasing to Mr. Wesley, when it was known. The only way then of keeping those minutes from falling under Mr. Wesley's eye, was to have them printed at some other press, if they were printed at all. If, upon the other hand Mr. Wesley did see them, it is evident that he disapproved of the Doctor's conduct, and would not allow the prayer book and minutes to be printed at his press. Had the Doctor informed Mr. Wesley that he had received information from America that there was not a sufficient supply of the prayer book for the societies; and had he intimated it would be necessary to have another edition printed, can any one suppose that Mr. Wesley would not have had it done at his press, provided the Doctor's conduct had been according to his instructions? Incredible. Mr. Wesley would not have driven Dr. Coke to the press of Frys and Couchman, and have compelled him to pay for the edition out of his own funds, if he approved of the title "the Methodist Episcopal Church."

6. To suppose that Mr. Wesley gave his consent that the prayer book and minutes should be printed at any other press than his own, would be incompatible with the interest he manifested towards the American societies. It would have been contrary to his usual custom. For as the profits of all the books printed at his press, were applied to the carrying on the blessed work in which he was engaged, it is not reasonable that he would, in this instance, relinquish his right of disposing of the proceeds of this edition, any more than he would those of any other: or if he intended to *give* this edition of the prayer book to the American Societies, that he would have thrown the payment of it upon Dr. Coke. Besides he must have been aware that by refusing to allow the prayer book and minutes to be printed at his own press, he would afford ground to impugn the motives and conduct of Dr. Coke in the organization of the Methodist Episcopal Church. And yet this consideration could not prevail on him to do a thing that might be construed to imply an approval of the proceedings of the Doctor and the American Conference. In fine, for Dr. Coke to have the prayer book and minutes reprinted in London, in a few months after he returned from the United States; before it could have been ascertained that a second edition was necessary; at the press of Frys and Couchman; and not at Mr. Wesley's; and all out of his own private "fortune,"

must be proof positive and irresistible to every impartial mind, that Dr. Coke had a peculiar object to obtain, that the obtainment of it could only be effected by the prayer book and minutes coming from England, and that that object was the apparent sanction of Mr. Wesley to the whole of the proceedings of the General Conference of 1784.

NUMBER XIX.

For some months past, our communications have been interrupted by circumstances which it is unnecessary to detail: but these circumstances having ceased to interrupt us, we are now left free to resume our labor, which, by Divine permission, we will do, by taking up the second item in the list of articles which, in a former number of your paper, we promised to review. And as this list may have been forgotten by many of your readers, we will copy the catalogue from our last letter.

"The facts and incidents which we shall notice as belonging to the second period of American Methodism, are — The prayer book of 1786 — The first section of the first chapter of the book of discipline — The notes to the Discipline, on which Dr. Durbin relied, among other things, to prove his position — The nomination of Richard Whatcoat to be superintendent — The rejection of Mr. Wesley's authority and leaving his name off the American minutes — The contention and strife between Dr. Coke and Mr. Asbury for power — The degradation of Dr. Coke and Mr. Asbury's vindictive triumph over him — The creation of the "council" — Dr. Coke's application to Bishop White to be received into fellowship with the Protestant Episcopal Church — The secession occasioned by the withdrawal of Rev. James O'Kelly, William M'Kendree, Rice Haggard and others from the M. E. Church — Dr. Coke's abandoning the American connexion, and his application to the Bishop of London to obtain ordination for some of the Methodist preachers in Great Britain; and failing twice in his application to the *church*, then turning to the *State*, and begging the Hon. William Wilberforce to use his influence with the Prince Regent to appoint him bishop for India. These are the topics which we mean to discuss as belonging to the second period of American

Methodism, to all which we invite the most profound attention of the reader."

Having commented on the prayer book of 1786 in our last letter, and having shown the object and design of Dr. Coke's having that prayer book printed at the press of "Frys and Couchman," and not at the press of Mr. Wesley, we now call particular attention to the first section of the first chapter of the book of discipline, the caption of which runs in these words — *"Of the Origin of the Methodist Episcopal Church."* And, believing as we do, that it fully sustains the charge of *fraud* which we have preferred against the rulers of the church, in order that the reader may have an opportunity of judging for himself of the truth of the allegation, we will take the trouble to transcribe the section without any abridgment.

"The preachers and members of our society in general, being convinced that there was a great deficiency of vital godliness in the Church of England in America, and being in many places destitute of the Christian sacraments, as several of the clergy had forsaken their churches, requested the late Rev. John Wesley to take such measures in his wisdom and prudence, as would afford them suitable relief in their distress.

"In consequence of this our venerable friend, who under God had been the father of the great revival of religion now extending over the earth by the means of the Methodists, determined to ordain ministers for America; and for this purpose in the year 1784 sent over three regularly ordained clergy; but preferring the Episcopal mode of church government to any other, he solemnly set apart by the imposition of his hands and prayer, one of them, viz. — *Thomas Coke*, Doctor of Civil Law, late of Jesus College, in the University of Oxford, and a Presbyter of the Church of England, for the Episcopal office; and having delivered to him letters of Episcopal orders, commissioned and directed him to set apart *Francis Asbury*, then general assistant of the Methodist Society in America, for the same Episcopal office; he, the said *Francis Asbury* being first ordained deacon and elder. In consequence of which, the said *Francis Asbury* was solemnly set apart for the said Episcopal office by prayer and the imposition of the hands of the said *Thomas Coke*, other regularly ordained ministers assisting in the sacred ceremony. At which time the General Conference held at Baltimore, did unanimously receive the said *Thomas Coke* and *Francis Asbury* as their bishops, being fully satisfied of the validity of their Episcopal ordination." On this section we will remark —

1. It was not written when the church was organized, for it is not found in the minutes of that Conference, nor is it in the book of discipline which was "printed in 1788 by Sheppard Kollock of Elizabeth Town." The fact is, it was not written until after Mr. Wesley's death, an event which took place *seven years* after the church was organized. The church was formed in 1784; Mr. Wesley died the 2nd of March, 1791, and this section speaks of him as "the late Rev. John Wesley," evidently carrying in itself internal marks of *fraud*. Now can anyone tell us why this section was not written until after Mr. Wesley's death? To us it is very plain, that the writer was conscious it does not set forth the *truth*, and that Mr. Wesley might contradict what it affirms, if it had been published in his lifetime. 2. In terms the most pompous, inflated and disgusting, it declares that "the late Rev. John Wesley in 1784, sent over three regularly ordained clergy: but preferring the Episcopal mode of Church government to any other, he solemnly set apart, by the the imposition of his hands and prayer, one of them, viz: — Thomas Coke, Doctor of Civil Law, late of Jesus College, in the University of Oxford, and a Presbyter of the Church of England, for the Episcopal office; and having delivered to him letters of Episcopal orders, commissioned and directed him to set apart Francis Asbury, the general assistant of the Methodist Society in America for the same Episcopal office."

We are pained in commenting upon this section to be obliged to declare, that in it, we believe, there are several palpable falsehoods. *First*, Mr. Wesley did *not* send over "three regularly ordained clergy," for he never applied the term "clergy" to any of those preachers in connexion with himself, unless they were ministers of the Church of England. And even if he had been in the habit of applying the term to his preachers, neither of those that he sent was regularly ordained, either according to the forms of the Church of England, or to ancient and primitive usage. The writer, therefore, in his ambition to be great, calls them "regularly ordained clergy," although he knew the whole three had been ordained in

Mr. Wesley's bed-chamber.

Second. It affirms that Dr. Coke was ordained to "the Episcopal office," and that Mr. Wesley "delivered to him letters of Episcopal orders." This we pronounce an absolute falsehood, and we regret that a "Doctor of the Civil Law," and a "Presbyter of the Church of England" should publish such untruths in the face of the documents. Dr. Coke was ordained "a *Superintendent;*" Mr. Asbury says, "I was ordained a *Superintendent,* as my parchments will show;" and what Dr. Coke calls "letters of Episcopal orders," may be found in Drew's Life of Coke, p. 66. On the truth of this published document we defy the advocates of Methodist Episcopacy to find one word about "Episcopacy or Episcopal office" in the document itself. But should it be said that Mr. Wesley, by ordaining Dr. Coke a *Superintendent,* intended to make him a bishop, we deny this too, and offer Mr. Wesley's letter to Mr. Asbury to prove the falsity of the assertion. "But in one point my dear brother, I am a little afraid both the Doctor and you differ from me. I study to be *little,* you study to be *great.* I *creep,* you *strut* along. I found a school, you a *college.* Nay, and call it after your own name! O beware! Do not seek to be *something!* Let me be nothing, and Christ be all in all.

"One instance of this your greatness has given me great concern. How can you, how dare you, suffer yourself to be called a bishop? I shudder, I start at the very thought. Men may call *me* a *knave,* or a *fool,* a *rascal,* a *scoundrel,* and I am content, but they shall never by my consent call me a *bishop.* For my sake, for God's, for Christ's sake, put a full end to this."

Third. There is not a word about Mr. Wesley's *preference* for the Episcopal mode of Church government to any other, in the genuine minutes of the conference of 1784. The *third* question of those minutes and its answer are in these words — *Ques.* 3. As the ecclesiastical as well as civil affairs of these United States have passed through a very considerable change by the revolution, what plan of church government shall we hereafter pursue? *Ans.* We will form ourselves into an Episcopal church, under the direction of superintendents, elders, deacons, and helpers, according to the forms of ordination annexed to our liturgy, and the form of discipline set forth in these minutes." Nor are we able to find in the book of discipline, until that work had passed through the "fifth edition" (which was in 1795) one word about Mr. Wesley's "preferring, or commending," this mode of government. Thus, for ten long years had the church been organized, before these would-be bishops were able to muster up sufficient courage to tell the members that "Mr. Wesley preferred the Episcopal mode of Church government to any other" — that "he recommended this mode to the societies," and that in compliance with his "recommendation" they had adopted it. Mr. Wesley's alleged "recommendation" was an afterthought, which it was supposed would silence the objections of Mr. O'Kelly and others against Mr. Asbury's assumption of such "Episcopal powers" as caused the split in the church in 1792, and would establish the right of Methodist bishops to exercise these powers *in extenso*, however oppressive or tyrannical they might appear. And to make the credulous and unsuspecting members believe that Mr. Wesley did "recommend" such a form of government as they had adopted, the genuine minutes, (taken when the church was organized,) were thrown aside, and spurious ones were published in their stead. For the proof of this fact we refer to the "volume of minutes from 1773 to 1813, published by Daniel Hitt and Thomas Ware for the connexion." This forged document, after inserting Mr. Wesley's letter dated "Bristol, Sept. 10th, 1784," says — "Therefore at this conference we formed ourselves into an Independent church, and following the counsel of Mr. John Wesley, who recommended the Episcopal mode of church government, we thought it best to become an Episcopal church." We see now what a Methodist bishop will do to keep himself in his ecclesiastical saddle that he may ride the members "legitimately," if not "by the grace of God," at least by the "recommendation and counsel" of an aged and greatly injured servant of Christ, the Rev. John Wesley. But if the transaction was of a civil nature and a sum of $100,000 had been unjustly obtained by such an operation, we think the perpetrators would suffer at common law; nor would a pettifogging lawyer, nor "Belesarius" himself be able to save them from sharing the fate of Monroe Edwards.

Fourth. The closing sentence of this noted section is in these words: — "At which time the General Conference held at Baltimore did unanimously receive the said Thomas Coke and Francis

Asbury as their bishops, being fully satisfied of the validity of their Episcopal ordination." Now this we know is not so. So far was the General Conference from "*unanimously*" receiving Dr. Coke and Mr. Asbury as their bishops, that they were not received as *bishops* at all. Indeed it is apparent to us that the writer betrays a consciousness of the invalidity of their Episcopal ordination by his over-anxiety to establish the validity of it: as some men, conscious that they are uttering an untruth, accompany their statement with an oath, lest their declaration should not be believed. Upon the whole, then, we think we have sufficiently established the truth of the position with which we set out, namely, that this section contains several palpable falsehoods, and that our position is too strongly fortified by proof to be set aside by any interested partisan or sycophant, exclaiming SHOCKING! And as the names of the bishops have been affixed from time to time to the discipline which contains these untruths, we call upon those of them who are alive, as *honest* men, and men of *truth*, to show wherein we have been "mistaken," or to prove wherein we have been guilty of "misrepresentation." Should they pass over this call in sullen silence, they shall be held up before the American public as favoring and countenancing these falsehoods, and as contributing by their names and influence to perpetuate an abominable fraud.

NUMBER XX.

Thanks to Dr. John P. Durbin for the "after-dinner speech" which he delivered on May 29, 1844, before the General Conference in the case of bishop Andrew. Were it not for that speech we might have continued under erroneous impressions respecting the doctor's literary attainments, and his acquaintance with general history — or with that part of it at least which relates to the history of the "Romish Church." But the very first paragraph of that speech has completely dissipated all our former opinions, founded on report, and has convinced us, that the doctor's knowledge of the history of the "Romish Church," with which, as President of a Protestant College, he ought to be well acquainted, is very limited indeed. Were it not for that speech, we might have supposed that the reverend gentleman, being a doctor of divinity, had made himself acquainted with what the Scriptures say on the subject of domestic slavery, for being "connected" with which, the conference sought to depose Bishop Andrew. But we are now convinced that the doctor is *not* acquainted with the teachings of the Bible on that subject; or if he is, for reasons best known to himself, he has neglected to sustain his position by proofs drawn from its pages. Perhaps, in the vanity of his heart, he may have thought it was not necessary for *him* to quote scripture to establish the doctrine of abolition, that it was quite enough to show *his* hand in its favor, and that poor old Mr. Dunwoodie's person and arguments merited nothing more from *him* than a contemptuous sneer. Were it not for that speech we might have overlooked "the Notes to the discipline;" or if we did remember to bring them forward in our review, we would not have had as fair an opportunity of animadverting on them as we now have, or of offering them as proof of the fraud which have been practiced on the members of the church.

In this speech, remarkable for its absurd, unjust, and tyrannical doctrines — doctrines which are discreditable to an American citizen — the doctor says: "It has been maintained here, *Sir*, that the General Conference has no power to remove a bishop, or to suspend the exercise of his functions, unless by impeachment and trial in regular form, for some offence regularly charged. If this be true, Sir, I have greatly misunderstood the nature of our episcopacy." And to prove that the General Conference has this power, he offers "the Minutes of Conference of 1785" — "the Notes to the Discipline" — and "a pamphlet published in Philadelphia in 1792." But when the doctor referred to the Minutes of Conference of 1785 — what minutes did he refer to — the *genuine* or the *spurious* ones? For it ought to be known, that there are two sets of minutes purporting to be minutes of conference of that year; the one set taken at the time the conference was held — the other set which was subsequently published and slipped in slyly among the records of the church, as the minutes of 1785. There are two sets the following facts will prove:

1. The title of the genuine minutes, (and by this expression we mean the minutes which were taken when the church was organized) runs thus: "The General Minutes of the Methodist Episcopal Church in America, forming the constitution of the said church."

The title of the spurious minutes is in these words "Minutes taken at the several annual conferences of the Methodist Episcopal Church for the year 1785." See the bound volume of minutes published in New York, 1813, by Daniel Hill and Thomas Ware, for the Methodist connexion.

2. The genuine minutes contained 76 questions and their answers. In the spurious minutes not one of these questions or answers is to be found.

3. The genuine minutes were printed in Philadelphia, by Charles Cist, immediately after the rising of the General Conference. From the 8th to the 15th of January, 1785, Dr. Coke was in Philadelphia, and there published the minutes of that conference, the title of which was, "The General Minutes of the Conference of the Methodist Episcopal Church in America." Defense of our Fathers, p. 42. The spurious ones were published long afterwards.

4. The genuine minutes were bound up in the prayer book of 1786, which were printed in London for Dr. Coke, by Frys and Coachman. We do not know when or where the spurious minutes were first printed. We have no recollection of having ever seen them until we saw them in the bound volume of 1813.

5. The spurious minutes contain *prima facie* evidence of their falsity; for throughout they speak in the past tense. "It *was* unanimously agreed — that circumstances *made* it expedient — therefore we *formed* ourselves — we *thought* it best to become an Episcopal Church, *making the episcopal office elective, and the elected superintendent or bishop amenable to the body of ministers and preachers.*"

But when Dr. Durbin referred to these minutes, did he know that this document was a spurious or false document? If he did not know that it was a false document, his ignorance of Methodism and "the nature of our episcopacy," is greater than we had reason to suppose. But if he *did know* that this document was a spurious or false document (and we believe he did) — if *he did know* that it does not contain the minutes of the conference of 1785 — if *he did know* that the words which we have italicized are not in the genuine minutes, what shall we say of this Doctor of Divinity — this *quondam* President of a Methodist College — this traveller into foreign lands — this writer for Magazines, &c., &c., &c.,

when he asserts "The minutes of 1785 declare that at the organization of the church, the episcopal office was made elective, and the elected superintendent or bishop amenable to the body of ministers and preachers." Now we say that the genuine minutes of conference for 1785 do not contain the above *italicized* words, and we defy Dr. Durbin, or any other man, to find them there. Is it fair then for the doctor to endeavor to pass off on the church a spurious document as genuine, with a view to depose Bishop Andrew? We presume the doctor would not attempt to pass off a *counterfeit* twenty dollar bill *knowing it to be a counterfeit.* Why he would do the one, and not the other, remains for him to explain.

III. Of "the Notes to the Discipline." Few Methodists of the present day have heard of the "Notes," and if the enquiry were made who were the authors, and for what purpose were they written? not many would be able to tell. A few words, however, will make known the authors, and their object. From the time the church was organized up to 1796, frequent and loud complaints were made respecting the powers possessed by the bishops. These complaints were not confined to a few of the preachers; for in 1792, thousands of the members of the church, with the Rev. James O. Kelley, William McKendree (who was afterwards made a bishop in the M. E. Church) and others, at their head, withdrew from her fellowship on account of those powers, which were then pronounced "despotic" and "tyrannical." To stop the dissatisfaction which prevailed from the centre to the circumference of the work, the bishops were requested by the General Conference of 1796 to draw up these "notes." They did so: but the work never received the approbation of that conference or of any other. The "Notes" were drawn up by Dr. Coke and Mr. Asbury, and were published in 1798, and as they were written to silence the opposition of the disaffected, and to vindicate the bishops in the exercise of their episcopal powers, the reader may be sure that everything was said in them, that could be said, to make these powers appear reasonable, just, and proper. Hence, the language of these "Notes" is as *mild* as the language of any young Miss, who had not entered into her *teens* could be, when speaking of her being "*subject*" to her mamma. But, O, when the lion was roused — when any dared to complain of being oppressed by the exercise of those powers —

when any dared to hint that these powers were too great to be entrusted to any one man, or to intimate that they ought to be
abridged or lessened — then were these poor unfortunates made
to feel with a vengeance, that the authors advanced one doctrine in
their "notes" whilst they acted out another doctrine in their practice. The history of Methodism, and of the men who have filled the
episcopal office from the expulsion of the Virginia preachers in
1779, by Mr. Asbury and a few tory preachers, to the expulsion of
Reformers in Baltimore and other places in 1827, will abundantly
confirm this statement. Great stress was laid on these "notes" by
the author of the "Defense of our Fathers;" for when he wrote that
pamphlet, he had an expectation of being raised to the episcopate;
and to his writing his "Defense" was he indebted for being made a
bishop. Knowing this to be a fact, Dr. Durbin may have thought it
would help the cause of another aspirant after episcopal honors,
were he to lug them into the debate, and give them that prominence
and importance which the bishops thought they deserved.

The third thing on which Dr. Durbin relied to prove his point is
a pamphlet, said to be "written by the Rev. John Dickens, and published by the unanimous request of the conference held at Philadelphia, Sept. 5, 1792." Now, although this pamphlet was brought
into the world under such high authority, and sent out into it under
such imposing influence and patronage; and although the conference is represented as approving of its contents, and is made answerable for its doctrines, yet we are not told whether the conference had the work before it, or not, whether any committee had examined it and reported favorably, or not: or whether the conference
had ever seen it at all. The writer of this communication has been
personally, and he may say intimately, acquainted with the M. E.
Church since 1791, and has been in the travelling connection before the "Notes" were published, yet he never heard of this noted
pamphlet until he read of it in the "Defense of our Fathers." He
cannot, therefore, say what it does contain, or what it does not. Nor
can he tell whether the quotations from it, like many other things in
that work of "our beloved Bishop Emory," are absolutely false, or
are greatly perverted: all he will say is this — the cause must be a
bad one, which requires forged documents to be brought into court
to sustain it, and the *lawyer* who could resort to such a mode of de-

fense must be sensible of the badness of his cause and be radically a bad man himself.

But let us see what the pamphlet says: "The superiority of our bishops is not derived from their separate ordination, but from the suffrages of the body of ministers." "If this gave them their superiority, how came they to be removable by the conference? How can the conference have power to remove Mr. Asbury and ordain another to fill his place, if they see it necessary on any other ground?" "We all know Mr. Asbury derived his official power from the conference, and therefore his office is at their disposal." "Mr. Asbury was thus chosen by the conference, both before and after he was ordained a bishop; and he is still considered the person of their choice, by being responsible to the conference who have power to remove him, and fill his place with another, if they see it necessary. And as he is liable every year to be removed, he may be considered as their annual choice."

Such is the doctrine of this celebrated pamphlet, but do these quotations contain the truth — the whole truth — and nothing but the truth? We think they do not. That Mr. Asbury was elected by the votes of the members of the conference of 1784, to the office of superintendent, is an established historical fact, nor would he receive the office to which he had been appointed by Mr. Wesley, and which he had long earnestly coveted, until he was elected by the conference. The question may be asked, then, why was he so particular on this point? Was he not appointed to that office by Mr. Wesley, in his circular letter of Sept. 10th, 1784? He was. Was not Dr. Coke, who had been constituted a superintendent by Mr. Wesley, willing that Mr. Asbury should be a "joint superintendent" with himself? He was. Did not Mr. Asbury know that no opposition would be made, by either preachers or people, to his taking on him the office of a superintendent without the formality of an election? He did. Why, then, did he insist on being elected? Now we come to the "*gist*" of the business. Mr. Asbury was apprehensive of being recalled to England by Mr. Wesley, no matter for what cause, and he was determined that he would not obey the call. Being determined to throw off Mr. Wesley's authority and to stand at the head of the American Methodists, he insisted on being elected by the preachers, and then with a show of affection for them, he could disobey Mr. Wesley. This we consider the first step to the rejection of Mr. Wesley's authority which was completed a few years afterwards, by leaving his name out of the American minutes. Any man, therefore, who will affirm, that Mr. Asbury insisted upon being elected, that every succeeding conference might have it in their power to remove him, if they saw it necessary, and ordain another in his place," must be as ignorant "of the nature of our episcopacy," as of Mr. Asbury himself. Dr. Durbin would not have dared to quote the passages he has given us in his speech, if Mr. Asbury were alive and in the conference at the time. One look from eyes, half concealed and half disclosed, would have pierced the doctor through and through, and would have caused him to cry out in the agony of despair — I'm lost — I'm ruined — I'm undone forever.

NUMBER XXI.

The Methodist societies in America being formed into an "independent Episcopal Church," under the alleged instructions of Mr. Wesley, and everything being settled, on this side of the water, to the satisfaction of the parties concerned in its organization, one small matter, which shall be noticed hereafter, excepted, it may not be amis to follow Dr. Coke to Europe and see how it fared with him there, for his official conduct whilst in the United States. The history of the treatment he received at the first conference he attended, after his return to England, shall be given in "our beloved Bishop Emory's" own words, taken from his "Defense of our Fathers," a work, for the writing of which he was raised to the episcopate. And as Dr. Durbin, in his *after dinner speech*," has eulogized the bishop highly, and has presented him as "a *standard* writer," we shall ask the doctor to explain such things in the bishop's account as we cannot understand. Mr. Emory says —

"The General Conference commenced its session on the 24th of December, and closed on the 1st of January, 1785. On the 3rd of January Dr. Coke left Baltimore. From the 8th to the 19th, he was in Philadelphia and there published the Minutes of that conference, the title of which was, 'The General Minutes of the Conferences of the Methodist Episcopal Church in America.' And in the answer to the third question it was declared, that they had formed themselves into an Episcopal Church. See Dr. Coke's Journal of the above dates, and Jan. 22, 1785. On the 2nd of June following, Dr. Coke sailed from Baltimore for England, and was present at the ensuing British Conference, which commenced in London on the 26th of July of that year. Mr. Wesley was also present at that conference." Page 42. Every thing here is clear, circumstantial, and intelligible. Mr. E. goes on.

"According to Mr. Drew the charge alleged against Dr. Coke in the British Conference was neither 'the manner in which he discharged the duties of the new office he was appointed to fill,' nor his having assumed 'the title of bishop:' but simply that he, *being a British subject*, had expressed to Gen. Washington sentiments in relation to the American revolution, which, as *a British subject*, they conceived he ought not to have expressed. Mr. Drew, though himself a British subject, has vindicated both the conduct and the motives of Dr. Coke on that occasion, with a triumphant ability which leaves us nothing to add." Page 60.

As there is something in this paragraph which the writer of these historical sketches cannot understand, he has to request Dr. Durbin, who is a great scholar, and deeply versed in Methodist lore, to explain the matter. It is affirmed by Mr. Emory, that "the charge preferred against Dr. Coke" was neither the manner in which he discharged the duties of the new office he was appointed to fill, nor his having assumed the title of bishop, but simply, that he being a *British subject*, had expressed to *Gen. Washington* "sentiments in relation to the American revolution, which as a *British subject*, he ought not to have expressed." Now we want to know *when* and *where* did Dr. Coke express those exceptionable sentiments to Gen. Washington? We never read, or heard, of but one address presented by the bishops, or either of them, to this great man, and the fact is established, that the date of their address is May 29, 1789: and this charge was preferred at the conference of 1785. How is this?

"A copy of this address," says Mr. Emory, "was introduced into the British Conference as a ground of censure against the doctor. The doctor heard these charges against him in PROFOUND SILENCE. Under these circumstances, as some decisive steps were necessary to be taken in this critical affair, it was finally determined, that the name of Dr. Coke should be omitted in the Minutes for the succeeding year. This prudent resolution had the desired effect, and the business of conference proceeded and terminated in peace. Such was the 'punishment,' then, of Dr. Coke. Such the cause that led to it. Such the 'profound silence' with which he heard the charge." Page 61. But as the address of the bishops was not presented to Gen. Washington until May, 1789, it could not be made the ground of any charge in '85. The impeachment, therefore, must have been for some other cause, and if it was not for forming the Methodist societies into an "independent Episcopal Church," will Dr. Durbin please tell us what it was for?

Leaving Dr. Coke to get along, in England, as well as he can under the punishment inflicted on him by Mr. Wesley, let us turn our attention to the United States and see how it was with Mr. Asbury, whilst his colleague in the episcopacy was suffering in disgrace. We stated above, that one of the parties concerned in the organization of the church was not satisfied with the proceedings of the conference of '84. The cause of this dissatisfaction was the answer to the second question in the Minutes, which answer is in these words — "During the life of the Rev. Mr. Wesley, we acknowledge ourselves his sons in the gospel, ready in matters belonging to church government to obey his commands." To the adoption of this answer Mr. Asbury was violently opposed. His insatiable thirst for power, which showed itself in every part of his conduct, from his arrival in America to the General Conference of 1784, could not brook the idea of his being in subjection to Mr. Wesley, or any other man, any longer than such subjection would contribute to the attainment of his darling object. In proof of this position let it be recollected, that for 13 years after his arrival in America Mr. Asbury was subject to Mr. Wesley; but when he was ordained in 1784, it was not 13 days, perhaps 13 hours, before he showed his opposition to Mr Wesley's authority, and was anxious to throw off this yoke: Indeed before the ordination was obtained, he intimated his determination to do this as soon as he could. "Dr. Coke, in his letter to Mr. Wesley of Aug. 9, 1784, says — "I may want all the influence which you can throw into my scale. Mr. Brackenbury informed me at Leeds, that he saw a letter in London from Mr. Asbury, in which he observed, that *he would not receive any person deputed by you to take any part of the superintendency of the work invested in him.*" Moore's Life of Wesley. Vol. 2, p. 276.

It was owing to this ambitious principle, he would not consent to be ordained until he was elected by the preachers in conference, that thereby he might be independent of Mr. Wesley. On this principle he opposed the adoption of the minute which declares — "during the life of the Rev. Mr. Wesley we are ready to obey his commands in matters belonging to church government." For, notwithstanding he had arrived at the summit of episcopal honors, he *felt,* as another ambitious character formerly *felt,* "all this availeth me nothing, so long as I see Mordecai, the Jew, flitting at the king's gate." On this principle he wrote to Mr. Wesley, affirming, "that no person in Europe knew how to direct those in America." On this principle he told George Shadford, "Mr, Wesley and I are like Caesar and Pompey — he will have no equal, and I will bare no superior." Actuated by this principle, it is preposterous to suppose that Mr. Asbury was idle as it respects the attainment of his object, or that he would not avail himself of the first opportunity to throw off Mr. Wesley's authority. Such an occasion soon presented itself.

IV. *Of the nomination of Richard Whatcoat.* We are now come to a period in the history of American Methodism, respecting the transactions of which, much has been written; and as it was at this period, that the *open* and *implacable hostility* of Mr. Asbury began to show itself against Mr. Wesley, and we may add, against Dr. Coke also, it will be our endeavor to place the occurences of those times, impartially, fairly, and fully before the reader, so that he may have a full and perfect understanding of the causes, the progress, and the issues of this unnatural and unchristian war.

The General Conference, at the organization of the church, had formally passed the following minute — "During the life of the Rev. Mr. Wesley, we acknowledge ourselves his sons in the gospel, ready in matters belonging to church government to obey his commands." Under the belief that the conference meant what it said in this minute, Mr. Wesley wrote the following letter:

"LONDON, Sept. 6, 1786.

To the Rev. Dr. Coke:

DEAR SIR — I desire that you would appoint a general conference of all our preachers in the United States, to meet in Baltimore, on May the first, 1787. And that Mr. Richard Whatcoat may be appointed superintendent with Mr. Francis Asbury. I am, dear sir, your affectionate friend and brother, JOHN WESLEY."

Now what is there in this letter (remarkable for its brevity) that was calculated to give offence to any one? It was written by Mr. Wesley, the father of Methodism — who took deep interest in the prosperity of the work of God, whether on this side of the water, or on that — in the 84th year of his age, and when he was upwards of half a century in the ministry — and at what may be considered the request of the American conference, as "his sons in the gospel." The letter contains only two sentences — the first relating to the appointment of a general conference — the second to the appointment of Mr. Richard Whatcoat to be superintendent. Each of these subjects gave Mr. Asbury great offence; and he was determined, as he now stood at the head of the American connexion, to make Mr. Wesley and Dr. Coke *feel* his resentment to the utmost extent of his power. Mr. Asbury, therefore, opposed Mr. Wesley's authority, as the following document will show.

> "When Thomas Coke and Mr. Asbury met in Charleston, Thomas Coke informed him that Mr. Wesley had appointed Richard Whatcoat as a joint superintendent, and Mr. Asbury acquiesced in the appointment, as did the Charleston Conference when it was laid before them. Thomas Coke proposed the appointment to the Virginia Conference, and to his great pain and disappointment, James O'Kelly most strenuously opposed it, but consented that the Baltimore Conference might decide it, upon condition that the Virginia Conference might send a deputy to explain their sentiments.
>
> Signed, Thomas Coke."

Mr. Whatcoat says —

> "Mr. Asbury *was not opposed* to my being joint superintendent with himself. After receiving Mr. Wes-

ley's letter, he wrote to me from Charleston upon the subject. As I have not the letter by me at present, I cannot give the contents verbatim; but as well as I recollect, the conclusion was — "And if so, you must meet me at the Warm Springs, and we will make out a plan for your route through the continent."

Signed,

R. Whatcoat."

Happily, we have it in our power to lay before the reader Mr. Asbury's letter to Mr. Whatcoat, which the latter said he had not by him, when he gave the above certificate.

"CHARLESTON, March 25, 1789.[8]

My dear brother:

Hereby I inform you, that Mr. Wesley has appointed you a joint superintendent with me; I can therefore, claim no superiority over you: the way will be for you to come after me through the continent, if called, but through the States without all doubt. The best method will be to go out to the Ohio, upon a plan I have laid out for myself, and return to the Springs, there I will meet you and form a plan for our future work. The mode of appointment is not approved of, though many of us by no means object to the person. I am, with respect, as ever, FRANCIS ASBURY."

A few remarks for the better understanding of these documents. 1st. Dr. Coke says, "when he informed Mr. Asbury, Mr. Wesley had appointed Mr. Richard Whatcoat a joint superintendent, Mr. Asbury *acquiesced* in the appointment," — that is, in the *person* appointed, not in the *appointing power.* 2nd. "The Charleston Conference did the same when it was laid before them." But whether they "acquiesced" in the appointing power, or only in the person appointed, the certificate does not say. We believe they made no objection to Mr. Wesley's authority, and hence Mr. Asbury was greatly chagrined at their conduct. For here was one conference out of three that was willing to submit to Mr. Wesley's authority. 3rd. "Thomas Coke proposed the appointment to the Virginia Conference, and to his great pain and disappointment, James O'Kelly most strenuously opposed it." Whether Mr. O'Kelly was opposed

---

[8] This, we think is a typographical error. It ought to be 1787.

to Mr. Wesley's authority to appoint, or whether his opposition was confined to the person appointed, we are not informed. 4th. Here Mr. Asbury's hopes began to revive, that he would be able to throw off Mr Wesley's authority, for Mr. O'Kelly was opposed to Dr. Coke. But Dr. Coke appearing to have the advantage of Mr. O'Kelly in debate, Mr. Asbury proposed that the Baltimore Conference should decide the matter, to which Mr. O'Kelly consented, upon condition that the Virginia Conference might send a deputy to explain their sentiments. Mr. Asbury knew well, that he could rely on the tory preachers of that conference, for with their aid he had formerly expelled 27 preachers in Virginia. 5th. Mr. Asbury in his letter says — "The mode of appointment is not approved of, though many of us by no means object to the person." No objection to Mr. Whatcoat, but to Mr. Wesley's authority. Ah, that is the rub. It was *that* which galled Mr. Asbury. 6th. When the case was submitted to the Baltimore Conference it was asked, "if the conference was called on to ratify the appointment, or to vote discretionally according to their judgment?" This brought on a debate which resulted in annulling their former minute. 7th. This was done by the Baltimore Conference alone, without the concurrence of the Virginia or Southern Conference. 8th. The only matter referred to the Baltimore Conference to decide was, whether Mr. Whatcoat should be received as a superintendent, or not. But they went further — they annulled the minute of the General Conference — expelled Mr. Wesley — and struck his name from their minutes!!! Thus was Mr. Asbury's ambition gratified by the expulsion of his *father* and *friend*, the Rev. John Wesley.

NUMBER XXII

V. Of the expulsion of Mr. Wesley. The astounding fact with which we closed our last letter, will, no doubt, be denied by some ignorant and bigoted Methodists, or be attributed "to the malignity of the human heart." Such things have been done formerly, by some Methodist writers; but these facts are now too well established by documentary proof to be called in question or to be passed off on the community as the creatures of a disordered brain. The man, therefore, must be grossly and shamefully ignorant of

Methodist affairs, who will dare to deny them; or admitting their truth, he must be lost to every principle that enters into the composition of the character of the Christian, as laid down in the New Testament, who will attempt to *defend* them. Had some of the members of the General Conference of 1844, acted the part of honest debaters, they would not have appealed to the Minutes of '85 to sustain their position, knowing that the minutes, which are sent into the world as the records of the church for that year, are SPURIOUS. Mr. Wesley's name did stand on the genuine minutes of '85, and '86; but after the Baltimore Conference has rescinded the resolution of the General Conference of '84, "to obey Mr. Wesley in matters belonging to church government," all connexion with Mr. Wesley ceased, and his name was erased from the American records.

Let us now hear what Mr. Asbury says respecting these transactions. "I was amazed to hear, that my dear, aged friend, Benjamin Evans (now gone to glory) was converted to the new side, by being told by J. O'Kelly, that I had offended Mr. Wesley, and that he being about calling me to an account I cast him off altogether. But, *quere*, did not J. O'Kelly set aside the appointment of Richard Whatcoat? The writer of these sketches answers he did not. *He* could not do it. The most he could do, was to speak and vote against it. The *conference* 'decided.' And did not the conference in Baltimore strike that minute out of our discipline, which was called a rejecting of Mr. Wesley? and now does J. O'Kelly lay all the blame on me? It is true, I never approved of that binding minute, I did not think it practically expedient to obey Mr. Wesley at three thousand miles distance, in all matters relative to church government, neither did brother Whatcoat, nor several others." And yet, for 13 years before he received ordination, Mr. Asbury had no objection to the practical expediency of obeying Mr. Wesley at three thousand miles distance; nor did he scruple, with the aid of some tory preachers in 1779, to expel 27 preachers in Virginia, because they were not obedient to Mr. Wesley. Really, we are sorry that Mr. Asbury could not make out a better defense for his conduct than he has done; for we should like to see *consistency* in him as well as in other men. But he goes on.

"At the first General Conference, I was mute and modest when it passed, and I was mute when it was expunged." No necessity for the master spirit to move openly, or be conspicuous in the affair; he pulled the wires, and the puppets moved. "For this Mr. Wesley blamed me, and was dis pleased that I did not rather reject the whole connexion, or leave them, if they did not comply." Asbury's Journal, Vol. II., Page 270.

Let us next hear what Dr. Coke says. Mr. Asbury in his Journal of Friday, the 29th of April, 1791, writes thus: — "The solemn news reached our ears, that the public papers had announced the death of that man of God, John Wesley.[9] Dr. Coke accompanied by brother O____ and Dr. G____, set out for Baltimore, in order to get the most speedy passage to England, leaving me to fill the appointments. Next day I overtook Dr. Coke and his company at Colchester. At Alexandria Dr. Coke had certain information of Mr. Wesley's death. On Sabbath day he reached Baltimore, and preached on the occasion of Mr. Wesley's death, and mentioned some things which gave offense." And what did Dr. Coke say in his sermon, which gave offense? He said: — "The leaving of Mr. Wesley's name off the minutes was an almost *diabolical* thing. No history furnished any parallel to it — that a body of Christian ministers should treat an aged and faithful minister, as Mr. Wesley undoubtedly was, with such disrespect." And farther on, in this sermon he said — "two of those actors in Mr. Wesley's expulsion are dead and damned, and the others, with their patron, (Mr. As-

____

[9] We would have been glad to be able to discover, in this announcement of the death of "that dear man of God, John Wesley," either sympathy, sincerity, or affection; but truth obliges us to say, we cannot. If Mr. Asbury entertained either sympathy or affection for "that dear man of God," or if he was sincere in applying this phrase to Mr. Wesley, we cannot conceive why no record was made, in the American minutes, of the death of the father and founder of Methodism—of him, who had labored in the ministry for upwards of sixty years. This omission is the more remarkable, because in the minutes of conference for 1792, the year after Mr. Wesley's death, we have obituary notices of the following preachers — "Thomas Weatherford, an European, aged 56, upwards of four years a laborer in the vineyard of the Lord &c." "Peter Massic, who labored faithfully in the ministry upwards of three years &c." And "George Browning, two years and a half in the field of labor, &c." Besides, Mr. Asbury, in enumerating the sources of his authority as a bishop, omits Mr. Wesley's name, as if there was something in that name that inspired him with horror. See his Journals Vol. III, Page 168.

bury we suppose) will go to hell except they repent." And in a letter which the doctor wrote from Wilmington, Delaware, May, 4th, '91 he says: "I doubt much whether the cruel usage he received in Baltimore in 1787, when he was excommunicated (wonderful and unparalleled step) did not *hasten his death*. Indeed *I little doubt it*. For from the time he was informed of it, he began to hold down his head, and to think he had lived long enough."

And lastly let us hear what Mr. Wesley himself says. Here is his letter to Rev. Baverly Allen, dated,

> "LONDON, Oct. 31st, 1789.
>
> My dear brother:
>
> The point you desire my thoughts upon, is doubtless of no common importance. And I will give you my settled thoughts concerning it without the least disguise or reserve. Indeed, this has been always my manner of speaking, when I speak of the things of God. It should be so now in particular, as these may probably be the last words that you will receive from *me*.
>
> It pleased God sixty years ago, by me, to awaken and join together a little company in London, whence they spread throughout the land. Some time after, I was much importuned to send some of my children to America, to which I cheerfully consented. God prospered their labors; but they and their children still esteemed themselves one family; no otherwise divided than as Methodists on one side of the Thames are divided from the other. I was therefore a little surprised when *I received some letters from Mr. Asbury, affirming, that no person in Europe knew how to direct those in America.* Soon after he flatly refused to receive Mr. Whatcoat in the character I sent him.
>
> He told George Shadford, 'Mr. Wesley and I are like Caesar and Pompey — he will bear no equal, and I will bear no superior.' And accordingly he quietly sat by, until his friends, by common consent, voted my name out of the American minutes. This completed the matter, and showed he had no connexion with me."

Here let us pause for a moment, and contrast the characters that stand out most prominently in these transactions. The historian says — "So far as we can trace back any account of the family, Mr. Wesley's ancestors appear respectable for learning and conspicuous for piety." Of Mr. Asbury's, nothing is known beyond "his father, who was employed as a farmer and gardener by two of the richest families in the parish." Journals, Vol. II., Page 133. Mr. John Wesley, M.A., was fellow of Lincoln College, Oxford. Mr. Asbury "was sent to school early, and began to read the Bible between six and seven years of age; but did not remain long at school;" for, "when about thirteen years of age," he went to learn the trade of a button maker. Mr. Wesley "joined together a little company in London in 1729, whence they spread throughout the land," (*sixteen years before Mr. Asbury was born*) and held his first conference with his preachers in 1744. Mr. Asbury applied at Mr. Wesley's 27th conference to be received, and sent as a missionary to America. Mr. Wesley received him, furnished him with money, "for he had not one penny in his pocket when he came to Bristol, and paid his passage. Mr. Wesley's friends supplied him with clothes, and gave him £10." Mr. Wesley made Mr. Asbury his general assistant in America, and contributed to his support. Mr. Wesley writes thus to Mr. Asbury — "You are the elder brother of the American Methodist; I am, under God, the father of the whole family. Therefore I naturally care for you all, in a manner no other person can do. Therefore, I, in a measure, provide for you all, for the supplies which Dr. Coke provides for you, he could not provide, were it not for me; were it not that I not only permit him to collect, but support him in so doing." Mr. Wesley appointed Mr. Asbury "joint superintendent with Dr. Coke," and Mr. Asbury was ordained according to Mr. Wesley's directions. In fine, Mr. Wesley resembles the countryman in the fable, who found the adder stiff and frozen in his field, who brought it to his house, placed it near the fire, did everything in his power to restore it to life. Mr. Asbury is like that adder, who, as soon as he was warmed and invigorated, began to *hiss,* and *strike* at all who stood in his way, until at last, he stuck his fangs in his benefactor to whom he owed his existence, and stung him to death. Let those then who can vindicate such base ingratitude and marked contempt, as Mr. Wesley received from

Mr. Asbury, do so. We envy not the fame or the honors they may derive from "this labored deed of hard-earned infamy." We have no doubt, but that those who will read this letter will pronounce the verdict, that the man who can bring himself to defend such conduct, must be *bad at heart;* and that the man who can eulogize such a defense is not a whit better than the other.

VI. *Of the degradation of Dr. Coke.* The reader will recollect that Mr. Wesley, in his letter dated Sept, 6, 1786 directed Dr. Coke to call "a General Conference of all our preachers in the United States to meet at Baltimore on May, 1st, 1787." "The calling of this conference by Dr. Coke," says Mr. Emory, "by the direction of Mr. Wesley, was the first ground of dissatisfaction in the conference of 1787. This proceeding was one of the chief causes which led to the signing of the instrument given by Dr. Coke at that conference." That this was made the ostensible ground of the impeachment of Dr. Coke we will admit; but we are far from believing it was the real cause.

1. Because, Dr. Coke was only acting according to Mr. Wesley's instruction, and therefore *he* was not blameable. 2. Because the Gen. Con. of '84 had promised "to obey Mr. Wesley in all matters belonging to church government," therefore he had violated no law. 3. Because, the Baltimore Conference was only one of three conferences, into which the whole of the work was then divided the Baltimore, the Virginia, and the Charleston Conferences. That conference therefore had no *right* to take up the charge. 4. Because the Baltimore Conference was not a *General Conference.* No preachers from the Charleston district being present — and none from Virginia, unless "a deputy to explain their sentiments." See the certificate of Dr. Coke. If it was a General Conference, all the preachers in full connexion had a right to attend it. 5. Because no charge had been preferred at either the Virginia, or Charleston Conference, where Dr. Coke was present and presided, therefore none ought to be made at Baltimore. But why, it may be asked, were the charges kept back and no intimation of them given until the doctor arrived in Baltimore? We answer, because Mr. Asbury did not believe he could carry his point, either in the Virginia or Charleston Conferences. He knew, in the Baltimore Conference, were the men on whom he could rely. There were the tory preach-

ers who had aided him to expel 27 preachers in Virginia at a sweep. In accordance with his wishes they had just expelled Mr. Wesley, and they are next called on to bind Dr. Coke in chains. Here is the binding "instrument."

"I do solemnly engage, by this instrument, that I never will, by virtue of my office as superintendent of the Methodist Church, during my absence from the United States of America exercise any government whatever, in the said Methodist Church, during my absence from the United States. And I do also engage, that I will exercise no privilege in the said church when present in the United States, except that of ordaining according to the regulations and laws already existing, or hereafter to be made in the said church, and that of presiding, when present in conference, and lastly that of travelling at large. Given under my hand, the second day of May, in the year 1787. THOMAS COKE."

John Tunriel,
John Hagerty,
Nelson Reed.
Witnesses.

NUMBER XXIII.

We had not space in our last letter to make any remarks on the prominent points in the "instrument" of degradation which Dr. Coke gave the Conference. We will make a few now, 1. The Doctor says — "I never will, by virtue of my office as superintendent of the Methodist Church exercise any government whatever in the said Church, during my absence from the United States." As Mr. Wesley was excommunicated at this Conference, and as the Doctor engages not to exercise any government in the said Church when absent from the United States, it is plain, that, in the Doctor's absence, Mr. Asbury will have all the power of governing in his own hands. 2. He says farther — "I will exercise no privilege in the said Church when present in the United States, except that of ordaining — presiding when present in Conference — and lastly, travelling at large." By this, he gives up his right "to appoint presiding Elders, and to fix the appointments of the preachers for the several Circuits, &c." These privileges are now exclusively Mr. Asbury's;

and as long as he retains them he will never be at a loss for *tools*. 3. The Doctor gives a *written* instrument, as if his *word* could not be depended on, by those of his own fraternity; and even this *written instrument* must be signed by *three witnesses*. And is this what Thomas Coke, Doctor of Civil Law, late of Jesus College, in the University of Oxford, and a Presbyter of the Church of England has come to? Surely his Episcopal honors are prostrated in the dust; for Heaven knows it is low enough with a Methodist bishop, when his *word* will not pass with his *brother* bishop, or with the travelling preachers in Conference. Let the reader take notice that from this period, there never was anything like a good understanding, official harmony, or Christian love, between *bishop* Coke and *bishop* Asbury; and that the former never remitted his exertions to the day of his death, to be released from the state of servility and degradation, into which he was brought by the *trickery* and *management* of the latter.

VII. *Of the Council.* Mr. Asbury having achieved two such glorious victories at the Conference of 1787, as the expulsion of Mr. Wesley, and the degradation of Dr. Coke, it might be supposed, that with these he would have been satisfied. But those who entertain such an opinion of this "modest" bishop, give proof that they never knew the man. His thirst for power was insatiable; for, like the grave, its constant cry was, "give, give." Knowing that the travelling preachers who were the last to be subjugated, might thwart his measures if another Conference was held, he turned his thoughts and formed his plans, to prevent it, if possible. Accordingly, "in 1789 a plan was laid for holding a council. The bishops said they had made it a matter of prayer; and they believed it was the best plan they could think of." Lee's Hist. of Methodism, p. 149. "*Best*" it no doubt was, for the object which Mr. Asbury had in view, which was to prevent the preachers from coming together at Conference; for he well knew the narrower the circle, the easier it could be covered, and the smaller the numerical force, the sooner it could be overcome. He therefore preferred a council to a Conference, although this "plan" was a departure from original Methodism both in Europe and America. Mr. Wesley held a Conference every year with his preachers in England; and Annual Conferences had been held in America from 1773 to the present year. And what of that? Mr. Asbury could find it convenient, and "expedient," to depart from established usage, when it suited his purpose. The council therefore met on the 10th of October, 1789, in Baltimore — a city celebrated in Methodist history — formed its constitution and declared its powers. Should any ask, how was the council organized, of what number was it composed, and what were the powers it assumed? We answer — 1. It was composed of *nine presiding Elders*, with Mr. Asbury at their head, as president of council. 2. These nine presiding Elders were all appointed to that office by Mr. Asbury; of course they were all his creatures, and if any one of them dared to oppose any of his measures, he could lay him aside, and appoint another more subservient. 3. Mr. Asbury was president of council, and had a *negative* on its proceedings. 4. The council declare, "they have power to mature and resolve on all things relative to the *spiritual* and *temporal* interests of the Church." Such was the composition of this celebrated council, and such were the powers they modestly claimed. But "their proceedings," says Lee in his history of Methodism, p. 158, "gave such dissatisfaction to our connexion, in general, and to our travelling preachers in particular, that they were forced to abandon the plan, and there has never since been a meeting of the kind. And so offensive was the name, that "the bishops requested that the name of the council might not be mentioned in the Conference again."

Here we were about to close a subject, of which we confess we were ashamed, when casting our eye over the "Appendix to the Defense of our Fathers," our attention was arrested by the following remarks of the Author of that work, which we shall transcribe, and place in italics. "*The council was proposed as an expedient; but not being found to answer the purpose, it was discontinued, after only two sessions, in* 1789 *and* 1790." Let the reader bear in mind, that the travelling preachers in 1784 excluded the members of the Church from having any part in its organization. The council of nine presiding Elders in 1789 excluded the travelling preachers from participating in their proceedings. And Mr. Asbury, now the *pontifex maximus* of American Methodism, as president, had a negative on the proceedings of council. Is it any wonder, then, that Mr. O'Kelly and other American preachers were opposed to such a system of despotism? We think not. "*In that measure*" (the discontinuance of the council) *"Dr. Coke did not concur."* This we deny. We know it is not true. Bishop Emory, who, we are told, "was a chief ornament and light of our Episcopacy," and who "brought to the investigation of all ecclesiastical subjects a cool, sagacious, powerful, practical intellect," was not born at the time of the council; and yet he speaks as confidently as though he was personally acquainted with those who bore a part in the transactions of those times, and was present when the occurrences of which he writes took place. Had he been acquainted with what took place at the Charleston Conference in '91, he would have known that Dr. Coke condemned Mr. Asbury's conduct to his face. Or was he acquainted with what passed at the Virginia Conference of the same year, he would have known that Dr. Coke addressed Mr. O'Kelly in the following manner: "Methodism is gone. But remember, when we meet together, and overthrow the new institution,[10] as I believe we shall, if Mr. Asbury is not satisfied with the government as it stood before, we will contend for a Republican government. Give me thy hand — fear not; I am a friend to America." *"The proceedings of Mr. O'Kelly produced great agitation."* They did so. They shook the powers of despotism to their very foundation. And here is *one* truth from that book of lies. But the author did not "mean so;" it was written for another purpose to calumniate Mr. O'Kelly. If the reader would wish to know how this gentleman produced such "great agitation," we will give him one of the tools with which he worked. He wrote to the District Conferences, thus — "Brethren and fellow-laborers — You are the only court we have to lay our grievances before. We are not petitioning as criminals, we have done no evil, but we demand of you the ordinance of justice. *We are not allowed to be present. We are cut off,* &c." It was in this way that "Mr. O'Kelly produced great agitation;" and for his opposition to those despotic measures, his name has been cast out as evil by the friends and advocates of despotism. The bishop goes on — *"Special pains were taken to enlist Dr. Coke in his views, and to produce disaffection between him and bishop Asbury."* Here the bishop writes like himself again, for there are two palpable falsehoods in less than two lines. The "special pains that

---

[10] The Council.

were taken," were not taken by Mr. O'Kelly "to enlist Dr. Coke in his views;" but they were taken by Dr. Coke, and by Mr. Asbury, to secure Mr. O'Kelly to their respective interests. The fact is, these two ecclesiastical leaders, in their struggles for power, were afraid of Mr. O'Kelly, and each took "special pains" that this gentleman's influence might be thrown into his scale. Hence Mr. Asbury writes to him as follows: — "Let all past conduct between thee and me, be buried, and never come before the Conference, or elsewhere, — send me the dove. I saw thy face was not towards me in all the council, therefore [I] did not treat thee with that respect due to one who had suffered so much for the cause of truth and liberty. I wrote to the Doctor (T. Coke) that if he came here again he would see trouble." And Dr. Coke writes to Mr. O'Kelly in this strain — "Wilmington May 4, 1791. To brother O'Kelly: — DEAR FRIEND — I have written a letter of a sheet and a half to you, but on consideration I believe I shall not send it to you till I reach Europe: then I shall probably write as much again to you. By this time, you probably have been informed of our great loss, in the death of Mr. Wesley. I am hastening to Europe at this important crisis. You may depend on my being with you, God willing, at the General Conference. I think no step will be taken during my absence, to prevent the General Conference; it would be so gross an insult on truth, justice, mercy, and peace, that it will not be, I think, attempted. If it be, and successfully, we will call a Congress. I expect you to be faithful. But as Mordecai said to Esther, think not with thyself that thou shalt escape more than others; for if thou altogether holdest thy peace at this time, then shall there enlargement and deliverance arise to the Jews from another place; but thou and thy father's house shall be destroyed." Oh, be firm, be very firm, and very cautious, and very wise, and depend upon a faithful friend in THOS. COKE."

And does this look like Mr. O'Kelly's taking "special pains to enlist Dr. Coke in his views?" It is a pity that when a Methodist bishop, "who is the chief ornament of our Episcopacy" writes, he will not confine himself to the truth. Besides the above letter, Dr. Coke issued a Circular of the same date, and from the same place in which he says — "Five things we have in view. 1. The abolition of the arbitrary aristocracy. 2. The investing of the nomination of the presiding Elders in the Conference of the districts. 3. The limitations of the districts to be invested in the general Conference. 4. An appeal allowed each preacher on the reading of the stations. 5. A general Conference of at least two-thirds of the preachers as a check upon everything.

But a good superintendent will not do the wrong you fear. I answer, a good superintendent is but a man, and a man is fond of power. But a good superintendent may become a tyrant, or be succeeded by one. Oh, stand up for liberty, be friends of mankind in all things."

Nor was Bishop Emory nearer the truth when he asserted, that "special pains had been taken by Mr. O'Kelly to produce disaffection between Dr. Coke and Mr. Asbury." From the time that these gentlemen were raised to be bishops there was no affection between them — as the preceding letters fully prove — and we will add there could be none. For, the one was constantly studying and plotting how he could enlarge his own powers, and abridge those of his rival. The other was struggling, as for life, to recover the former position he occupied in the Church; and if that could not be regained, to extricate himself from the state of thraldom and disgrace into which he had been reduced by the cunning and rancorous hatred of his opponent. These are unpalatable truths, we know, to the Methodist reader; but it is on these principles, and on these alone, we can account for Dr. Coke's conduct, in applying to Bishop White to be united with the Protestant Episcopal Church in the United States, whose clergy, in general, he had denounced from the pulpit and the press, a few years before, as being "the parasites and bottle companions of the rich and the great." Dr. Coke's letter to Bishop White shall be given in our next number.

NUMBER XXIV.

VIII. Of Dr. Coke's letter to Bishop White.

"Right Reverend Sir: Permit me to intrude a little on your time, on a subject of great importance.

You, I believe, are conscious, that I was brought up in the Church of England, and have been ordained a presbyter of that church. For many years I was prejudiced, even, I think, to bigotry, in favor of it: but through a variety of causes and incidents, to mention which would be tedious and useless, my mind was exceedingly biased on the other side of the question. In consequence of this, I am not sure but I went further in the separation of our church in America, than Mr. Wesley, from whom I had received my commission, did intend. He did indeed solemnly invest me, as far as he had a right so to do, with episcopal authority, but did not intend, I think, that our entire separation should take place. He being pressed by our friends on this side the water, for ministers to administer the sacraments to them, (there being very few clergy of the Church of England then in the States) he went farther, I am sure, than he would have gone, if he had foreseen some events which followed. And this I am certain of — that he is now sorry for the separation.

But what can be done for a re-union which I wish for? and to accomplish which, Mr. Wesley, I have no doubt, would use his influence to the utmost. The affection of a very considerable number of the preachers, and most of the people, is very strong towards him, notwithstanding the excessive ill usage he received from a few. My interest also is not small; and both his and mine would readily and to the utmost, be used to accomplish that (to us) very desirable object, if a readiness were shown by the bishops of the Protestant Episcopal Church to re-unite.

It is even to your church an object of great importance. We have now above 60,000 adults in our society in these States; and about 250 travelling ministers and preachers; besides a great number of local preachers, very far exceeding the number of travelling preachers; and some of these local preachers are men of very considerable abilities: but if we number the Methodists as most people number the members of their church, viz: by the families which constantly attend the divine ordinances in their places of worship, they will make a larger body than you possibly conceive. The society, I believe, may be safely multiplied by five on an average, to give us our stated congregations; which will then amount to 300,000. And if the calculation, which I think some eminent writers have made, be just, that three-fifths of mankind are un-adults (if I may use the expression) at any given period, it will follow that all the families, the adults of which form our congregations in these States amount to 750,000. About one-fifth of these are blacks.

The work now extends in length from Boston to the South of Georgia; and in breadth, from the Atlantic to lake Champlain, Vermont, Albany, Redstone, Holstein, Kentucky, Cumberland, &c. But there are many hindrances in the way. Can they be removed?

1. Our ordained ministers will not, ought not, give up their right of administering the sacraments. I don't think that the generality of them, perhaps none of them, would refuse to submit to a re-ordination, if other hindrances were removed out of the way. I must here observe, that between sixty and seventy only, out of the two hundred and fifty have been ordained presbyters, and about sixty deacons (only). The presbyters are the choicest of the whole.

2. The other preachers would hardly submit to re-union, if the possibility of their rising up to ordination depended on the present bishops in America. Because, though they are all, I think I may say zealous, pious, and very useful men, yet they are not acquainted with the learned languages. Besides, they would argue, if the present bishops would waive the article of the learned languages, yet their successors might not.

My desire of a re-union is so sincere and earnest, that these difficulties make me tremble: and yet something must be done before the death of Mr. Wesley, otherwise I shall despair of success: for though my influence among the Methodists in these States, as well as in Europe, is I doubt not increasing, yet Mr. Asbury, whose influence is very capital, will not easily comply, nay I know he will be exceedingly averse to it.

In Europe, where some steps had been taken tending to a separation, all is at an end. Mr. Wesley is a determined enemy of it, and I have lately borne an open and successful testimony against it.

Shall I be favored with a private interview with you in Philadelphia? I shall be there, God willing, on Tuesday, the 17th of May. If this be agreeable, I'll beg of you just to signify it in a note directed to me at Mr. Jacob Baker's, Merchant, Market street, Philadelphia; or if you please, by a few lines sent me by the rereturn of the post, at Philip Rogers', Esq., in Baltimore, from yourself or Dr. Magaw: and I will wait upon you with my friend Dr. Magaw. We can then enlarge on the subjects.

I am conscious of it, that secrecy is of great importance in the present state of the business, till the minds of you, your brother bishops, and Mr. Wesley, be circumstantially known. I must therefore beg that these things be confined to yourself and Dr. Magaw, till I have the honor of seeing you.

Thus you see I have made a bold venture on your honor and candor, and have opened my whole heart to you on the subject, as far as the extent of a small letter will allow me. If you put equal confidence in me, you will find me candid and faithful.

I have, notwithstanding, been guilty of inadvertencies. Very lately I found myself obliged (for the pacifying of my conscience) to write a penitential letter to the Rev. Mr. Jarratt, which gave him great satisfaction: and for the same reason I must write another to the Rev. Mr. Pettigrew.

When I was last in America, I prepared and corrected a great variety of things for our Magazine; indeed almost every thing was printed, except some loose hints which I had taken of one of my journeys, and which I left in my hurry with Mr. Asbury, without any correction; entreating him that no part of them might be printed which could be improper or offensive. But through great inadvertency, I suppose, he suffered some reflections on the characters of the two above mentioned gentlemen to be inserted in the Magazine, for which I am very sorry: and probably shall not rest till I have made my acknowledgments more public; though Mr. Jarratt does not desire it.

I am not sure, whether I have not also offended you, sir, by accepting one of the offers made me by you and Dr. Magaw, of the use of your churches, about six years ago, on my first visit to Philadelphia, without informing you of our plan of separation from the Church of England. If I did offend, (as I doubt I did, especially from what you said to Mr. Richard Dallam of Abingdon) I sincerely beg yours and Dr. Magaw's pardon. I'll endeavor to amend. But alas! I am a frail, weak creature.

I will intrude no longer at present. One thing only I will claim from your candor — that if you have no thought of improving this proposal, you will burn this letter, and take no more notice of it (for it would be a pity to have us entirely alienated from each other, if we cannot unite in the manner my ardent wishes desire) but if you will further negotiate the business, I will explain my mind still more fully to you on the probabilities of success.

In the meantime, permit me, with great respect, to subscribe myself, Right Reverend Sir, your very humble servant in Christ,

(Signed) Thomas Coke.

The Right Reverend Father in God, BISHOP WHITE.
Richmond, April 24th, 1791.
P.S. You must excuse interlineations, &c. I am just going into the country and have no time to transcribe."

We cannot dismiss this letter, notwithstanding it is very plain and intelligible, without observing, it exhibits Dr. Coke in his true character, as ambitious, changeable, and unfaithful. Let the reader take notice, that the doctor's attempts to wheedle Bishop White, as he had previously wheedled Mr. Wesley, and as he afterwards tried to wheedle the Bishop of London and the Hon. William Wilberforce, by representing *his* schemes as being promotive of the cause of Christ. But all these schemes were schemes of *darkness*, and intended to further his *self aggrandizement*. "He withdrew with Mr. Asbury, to a *private chamber*, to consult on the plan for the government of the societies;" although it is now said, Mr. Wesley recommended the episcopal form of government for the church. His "commission" never saw the light, until after his death. He destroyed the "little sketch" — mutilated Mr. Wesley's circular of Sept. 10, 1784 — forged a false section of Chap. 1, of the book of discipline — and in this letter he says — "secrecy is of great importance." All very "*candid* and *faithful*" to be sure. Was he "faithful" to Mr. Wesley in organizing the societies into an "independent Episcopal Church?" Was he "faithful" to Mr. Wesley's commands when he took the title of bishop? The Rev. Henry Moore, in his Life of Wesley says — "With respect to the title of bishop, I *know* that Mr. Wesley enjoined the doctor and his associates, and *in the most solemn manner*, that it should not be taken. In a letter to Mrs. Gilbert, the widow of the excellent Nathaniel Gilbert, Esq., of Antigua, a copy of which now lies before me, he states this in the strongest manner. In this, and *in every similar deviation*, I cannot be the apologist of Dr. Coke; and I can state in contradiction to all that Dr. Whitehead and Mr. Hampson have said, that *Mr. Wesley never gave his sanction* to any of these things: nor was he the author of one line of all that Dr. Coke published in America on this subject. His *views* on these points, were very *different* from those of his zealous son in the gospel." Vol II., Page 279. We wonder if Dr. Coke ever "found himself obliged (for the pacifying of his conscience) to write a penitential letter" to Mr. Wesley, for violating his most solemn injunctions? If he did not, "his conscience" was made of *queer* stuff — we will call it Methodist stuff. But seriously, how shameful — how detestable are such deeds of darkness, for a man who claims to be a Christian bishop. Will Dr. Durbin defend them?

This letter exhibits also a delightful example of the mutual confidence and cooperation, which Mr. Emory tells us always existed between the two Methodist bishops, Dr. Coke and Mr. Asbury. A fine specimen indeed of episcopal affection!! Interest opposed to interest. Influence working against influence. One bishop trying to counteract, and get away from the power of the other. Well may some of the Methodist Episcopal Church be ashamed of their bishops, and express surprise, that any man would dare to write "a defense" of such conduct. For what would any man, who was associated with another in mercantile pursuits, think of his partner, if that partner were to conduct himself towards him, as Dr. Coke conducted himself towards Mr. Asbury?"*Burn this letter*" would be sufficient to excite indignation in the breast of any man against his partner. But instead of contemplating these men as men of the world, bound to each other by the ties of interest and honor, they must be considered in a higher point of view, as *joint superintendents* in the Methodist Episcopal Church. Standing in this relation to each other, they travel together for several days after the letter was written. They converse together, pray together, preach together, eat and sleep together, and the one does not utter a syllable to his colleague about the reunion!! Is there anything in the history of the Popes to surpass this? How must Mr. Asbury have felt, when he received, opened, and read Bishop White's answer to Dr. Coke's letter which fell into his hands? Is it not reasonable to suppose he was thunderstruck with surprise, and that he was indignant at the doctor's conduct? That he was ready to cry out treachery, deception, intrigue, and a thousand things beside? Nor is it strange, that in a letter written subsequently, and now lying before me, he should say — "I cannot confide in ecclesiastics passing through the degrees and *intrigues* of a University, as I can trust a ploughman."

NUMBER XXV.

In February, 1791, the Southern Conference met in Charleston, at which Dr. Coke was present. Here, learning that the proceedings of the "council" had giving great dissatisfaction to preachers and people, he insisted on a call of the General Conference, "to overlook," as he said, "the proceedings of council." To this measure Mr. Asbury was opposed, knowing that his conduct would not bear the light; but at last, reluctantly consented. From Charleston the two bishops travelled together to the Virginia Conference, which was held in Petersburgh that year; and after conference pursued their journey to the North. At Richmond, on their way, Dr. Coke wrote his letter to Bishop White, on the 24th of April, and on the 29th, five days afterward, he received information of the death of Mr. Wesley: a proof that he did not know of the death of Mr. Wesley at the time he wrote to Bishop White. As soon as he obtained information of this event, he immediately took steps to return to England — preached on the 1st of May on the occasion, in Baltimore, and on the 4th wrote the letter to Mr. O'Kelly, and issued the "circular" from Wilmington, Delaware, which have been given in a preceding number.

It is more than probable, that as soon as Dr. Coke had heard of Mr. Wesley's death, he entertained sanguine expectations of being elevated to higher places of distinction in the British conference, than he had occupied in Mr. Wesley's life time. He may have entertained these expectations, knowing with what success he had practiced his schemes upon Mr. Wesley, an instance of which we shall give from Whitehead's Life of Wesley, to show the arts to which the doctor had recourse to raise himself to influence and power. True, Dr. Whitehead does not mention Dr. Coke's name; but believing him to be the person intended, we place to his account the *discredit* of the transaction.

Dr. Whitehead says: "In the latter end of the summer preceding Mr. Wesley's death, a certain person, who had long been trying various schemes to acquire a superior influence over both preachers and people, endeavored to persuade Mr. Wesley, that if he disposed of his literary property by his will only, his next of kin would claim it; that a deed of assignment was necessary to prevent their claims. Mr. Wesley denied that this would be the case, and resisted the proposition of making a deed of assignment. Being, however, frequently worried on the occasion, he at length, in company with this same person, applied to his confidential solicitor on the question; who told them, that as his literary property was personal estate, his Will was a competent instrument to convey it, and that no deed of assignment was necessary. The party who wished for a deed of assignment that might answer this purpose, was not discouraged by this repulse, but afterwards wrote to the same solicitor for his further opinion on the subject; and received the same answer in writing. Finding Mr. Wesley's solicitor not of an accommodating disposition where integrity must be sacrificed, he applied to another, a total stranger to the Methodist economy, and therefore more under his direction. A deed of assignment was drawn up, to answer the purpose intended, conveying Mr. Wesley's literary property to seven persons therein named," Thomas Coke's name stands first, and that of Alexander Mather, perhaps the preacher to whom Dr. Whitehead alludes, as being in *league* with Thomas Coke, stands next, ("among whom the executors of Mr. Wesley's Will were not included) upon special trust, that they should apply all the profits of the books, &c., to the sole use and benefit of the conference, in such manner as to *them* shall seem most proper and expedient. Things being thus prepared, the old gentleman was carried privately to a friend's house, to execute this deed, five months before he died; a time when his weakness was so great, that we may venture to say, he could not sit five minutes to hear any thing read, especially in the forms of law, without falling into a doze, so that there is not the least probability that Mr. Wesley knew the contents of the deed he executed, or had any suspicion of its tendency or the design of its author. It is very certain the body of the preachers were ignorant of this scandalous transaction; in which an advantage was taken of age and infirmities by one or two individuals, to gain the management of a large and increasing annual revenue, to serve the purposes of their own influence and ambition.

I mention one or two individuals, because it has been said that one of the preachers named in this deed was in league with *him* who ought to be considered as the author of it. But I say no more on a subject that will not bear to be fully examined." Life of Wesley, Boston, Ed. Vol. II., p. 284.

There is an Edition of Whitehead's Life of Wesley, printed in Dublin in 1806, by JOHN JONES, which now lies before us. In this edition the publisher says: "In the fear of the Lord, and from a love of truth, I have labored to render this undertaking both useful and interesting, to effect which, the additions to Dr. Whitehead's original work, will be found very considerable." One of these "additions" will supply what was omitted in Dr. Whitehead's account,

— the names of the persons that were inserted in the "deed of assignment;" and will inform us of the issues of this "scandalous transaction." Mr. Jones says: "About a year and a half after making this Will, Mr. Wesley executed a Deed, in which he appointed seven gentlemen, viz.: *Dr. Thomas Coke, Messrs. Alexander Mather, Peard Dickerson, John Valton, James Rogers, Joseph Taylor, and Adam Clarke*, Trustees for all his Books, Pamphlets, and Copyrights for carrying on the work of God by itinerant preachers, according to the enrolled Deed, which we have already mentioned. But Dr. Coke being in America at the time of Mr. Wesley's death, the deed was suffered to lie dormant till his return. The three Executors then took the advice of two of the most eminent counsellors in the kingdom, who informed them that the Deed was of a *testamentary* nature, and therefore superseded the Will, with respect to the books, &c. The Deed was then presented to the Judge of the Prerogative Court of *Canterbury*, who received it as the third Codicil of Mr. Wesley's Will; on which the three Executors delivered up their general Probate, and received a new one limited to those particulars which were not mentioned in the Deed. At the same time a Probate was granted to the seven Trustees constituting them Executors for all the books, pamphlets, and copyrights of which Mr. Wesley died possessed; and empowering them to pay all his debts and legacies." Vol. II. p. 444.

And thus was Mr. Wesley's Will nullified, so far as the management of the revenue arising from all his books, pamphlets, and copyright were concerned, the power to manage this revenue taken from his "three executors, *John Horton*, Merchant, *George Wolff,* Merchant, and *William Marriott*, Stock Broker, all of London," and placed in the hands of Thomas Coke, Alexander Mather and others (without, we believe, the knowledge or sanction of the others) by the deep-laid scheme of Dr. Coke, a bishop of the Methodist Episcopal Church in America. Now, have we any reason to suppose that he that would play such tricks before High Heaven on a man enfeebled by age, and just about to step into the grave, would hesitate, for a moment, to destroy documents that were intended to curb and abridge his ambitious projects, and forge others favorable to advance his ardent aspirations? No, never. Let the rulers of the Methodist Episcopal Church say what they may, in "defense" or in extenuation of the turpitude of the above recited in-famous conduct, were a General Conference to elect us a bishop tomorrow, we should decline the *honor;* lest, as we walked the streets, the boys should cry out as we passed along — there goes a successor of *bishop* Coke, who set aside Mr. Wesley's Will, that he might have the power in his own hands, that was intended by the testator to be placed in the hands of others. Well might the Poet say —

"An honest man is the noblest work of God."

It cannot be supposed for a moment, that the author of such a scheme as the above, would find favor with the British Confer-ence; nor should he with the American Conference — nor with honorable and honest men anywhere. Failing in his expectations in England, Dr. Coke returned to the United States, to be present at the Gene ral Conference of 1792; and on the day before it com-menced its session, arrived in Baltimore. Mr. Asbury, who knew the vanity of the man, and that he could be "tickled with a straw," forgetting, or seeming to forget, the indignation he had felt against the doctor, for his secret application to Bishop White to be re-united to the Protestant Episcopal Church, proposed that the doctor should be the President of the Conference. This mark of respect coming from *bishop* Asbury, was very gratifying to the doctor's feelings, considering that sharp words had passed between these bishops at a Conference in the preceding year. The doctor accord-ingly agreed to the proposal. Whereupon Mr. Asbury selected a few preachers (men that he could depend upon you may be sure) and directed them to meet him and Dr. Coke in the evening at a private house. These preachers met the bishops as directed, and in-stead of taking any steps to review "the proceedings of council," the very thing for which the Conference was called, they declared themselves a committee to prepare the business of conference, and determined that nothing should be allowed to come before that body but what had been previously chalked out for it by that com-mittee. Now was not this an excellent device, a master stroke of policy — to keep Mr. Asbury's conduct, and "the proceedings of council," out of sight? Accordingly whenever a preacher in Con-ference would call for "the proceedings of council," Dr. Coke would stop him, and command him to be silent, saying nothing could come before them but what had been prepared by the committee. And to give the more weight and importance to the acts of the Conference, he affirmed — "THE MEMBERS OF THIS CONFERENCE ARE THE REPRESENTATIVES OF THE PEOPLE, AND WE ARE TO ALL INTENTS THE LEGISLATURE OF THE METHODIST EPISCOPAL CHURCH, AND THE GOVERNMENT IS ARISTOCRATICAL. YOU MAY CALL ME A WEATHERCOCK."

VIII. *Of the secession occasioned by the withdrawal of Rev. James O'Kelly, William M'Kendree, Rice Haggard, and others from the connexion.* Finding that the General Conference would not be allowed to review the proceedings of the council, and that he was baffled by the management of Mr. Asbury, and by the treachery of Dr. Coke in his efforts to abridge the exorbitant powers of the bishops, Mr. O'Kelly offered the following resolution — "Resolved, that after the bishop appoints the preachers at conference to their several circuits, if any one think himself injured by the appointment, he shall have liberty to appeal to the conference, and state his objections: and if the conference approve his objections, the bishop shall appoint him to another circuit."

For the information of those who are not acquainted with the Methodist economy, it may be proper to say, that from the time the preachers assumed the name of the Methodist Episcopal Church, it had been customary for Mr. Asbury to appoint each preacher to his station or circuit; and no man had any right to question the propriety of the exercise of this power, or to oppose the execution of this part of our discipline. This prerogative Dr. Coke renounced in the certificate he gave the conference in 1787; nor was he ever afterwards suffered to resume it. But with Mr. Asbury the exercise of this power was never interrupted. He held this rein of government firmly in his own hands, sensible that as long as he had it in his sole power to give places to preachers, and preachers to whatever places he chose, he never would want men to carry into execution whatever measures he wished. To him it belonged to send a preacher where he pleased; and it was immaterial to him, whether the preacher chose to go or not; whether it was convenient for him to go or not — or, whether the place to which he was appointed to go would agree with his health and constitution or not. This tremendous power over the comfort, the supplies, the health, nay the life of the preacher, began to be considered by the travelling preachers themselves, as too mighty to be exercised by any one man. If the objections entertained by the preacher against his appointment were ever so reasonable or just, it was optional with Mr. Asbury whether he would hear them or not. If he heard them, well; but if he did not choose to alter the appointment, the preacher had no alternative but to go to his circuit, or go home. To prevent the abuse of this tremendous power, and to afford the preacher security against the exercise of it, Mr. O'Kelly offered the above resolution. Mr. Lee says, in his History of Methodism, — "This motion brought on a long debate; the arguments for and against the proposal were weighty, and handled in a masterly manner. There never had been a subject before us which so fully called forth all the strength of the preachers." p. 179. But after discussing the subject three or four days, when the vote was taken, the resolution was rejected by a large majority; upon which Mr. O'Kelly and others left the connexion.

NUMBER XXVI.

There are but few now alive who were members of the Methodist Episcopal Church, when the resolution giving to a travelling preacher, when he thought himself aggrieved, a right to appeal to his conference from the appointment of the bishop, was offered at the General Conference of 1792, and for the rejection of which Mr. O'Kelly, with others, withdrew from the connexion. Of course the present race of Methodists cannot be supposed to understand the causes, the merits, or the objects of that resolution; nor have they any idea, that the rejection of it has had a tendency to bring about the present calamitous and deplorable condition of the church.[11] How could they have such an idea, when the greatest

---

[11] "The first of these cords which snapped, under its explosive force, was that of the powerful Methodist Episcopal Church. The numerous and strong ties which held it together are all broken, and its unity is gone. They now form separate churches; and instead of that feeling of attachment and devotion to the interests of the whole church which was formerly felt, they are now arrayed into two hostile bodies, engaged in litigation about what was formerly their common

pains have been taken by those who have shaped the destinies of the church, not only to conceal the occurrences of the times of which we write, but to blacken the characters of those who resisted the arbitrary power of the bishops and were not base enough to be bought back to their fealty. From travelling preachers, therefore, no correct information ought to be expected; their hopes, their fears, their interests, their prospects, their subserviency to men in power, and their official relation to those who fill the episcopal office, all forbid them to give a true account, either of the measures that were adopted, or of the men who attempted to overthrow Episcopal despotism. Correct information, on these points, should, therefore, be placed before the public; and as this is the object we have in view in drawing up these historical sketches, we shall submit to the reader, briefly and impartially, what we know of the advocates of that resolution. And first of Mr. O'Kelly.

Of this gentleman's parentage, birth, education, and manner of life, before he joined the Methodist societies, we know nothing. The first knowledge we have of him is, that his name stands on the minutes of conference for 1778, as a preacher *"remaining on trial."* According to this account, he had been fifteen or sixteen years in the travelling connexion when he offered his resolution for an "appeal." We have seen this gentleman, but we have had no personal acquaintance with him; but wherever we have been, we have never heard any speak against him, except the Methodist Episcopal preachers. The testimony of all others was to this amount: he was a pious and good man — a powerful and successful preacher. That as an *American* citizen, he was opposed to *English* ideas of liberty, there can be no doubt, and that he was zealous and uniform in his opposition to the arbitrary power of the bishops, Dr. Coke and Mr. Asbury *felt* and knew full well. The Virginia preachers greatly regretted his leaving the connexion, and sent him the following offer — "Whereas it appears that James O'Kelly's absence intimates an intention in him to stop travelling at large, as we suppose, on account of his not being allowed an appeal — We the Manchester Conference conclude, that if the rejection, of the motion for the ap-

---

property"— Speech of Hon. J. C. Calhoun in the Senate of the U.S., March 4th, 1850.

peal be his only objection, and if he will travel, we will grant him the exclusive privilege of travelling where he pleases, of preaching where he pleases, and his £40 per annum as usual. Provided nevertheless, that he shall be amenable to the Conference for his moral and ministerial character." Now, although this document bears testimony to the goodness of Mr. O'Kelly's character, yet travelling preachers would, one after another, daub him with a coat of paint, until at last they had him as black as midnight. He, however, went on preaching and forming societies which continue to the present day; and as long as he lived, he was respected and beloved by his brethren.

Of the Rev. Rice Haggard we have no knowledge farther than that he was one of the travelling preachers who withdrew from the connexion with Mr. O'Kelly: we shall, therefore, pass on to the Rev. William McKendree, another of the seceding ministers, who bore a very conspicuous part in the struggles for the appeal. And as this gentleman deserted his friend, Mr. O'Kelly, and the cause in which they had been engaged, and as he was subsequently made a bishop in the Methodist Episcopal Church, we must be allowed to bestow on him something more than a mere passing remark; and this is the more necessary and proper, as we have the authority of Bishop Soule for saying, "Mr. McKendree's life was connected with the history of Methodism, and the most important eras and events in the history of the Methodist Episcopal Church." We shall not be so disrespectful, therefore, as not to give him a due share of our attention; and that we may not be charged with unfairness, we shall form our statements from what has appeared in print.

In a secular paper of March 27th, 1835, speaking of his death, the writer who drew up the obituary panegyric of the bishop says — "Mr. McKendree was born in Williamsburgh, and was an Adjutant during the revolutionary war — that he preached his last sermon in Nashville on the 23rd of November, 1834 — that on Dec. 22nd he went to visit his brother, Dr. James McKendree — that at this place his mind seemed to be in a state of severe trial, arising chiefly from the thought that his days of usefulness and labor for the church were over, and that he could, in future, expect to be nothing but an unprofitable servant. A spirit of worldly anxiety assailed him, with which he buffetted for a season, struggling in prayer against it. Here the senior Prelate of our episcopacy surrendered the parchment of superintendency which he had held of God and the church since 1808 — he returned it stainless as the mountain snow. In conformity with the wishes of the deceased, he was shrouded in a grave robe of black silk, and enclosed in a plain, but substantial, walnut coffin, and on Saturday was interred at the left hand of his father, only a few rods from his family mansion where he died."

This account was evidently drawn up by a friend of Mr. McKendree, and was intended to set off the bishop as an almost superhuman being. But notwithstanding the pomposity of his style, the the writer has certainly done the bishop an injury, by giving room to those who might read the account, to think that the dying man was conscious of having done something enormously bad which he ought not to have done, the guilt of which now pressed upon his mind with great weight. This supposition we think is far more natural and reasonable to the philosopher and true Christian than that which is assigned by the writer as being the cause of this "severe trial." For what Christian man, who was almost eighty years old, much less what Christian bishop, would be severely distressed because he could not live longer than the utmost limit of human life? The idea is absurd, and is a libel on Christianity. Perhaps the "severe trial" which Mr. McKendree endured in his last moments, may have arisen from a review of the part he acted in the occurrences of which we are treating — or it may be, from a recollection of his agency in the expulsion of "Reformers" from the church in latter years. Be it as it may, we are greatly mistaken if we will not be able to show hereafter, that "the parchment of the senior prelate of our Episcopacy" was *not* "surrendered as stainless as the mountain-snow;" and that if it was not "red with the blood of the saints," it was at least, plentifully bedewed with their tears.

The next that we shall introduce as eulogising bishop McKendree, is the man who has been called "the light and chief ornament of our Episcopacy — our beloved bishop Emory." He says — "The venerable bishop McKendree, the senior bishop of the Methodist Episcopal Church, is at present (1830) about seventy-three years of age. His *allowance* has, at no time, exceeded *one hundred dollars* per annum, and his actual expenses in travelling.

The latter, too, have, for some years past, been voluntarily *limited* to one hundred dollars: so that, if he expended more, it must be his own cost. It is only occasionally, and when necessity obliged him, that he has incurred the expense of a travelling companion, though authorized by the conference to do so; and has not always drawn even the small appropriations made for the purpose. Within the last two years, we know that he has actually bestowed on charitable objects, not less than $200 of such appropriations; and there is good reason to believe, that his private and personal benefactions fully equal, if not exceed, his salary annually."

Here again we have a fine coat of white paint put on "our venerable bishop McKendree." But we have an objection to it — it is put on too thick, and will crack with the rays of the sun. Let us look at it. Bishop McKendree's yearly *allowance* was $100. His travelling expenses were *limited* to $100. These are the sums he received annually, which in "two years" amount to $400. *Of such appropriations* he gave "two years" for charitable objects $200. His personal benefactions fully equalled, if they did not exceed his annual salary, which in two years, amount to $200. So that he received in "two years" $400 — gave away in the same time $400 *or more*, which would leave the bishop nothing to supply his personal wants. This places him at once in the rank of angels, who, when they visit our globe, can pass through the world without victuals or clothes.

But why all these extravagant encomiums to place this man in a false position which we certainly think greatly injures him? We may be told his private purse supplied all his wants; and to those who are total strangers to his history, this answer may be satisfactory. But to us is far from being so; for it suggests the inquiry — *when* and *how* did he obtain such an amount of wealth as enable him to be so extremely beneficent? He never was book-agent — nor had he, like others, the handling of the funds of the "book concern;" if he had, we would not be at loss to comprehend *how* he got his wealth — but he was not.

Now it happens, that "we know" something of this man's parentage, that his episcopal trumpeter did not know. Old Mr. Macintree the father — for it was by this name he was called and known, and by this name the family was called and known, when the writer knew them in Greenville County, Va., near fifty years ago — was a very poor man, not having either land, or any stock whatever, that we have heard of. "We know," that we have staid all night at the house of one family, and "we know" we slept on a chaff bag. "We know," also, that we took sister Nancy into society, and entered her name on the class paper as Macintree. And "we know" that when we heard the Rev. William McKendree was elected bishop in 1808 — we could not conjecture who he was, for we did not suppose that he was the same man that was spoken of as "Billy Macintree," when we travelled in Virginia. Yet, *McKendree* may have been the name, and *Macintree* a wrong pronunciation of it. We think we have seen in some of Lorenzo Dow's writings, an allusion to the fact we have mentioned; for he com pares the bishop, if we remember right, to a "runaway negro who changes his name when he runs away." We may, however, be mistaken in this. These remarks we would not have made, were it not for the labored efforts of others to place this man on the apex of honor and power; nor do we make them now, with a view to represent *poverty*, in the abstract, as an insuperable impediment to the attainment of the grace and favor of God; for we read, that "when the beggar died, he was carried by angels into Abraham's bosom."

The third and last we shall introduce as eulogising bishop McKendree is the Rev. Bishop Joshua Soule. He says — "It is well known that at the death of our venerable and beloved Bishop McKendree, it was found that in his will he had bequeathed to me personally and individually, all his papers and manuscripts. . . . Consequently I am left, by virtue of that will, in the sole possession of Bishop McKendree's papers and manuscripts of every description. I have them in my possession. It will be recollected that at the General Conference, held in Cincinnati in 1836, I was requested by that body to preach a sermon on the death of Bishop McKendree. I did so, in compliance with the request, which by order of conference was published. . . . After the delivery of that discourse I was requested by the General Conference to prepare a Life of Bishop McKendree, which I was disposed to do according to the best of my ability ... but I have not been able to meet the request of the General Conference; and the most I can say with respect even to a preparation for accomplishing the work is that I have passed through a vast mass of Bishop McKendree's papers. ... I have no hesitation in saying that I cannot write the Life of Bishop McKendree — connected as that life is with the history of Methodism, and the most important eras and events in the history of the Methodist Episcopal Church — I cannot write the life of Bishop McKendree in such a manner as I conceive that such a work should be written. ... it is impossible for me, in the view that I take of the importance of such a work as the Life of Bishop McKendree, to write it while I am travelling around this continent.

I confess to you that were it not for my inability to perform the work, it would afford me pleasure to make the attempt. It would bring before me many important and interesting occurrences in the history of the church which all so much love, and to which I am so much attached. But I think the brethren who look abroad to such a vast field will perceive, that it should be no ordinary, commonplace publication." See the debates of the General Conference of 1844, p. 74.

NUMBER XXVII.

"*Audi alteram partem*," was an advice given by a heathen, which every Christian, who would form a correct judgment of the character of men, would do well to observe. We have given the panegyric which Mr. McKendree's personal friend drew up respecting him; and we have given what two Methodist bishops have said in his favor. We will now give the other side, and by this means, the reader will be able to make up his opinion, as to the merits or demerits of this man's conduct.

Our first inquiry must be, did Mr. McKendree take any part in the "appeal" case at the General Conference of '92? We answer he did take a very decided and active part, in support of the resolution for the appeal, which was intended to reduce and limit the power of the bishop. And when he was delivering his sentiments respecting this power, he expressed himself in these words — "*It is an insult to my understanding, and is such an arbitrary stretch of power, so tyrannical [and] despotic, that I cannot, [I] will not submit to it.*" This is the testimony of the Rev. Ezekiel Cooper, whose word no bishop's man will dare to contradict.

2nd. What did Mr. McKendree do when the resolution for the appeal was negatived? He, with Rev. James O'Kelly, Rice Haggard, and others, withdrew from the connexion. On this point Mr. Asbury testifies thus — "Sunday, 25th, came to Manchester. W. McKendree and R[ice] H[aggard], sent me their resignation in writing." — Asbury's Journals, Vol. II. page 148. We see from this circumstance, that Mr. McKendree's resignation was not a hasty or precipitate act, done in the moment of passion, or in the warmth of debate; but was a calm and deliberate deed, reduced to writing in the hours of reflection, and sent to Mr. Asbury several days after the close of the General Conference.

3rd. Did Mr. McKendree ever return to the church, and if so, in what way, or on what terms? He did return to the church, and was stationed in Norfolk, Va., the next year; but we believe he was not received by any conference. And as for the *terms* we know not that they ever transpired. We do not know whether he changed his principles — whether he made a satisfactory apology to the bishop for resisting his despotic power — or whether he was *bought* to silence. On these points we have no information, and, perhaps, never shall have any. One thing however is certain: he went back, and was made a bishop in the church, and was invested with all the essentials of power that he had resisted and condemned.

4th The next thing is to consider, was Mr. McKendree's conduct, *in these particulars,* right or wrong, creditable or discreditable, praiseworthy or infamous? On these points we are convinced there will be different opinions. Some will say that in returning to the church, and ultimately receiving all the *honors* that belong to this episcopacy, Mr. McKendree did right — nothing but right. Others who are not willing to go so far, will say: he did wrong, but as the act was only a slight offence, it ought to be forgiven, or covered with the mantle of charity. Whilst others will say, his conduct was infamous for a minister of the gospel, of which number the writer of this article declares himself to be one. Now for his reasons.

1. Mr. McKendree at the General Conference of '92, had been several years in the itinerant connexion, and was, at the time of the conference, an Elder in the church of God. As such, it is fair to conclude, that he had thought and conversed on the subject with

the Virginia preachers; and after examining it thoroughly, he pronounced it *"an arbitrary stretch of power, so tyrannical and despotic, that it was an insult to his understanding, and he would not submit to it."* Now will those who say Mr. McKendree did right in returning to the church, with these views of the power of the bishop tell us — Is it not a first truth of scripture, that there is a natural and necessary difference between right and wrong, just and unjust, good and evil, truth and falsehood — a difference which all mankind, even without the scripture, are forced, by their own feelings, to avow? — Romans 2:15. Will they tell us that Mr. McKendree, in order to get rid of the uneasiness attendant on his views, could abrogate the law connecting the intellectual and the moral faculties? Or will they tell us, that the Almighty Maker of *mind* has made it of such flexible stuff, that it will accommodate itself to the wishes or sinful propensities of men? Truly this would be to place *mind* on a level with the kaleidoscope, which takes and presents a new form and figure at every turn, and with every shake. But it may be said, the mind may be convinced of error today, and then it will change its decisions. True, but was that the case with Mr. McKendree? If it was, he is the first man that we ever heard of that was CONVINCED *right was wrong — justice* was *injustice — good* was *evil —* or *truth* was *falsehood.* His friends, therefore, cannot avail themselves of the benefit of the argument of a change of mind.

2. The General Conference of '92, was convened "to overlook the proceeding of council," and to abridge the power of the bishop, if they could not overthrow it. See Dr. Coke's circular letter dated Wilmington, Delaware, May 4th, 1791. With these objects in view, it would be strange if Mr. McKendree, to whom this power appeared so unreasonable and alarming, and who expressed himself so fearlessly respecting its nature, in the presence of the man who exercised it, would be backward to pledge himself to Mr. O'Kelly and the other Virginia preachers, that he would aid them in putting it down. It had been discussed among themselves for years. It had been denounced as oppressive to the preachers and detrimental to the work of God and the increase of the members. As such it was an object of their special hate, and therefore as a band of brothers, they came up to the conference, determined, if possible, to abridge

it. But they failed. Now it is worthy of remark, that of all those who left the church on account of this tyrannical power, Mr. McKendree was the only one who deserted his companions, and went back.

3. Mr. McKendree, as a minister of the gospel, must be supposed to have examined this subject, with reference to the precepts and principles of the gospel, otherwise he was not fit to fill the sacred office. This was his imperative duty, and no Methodist minister can be excusable before man, or be guiltless before God, who neglects this part of his duty. Now this "tyranny, this despotism, this arbitrary stretch of power which he declared was an insult to his understanding and to which he said he would not submit," is in accordance with the spirit of Christianity, or it is not. If it is agreeable to Christianity, and is sanctioned and authorized by the gospel, then was Mr. McKendree wrong in opposing it, for in so doing, he was "fighting against God." But, on the other hand, if the thing which he resisted is contrary to the nature and genius of Christianity, and if it is forbidden and condemned in the gospel, then was Mr. McKendree not only justifiable in his opposition to it, but he was under the most sacred obligations never to remit his exertions until it was extirpated from the church, both root and branch. For him then to renounce the principles by which he was governed in the conference of '92, and to act under another set of principles diametrically opposite, as if they were the real sentiments of his heart, and as if he believed they were the principles of the gospel, make him an *apostate* and a *hypocrite*, and *his* return to the church an infamous transaction.

4. This reasoning will apply with greater force to Mr. McKendree, when the fact is taken into consideration, that a later period of his life, he was made a bishop in the Methodist Episcopal Church, and was invested with all the essentials of that "arbitrary power," against which he so justly and vehemently exclaimed in the conference of '92. Nay, that he went farther than Mr. Asbury ever went in the exercise of it: for it was under his administration, and with his sanction, if not by his express directions, that hundreds of good men were excommunicated from the church — their characters blackened — and their temporal interests destroyed — for no other offence than for advocating a lay representation in the

legislative department of the church. Is it any wonder then, that in the dispensations of Providence, this man's mind should suffer a "*severe trial*" in his dying moments? — such a "severe trial," that we pray to God our last moments may *not* be like his. O how different was his end from that of Mr. Wesley! His mind was covered with the blackness of darkness — Mr. Wesley's was, to use the simile of Longinus, "like the sun in its evening declination, he remits his splendor, but retains his magnitude, and pleases more though he dazzles less."

5. Having pledged himself to Mr. O'Kelly and the other Virginia preachers, that he would stand by them and their cause, and having assured them that he would, with them, conquer or fall gloriously in the struggle, was he not bound to those men who confided in his veracity, and who considered his being marshalled in their ranks as a guaranty of his fidelity? He was; and yet he severed the connexion, by violating his sacred engagements, and deserting them and their cause forever. Now we appeal to politicians as men of the world, who do not profess to be bound to each other by *religious ties*, to say — in what light would they consider one of their party who would abandon them and their cause, and go over to their opponents in some warm political struggle? Would they not call him an apostate, a turncoat, a renegade, a deserter? Nay, would not they despise him in their hearts? They would. And so do we despise in our heart, the whole tribe of apostate "reformers," from B_____ W_____, the man who fills the episcopal chair, to the man who whips the dogs out of the meeting-house. O beware! Think of retributive justice, and in time, be wise. Indeed we would appeal to Mr. McKendree himself, if he were alive, to say — what would have been his fate, if, when he was "an Adjutant in the revolutionary war," he had deserted from the Americans and had gone over to the British? He would say, what every man will say, — if taken, he would have been shot. And this is the man whose Life bishop Soule is about to write, and to send out to the world, as a man every way worthy of imitation. As well might somebody write the Life of Benedict Arnold, and represent him as a patriot worthy of imitation. We confess when we first saw this announcement, we thought Mr. Soule was crazy; but now we think he imagines, that the omnipotence of Methodist Episcopacy can change the nature of

things, and that the admirers of the system do believe, that whatever *he* touches will be turned into gold. We, however, do not think so. And now we declare, in the face of the thousands who may read these sketches, that we think the announcement of the Life of such a man as William McKendree, by a Methodist bishop, is an insult to the churches of Christ in these United States.

6. With a view to show that Mr. McKendree's conduct is indefensible, and that similar conduct has been condemned on the page of ecclesiastical history, we will transcribe what Dr. Mosheim says respecting one of the pontiffs. "AeNEAS SYLVIUS PICCOLOMINI who succeeded him in the pontificate that same year, under the title of Pius II., rendered his name much more illustrious, not only by his extraordinary genius and the important transactions that were carried on during his administration, but also by the various and useful productions with which he enriched the republic of letters. The lustre of his fame was, indeed, tarnished by a scandalous proof which he gave of his fickleness and inconstancy, or rather, perhaps, of his bad faith: for after having vigorously defended against the pontiffs, the dignity and prerogatives of general councils, and maintained with peculiar boldness and obstinacy the cause of the council of *Bazil* against EUGENIUS IV., he ignominiously renounced these generous principles upon his accession to the pontificate, and acted in direct opposition to them, during the whole course of his administration. Thus in the year 1460, he denied publicly that the pope was subordinate to a general council, and even prohibited all appeals to such a council under the severest penalties. The year following he obtained from Louis XI. king of *France*, the abrogation of the *Pragmatic sanction* which favored, in a particular manner, the pretensions of the general councils to supremacy in the church. But the most egregious instance of impudence and perfidy that he exhibited to the world was in the year 1463, when he published a solemn retraction of all he had written in favor of the council of *Bazil*, and declared without shame or hesitation, that as AENEAS SYLVIUS he was a damnable heretic, but as Pius II., he was an orthodox pontiff. This indecent declaration was the last circumstance worthy of notice that happened during his pontificate, for he departed this life in the month of July, in the year 1464." Mosheim's Eccl. His. Vol. III., page 416.

We have been so long detained with the "council," and the General Conference of '92, which was assembled "to overlook its proceedings," and to abridge, if it could not overthrow the arbitrary power of the bishop, that we have almost lost sight of Dr. Coke in the crowd of incidents that have pressed upon our attention. We shall, however, turn to him as soon as we shall have noticed one remark, which we consider of great importance in these sketches, although it was only incidentally made by the speaker, and was intended to have a bearing on a subject different from the one on which we write.

In the Debates of the General Conference of 1844, Dr. William Capers of South Carolina, (now a bishop of the Methodist Episcopal Church, South) expressed himself thus — "I must say here, I am in possession of a piece of information about his (Mr. Wesley's) anti-slavery principles, which, perhaps, other brethren do not possess. The gentleman mentioned yesterday by Dr. Durbin, (I mean Mr. Hammett,) was, for some time, my schoolmaster. My father was one of his first and firmest friends and patrons, and a leading member of his society, first in Charleston, and afterwards, in Georgetown, where, for a while, I was his pupil. Owing to this, I suppose, at the death of his only son, not many years ago, I was given his correspondence with Mr. Wesley, during his residence as a Wesleyan missionary in the West Indies, and afterwards in Charleston, till Mr. Wesley's death. The handwriting of Mr. Wesley is unquestionable, and I state on the authority of this correspondence, that Mr. Wesley gave Mr. Hammett his decided countenance and blessing while he was in Charleston, no less than when he was at St. Kitts. Here in South Carolina, then, *Mr. Hammett formed a religious society with Mr. Wesley's sanction, and for the avowed purpose of being more Wesleyan than what was called Mr. Asbury's connexion was thought to be.*" Page 179. The italic is our own.

We have asserted more than once in the course of these letters, that the organization of the Methodist societies in America, into an "Independent Episcopal Church," was not in conformity with Mr. Wesley's instructions, nor did he ever approve of Dr. Coke's or

Mr. Asbury's conduct in this matter. And among other causes for this opinion is the fact, that some of the documents which had a direct bearing on the subject were withheld — others were mutilated — and others were destroyed. Indeed, we have affirmed in the most plain and unequivocal terms, that Methodist Episcopacy is a palpable fraud, and that the system has been perpetuated by the most shameful forgeries and falsehoods. Now who would suppose that the truth of these assertions would receive confirmation from a Methodist bishop? He is the last man in the world that might be supposed to take up his pen, or move his tongue, to establish these facts, and yet bishop Capers does it most effectually. He asserts — and we believe him to be a man of truth, though we would be very far from saying that of another Methodist bishop that we could name, — that "Mr. Wesley did correspond with Mr. Hammett" that "the handwriting of Mr. Wesley is unquestionable" — that "Mr. Wesley gave Mr. Hammett his decided countenance and blessing while he was in Charleston no less than when he was in St Kitts" — that "*Mr. Hammett formed a religious society in Charleston with Mr.*

Wesley's sanction, and for the avowed purpose of being more Wesleyan than what was called Mr. Asbury's connexion" — by which was meant the Methodist Episcopal Church. Thank you doctor — "thank you much," for this testimony in support of the truth of our position. We confess we did not expect it from a Methodist bishop, but it is not the less acceptable to us, and the sincere enquirer after the truth of Methodist history, on that account. All we regret is, that we cannot have access to this correspondence, as we think, if we had, we should find, not only these documents, but "a few more of the same sort."

To return to Dr. Coke. In order to keep all these things together which were connected with the council &c., we were obliged to pass over the letter which the bishops addressed to the President of the United States. This letter, in point of time, ought to have come in before that which Dr. Coke wrote to Bishop White. But as we passed over the chronological order, we will give it now.

"To the President of the United States:
Sir — We, the bishops of the Methodist Episcopal

Church, humbly beg leave, in the name of our society, collectively, in these United States, to express to you the warm feelings of our hearts, and our sincere congratulations on your appointment to the presidentship of these States. We are conscious from the signal proofs you have already given, that you are a friend of mankind; and under this established idea, place as full a confidence in your wisdom and integrity, for the preservation of those civil and religious liberties which have been transmitted to us by the providence of God, and the glorious revolution, as we believe ought to be reposed in man.

We have received the most grateful satisfaction, from the humble and entire dependence on the Great Governor of the Universe, which you have repeatedly expressed, acknowledging him the source of every blessing, and particularly of the most excellent constitution of these States, which is at present the admiration of the world, and may in future become its great exemplar for imitation, and hence we enjoy a holy expectation, that you will always prove a faithful and impartial patron of genuine, vital religion; the grand object of our creation and present probationary existence. And we promise you our fervent prayers to the throne of grace, that God Almighty may endue you with all the graces and gifts of his Holy Spirit, that may enable you to fill up your important station to His glory, the good of His church, the happiness and prosperity of the United States, and the welfare of mankind. Signed in behalf of the Methodist Episcopal Church.

THOMAS COKE.
FRANCIS ASBURY.
New York, May 29th, 1789."

Pursuing our usual method of making insulated remarks on documents which we think are deserving the attention of the reader, we beg him to notice the pompous manner in which this "address" commences. "We, the bishops." Now the assumption of this title was in positive disobedience of Mr. Wesley's instructions to Dr. Coke, and in contempt of his advice to Mr. Asbury. Mr. Wesley says — "how can you, how dare you, suffer yourself to be called a bishop? I shudder, I start at the very thought. Men may call me a *knave*, a *fool,* a *rascal,* a *scoundrel*, and I am content; but they shall never, by my consent, call me a *bishop.* For my sake, for God's sake, for Christ's sake, put a full end to this." From these entreaties, it is plain — yes, as plain as the sun in the heavens of a cloudless day — that "*episcopal*" Methodism is not "*Wesleyan*" Methodism — nor is it Christianity, nor is it according to the gospel of Christ.

2. At the Conference of 1787, when Mr. Wesley's name was struck off the American minutes, and his authority disowned, the title "bishop" was assumed by our "superintendents." At that conference, Dr. Coke was disgraced, and deprived, in part, of his official authority, all which we have noticed in a former letter. The doctor went to England and soon after returned; and now, on his return to the United States, he draws up and presents an address to the President, commencing with — "We, the bishops." What efforts will a drowning man make to save his life? He will even catch at a straw. These facts in Methodist history remind us of another remarkable fact, somewhat like the assumption of the title bishop, namely — that Mahomet began his imposture in the very year that the bishop of Rome, by virtue of a grant from Phocas, first assumed the title of universal pastor, and thereon claimed to himself that supremacy, which he hath been ever since endeavoring to usurp over the church of Christ. This was in the year 606, when Mahomet retired into his cave to forge his impostures; so that Antichrist seems at the same time to set both his feet upon Christendom; the one in the east, and the other in the west.

3. Is it not strange, that the address to the President of the United States does not appear in "Drew's Life of Coke?" This is the more remarkable, as the doctor's biographer inserted the President's answer. Did Mr. Drew think that the language of the address was too republican, or if you please, too American, for a subject of the King of Great Britain to use to a President of the United States? Or did he think, that if the doctor's encomiums "of those civil and religious liberties which have been transmitted to us by the provi-

dence of God, and the *glorious revolution,*" were spread upon its pages — they might involve the doctor in trouble a second time with the British conference, and bring on him another mark of Mr. Wesley's displeasure? Be that as it may, the "address" is not in Drew's Life of Coke; and we now invite particular attention to the language which Dr. Coke used when approaching a President of the United States, with a view of contrasting it with the language he used in replying to some of the Methodist brethren in Europe, who were petitioning for a representation in the British conference. In his address to the President he says — "We have received the most grateful satisfaction, from the humble and entire dependence on the Great Governor of the Universe, which you have repeatedly expressed, acknowledging him the source of every blessing, and *particularly of the most excellent constitution of these States, which is at present the admiration of the world, and may in future become its great exemplar for imitation.*" Such is the language which the doctor uses when addressing the President of the United States; — now for his reply to some of his Methodist brethren in Europe.

> "Sirs, The conference considers the plan of electing by the votes of the people, and sending delegates to conference and district meetings, committees, delegates, is founded on the principles of Jacobinism; *principles which we abhor.* Such principles have an immediate tendency to bring into the church of God disorder and confusion, similar, in its way, to that which the same principles have brought into the State. We are certain that our late venerable father in the gospel detested those principles as much as any man on earth. The economy he established among the Methodists, his writings and public declarations from the pulpit, have been witness of this.
>
> We are therefore determined, in the most resolved manner, and with the most unanimous spirit, to reject the plan of delegates, in whatever shape or manner it may be proposed.
>
> Thomas Coke."

What episcopal Methodist, who may happen to read the above letters, will believe that Dr. Coke was capable of practicing such duplicity and falsehood as they exhibit? or what stronger proofs will be required to establish the truth of these things, than is given by the doctor's own pen? It is not, however, in a moral, but in a *political* point of light, that we would now present Dr. Coke to the American reader. Will episcopal Methodists bestow a little reflection on the Subject? Will they see — or will they refuse to see — in what light one of their bishops, whose praise has been trumpeted throughout the length and breadth of the land, represents the principle of the government under which we live? He declares, that he "considers the plan of electing delegates by the vote of the people, is founded on the principles of Jacobinism; principles which he abhors." He declares, that "the principles of electing and sending delegates, bring disorder and confusion into the State;" and that he "will resist these principles in whatever shape or manner they may be proposed." Now we put it to you as Americans, are you willing to hear these principles stigmatized by an Englishman, as the principles of Jacobinism? Are you willing to sacrifice these principles, which are the principles of the Constitution of the United States, and to preserve the integrity of which the nation is convulsed to her very centre, are you willing, we say, to sacrifice this Constitution and these principles at the shrine of Methodist Episcopacy? Are you prepared to give up all to support a system which theoretically denounces and "*abhors*" principles of which you justly boast, and for which your fathers bled and fell on the field of battle? You can make your election between the Constitution of the United States, and the system of Methodist Episcopacy; but you cannot support them both, and be consistent men; for their principles are diametrically opposite to each other. Turn away then from ecclesiastical demagogues — men who would sell their country to be made a Methodist bishop, and let those principles of "electing delegates by the vote of the people and sending them" to Conference as well as to Congress, be the principles which hereafter you will cherish and defend.

From the General Conference in 1792 to the General Conference in 1796, Dr. Coke's time was spent principally in superintending the missions to the West Indies and other parts of the world: But, at the General Conference in the latter year, he gave himself up to the Methodist Episcopal Church; and engaged, after he had settled his affairs in England, to return, and make the United States his future and permanent home. This transfer of himself to the American Methodists, has always appeared to us a very extraordinary step in the doctor's conduct; especially, when we reflected on the treatment he had received from the Conference of 1787, at which he was disgraced and deprived, in part, of his official authority. It may be, however, that the treatment he received from the British Conference, on his return to England, immediately after the death of Mr. Wesley, was not more pleasing to him, than that of the American Conference in '87: and that the conduct of the British Conference induced him to make a transfer of himself to the American Methodists. Many of the British preachers had long considered Dr. Coke as an ambitious and aspiring man; and it was supposed by several of them, that he indulged expectations of being raised to the head of the British connexion, after the death of Mr. Wesley. That the preachers attributed these ambitious views to him, seems to be pretty plainly intimated in Drew's Life of Coke, p. 233. Mr. Drew says — "The supposed occasion of Dr. Coke's arrival in England at this particular crisis of the Methodist connexion, though pleasing to some, was by no means gratifying to all the preachers. To the painful feelings which arose from this circumstance, he was not insensible." The Doctor, distinctly understanding by the conduct of the preachers on this occasion, that it would be idle in him to indulge any farther hopes of ever arriving at this honor, turned his thoughts to America, and gave himself entirely to the Episcopal Methodists. This is an important epoch in the doctor's history, and will require us to place before the reader some documents relating to this transfer. And first from Mr. Asbury:

"My very dear friend Dr. Coke, — When I consider the solemn offer you made of yourself to the General Conference, and their free and deliberate acceptance of you as their Episcopos," *(risum teneatis amici)* "I must view you as most assuredly bound to this branch of the Methodist Episcopal Church in the United States of America. You cannot, you dare not, but consider yourself as a servant of the church, and a citizen of the continent of America. And although you may be called to Europe to fulfil some prior engagements, and wind up your temporal affairs, nothing ought to prevent your hasty return to the continent, to live and die in America. I shall look upon you as violating your most solemn obligations, if you delay your return. If you are a man of a large mind, you will give up a few islands for a vast continent, not less than 1400 miles in length, and 1000 miles in breadth. We have sixteen United States for ingress and egress, rising, not like little settlements, but like large nations and kingdoms. I conclude, that I consider you are no longer a citizen of Wales, or England, but of the United States of America. I am, with great respect, your ever dear brother, FRANCIS ASBURY. Charleston, Feb. 8th, 1797.

P.S. I give you this to remind you, lest you should forget what you have done, and what the general Conference expects from you."

We shall drop the history of Dr. Coke's offer of himself to the Episcopal Methodists, for the present, in order to take up another of the doctor's secret projects; for it really appears to us, he was always plotting and scheming how he might advance his own aggrandizement. It will be remembered, that in 1791, Dr. Coke made a proposal to Bishop White, for himself and the whole body of the Episcocal Methodists to be united with the Protestant Episcopal church, without even consulting his colleague, Mr. Asbury, or any of the preachers, respecting the propriety of the measure. And now he has another scheme in his head, the principles and outlines of which are developed in the following letter to the Bishop of London:

> "May it please your Lordship,
> I have felt strong inclination for more than twelve months past, to take the liberty of writing to your Lordship on a subject which appears to me of vast importance; I mean the necessity of securing the great body of Methodists in connexion with the late Rev. John

Wesley to the Church of England.

The Methodist society in England only, consists of between eighty and ninety thousand adults in close connexion. Our regular hearers amount, I believe, to full six times as many, upon the average, inclusive of the societies; so that the regular hearers make up half a million. They are friends of the liturgy of the Church of England, and of its Episcopacy. But there is one thing which I greatly dread, and which I am afraid, if not prevented, will in the course of years have a very fatal tendency.

A very considerable part of our society have imbibed a deep prejudice against receiving the Lord's Supper from the hands of immoral clergymen. The word immoral they consider in a very extensive sense, as including all those who frequent card-tables, balls, horse-racing, theatres, and other places of fashionable amusement. I have found it in vain to urge to them, that the validity of the ordinance does not depend upon the piety or even the morality of the minister: all my arguments have had no effect. In consequence of this, petitions were sent, immediately after the death of Mr. Wesley, from different societies to our annual conferences, requesting that they might receive the Lord's Supper from their own preachers, or from such as Conference might appoint to administer it to them. For two years this point was combatted with success; but some of our leading friends conceiving that a few exempt cases might be allowed, opposition to the measure was overruled. These exempt cases, as had been foreseen, annually increased: so that now a considerable number of our body have deviated in this instance from the Established Church; and I plainly perceive, that this deviation, unless prevented, will, in time, bring about a universal separation from the Establishment.

But how can this be prevented? I am inclined to think, that if a given number of our leading preachers, proposed by our General Conference, were to be ordained, and permitted to travel through our connexion, to administer the Sacraments to those societies who have been thus prejudiced as above, every difficulty would be removed. I have no doubt that the people would be universally satisfied. The men of the greatest influence in the connexion would unite with me; and every deviation from the Church of England would be done away.

In a letter which a few months past I took the liberty of writing to your Lordship, on the business of our societies in Jersey, I observed, that for a little time I had been warped from the Church of England, in consequence of my visiting the States of America; but I return with a full conviction that our numerous societies in America would have been a regular Presbyterian Church, if Mr. Wesley and myself had not taken the steps which we judged it necessary to adopt.

Perhaps my lord, I may urge for the importance of the present proposition, that the promotion of union among Christians was never so necessary as in the present age, when infidelity moves with such gigantic strides. However its numerous votaries may disagree in their philosophical tenents, they cordially unite to oppose Christianity. It is only between the Methodists and the establishment, that we can hope for any cordial and permanent union to take place.

If this point be worthy of your Lordship's consideration, I could wish that something might be done as soon as convenient, as some of my intimate friends, to whom I have ventured to disclose this plan, are far advanced in years. These are men of long standing, and of great influence in our connexion. The plan meets their decided approbation, and cordial wishes for success; and I have no doubt they would gladly lay down their lives with joy, if they could see so happy a plan accomplished as I have now proposed. If an interview shall be thought necessary, on your Lordship's signifying it, I will visit London for the purpose, about the beginning of next month. About the end of April, my private plan will lead me to visit our numerous societies in Ireland, and I shall not return till the end of July, at which time our Conference will be held in Manchester. In September I intend setting off for America, to make a short visit of six or seven months to our societies on that continent, unless some business of the first importance prevent it.

I did myself the honor about a year ago, to lay this whole plan before the Attorney General, with whom I had the honor of being acquainted at Oxford, and so far as a cursory view of the business could enable him to speak, he greatly approved of it, and some months past encouraged me to lay the whole at the feet of your Lordship. This have I now done; and I pray you, my lord, whatever be your Lordship's judgment, to forgive, at all events, the liberty I have now taken. I have the honor to be, my Lord, &c. &c., *Manchester*, March 29, 1790.

T. COKE.

We cannot allow ourselves to pass over this letter although it seems to relate to the British Methodists exclusively, without making a few remarks on it. This letter, like the one to Bishop White, was hatched in secrecy; for the Doctor was as far from consulting with the British Conference respecting the object of his application to the Bishop of London, as he was from consulting with Mr. Asbury and the American preachers, with reference to their being united to the Protestant Episcopal Church, when he wrote to Bishop White. Mr. Drew says, in his Life of Coke, page 288. "It may perhaps be necessary to state, that this correspondence with the Bishop of London was of a personal nature as it respects Dr. Coke, the Conference knowing nothing of it at the time, and having no connexion whatever with the business." Now the principle of *secrecy* on which Dr. Coke acted so often, in affairs relating to others, renders it highly probable that *self* lay at the bottom of the plan, and that the object of his application was intended in some way or other, to forward his own ambitious views, rather than the interests of religion. If this was not the case, why was he so careful to conceal from his fellow-laborers in the gospel, on both sides of the Atlantic, his plans until they were brought to light without his agency? The principle of such secrecy which is so far removed from the principle of honor and honesty, ought never to find a place in the breast of a Christian minister. A married lady, no matter how high she moves in society, forfeits all claim to virtue, when she is detected carrying on a correspondence with a man, unknown to her husband. And the secret correspondence of Arnold, through the unfortunate Andre, has transmitted his name to posterity, covered with reproach.

But with what propriety could Dr. Coke lament over an event which he had a principal hand in bringing about? Mr. Drew tells us, page 358, that "At the Conference held this year in Leeds, Dr. Coke acted as Secretary, and took a distinguishing part in an important question that was agitated in this Assembly. Hitherto the Methodists had followed the advice and example of Mr. Wesley; and, with some few exceptions, had abstained from having preaching during church hours — from introducing baptism, and the Lord's Supper, and from burying their dead. From this rule many were now disposed to deviate. Both sides of this question had many able advocates; and perhaps few subjects have ever been debated in Conference, in which more force of argument, comprehensiveness of thought, and energy of expression have been displayed, than on the present occasion. Dr. Coke took the side which countenanced innovations on the old plan; and from the zeal and activity which on all occasions marked his conduct, rendered himself so conspicuous as to become unpopular with those whom he opposed." He now sees, or pretends to see, that "this deviation, unless prevented, will, in time, bring about an universal separation."

> "But how can this be prevented? I am inclined to think, that if a given number of our leading preachers, proposed by our General Conference, were to be ordained, and permitted to travel through our connexion, to administer the sacraments to those societies who have been thus prejudiced as above, every difficulty would have been removed."

Could Dr. Coke be so silly as to believe that he would be recognized a bishop over the newly ordained preachers? or did he suppose that if the Bishop of London had acceded to his plan, his Lordship could be prevailed on to ordain him a bishop? We cannot tell anything of his ulterior project; but we think the Doctor began to find he would not realize from the transfer of himself to the Methodist Episcopal Church, all the pleasure and honor he had fondly anticipated; he therefore made the foregoing application, like throwing an anchor ahead.

NUMBER XXX.

After Dr. Coke had made the foregoing application to the Bishop of London for ordination for some of the English preachers, and the Doctor's request had not been granted, he employed himself in various duties until the time arrived when he should sail for America. Accordingly when that time came he again quit Europe, and was present at the General Conference at Baltimore, which, in this year, began its session May 1, 1800, instead of the Fall, as it had done in former years. "Dr. Coke, on his embarkation," says Mr. Drew, "carried with him another Address from the English Conference, again soliciting the American brethren not to enforce with rigor the promise which he had previously made, but requesting them to permit his return to England, as they thought his presence necessary on various accounts. To this address the Conference at Baltimore returned the following reply:

"We have considered, with the greatest attention, the request you have made for the Doctor's return to Europe; and after revolving the subject deeply in our minds, and spending part of two days in debating thereon, we still feel an ardent desire for his continuance in America. This arises from the critical state of Bishop Asbury's health, the extension of our work, our affection for, and approbation of the Doctor, and his probable usefulness, provided he continued with us. We wish to detain him, as we greatly need his services. But the statement you have laid before us in your Address, of the success of the West India missions under his superintendence, the arduous attempt to carry the Gospel among the native Irish, requiring his influence and support, and the earnest request you have added to this representation, 'believing it to be for the glory of God,' hath turned the scale at present in your favor. We have, therefore, in compliance with your request, *lent* the Doctor to you for a season, to return to us as soon as he conveniently can, but at farthest by the meeting of our next General Conference. Signed by order and in behalf of the General Conference of the Methodist Episcopal Church in the United States of America.

Francis Asbury,
Richard Whatcoat.
Baltimore, May 9th, 1800."

Mr. Drew says:

"The General Conference, after viewing with due deliberation, the peculiar ground on which he stood, and weighing the solicitation which the English conference had made for his return, instead of forcing those claims which his promise had enabled them to urge, manifested a willingness to follow the example which the Virginia conference had set before them. They were willing to suspend their demands, but not to renounce their rights. The utmost, therefore, to which they would submit was, that Dr. Coke should remain in England and act under the direction of the British conference, so long as his presence in America was not essentially necessary. But in case they thought it needful to call him to the continent, his promise was still to be considered obligatory, and he was to obey the summons. Such was the final determination of the General Conference, and in this state of uncancelled suspension his promise remained until his eyes were closed in death." Page 286.

We will here offer another extract from Drew's life of Coke, with a view of supplying information upon some points, which it seems, that gentleman, with Dr. Coke's papers before him, was unable to give. Mr. Drew says — "Having made all necessary preparations for his voyage, Dr. Coke sailed in the autumn of 1803, on his ninth voyage to the Western World. But of this voyage no remarkable circumstances are known, as he either kept no journal, or else that journal is lost. From the following passage which occurs in a letter written by Mr. Asbury, it appears that the present voyage was accomplished with considerable expedition, which scarcely allowed room for many observations.

"I was a little surprised," says this venerable Apostle of the continent, "at the reception of a letter dated Petersburg, only about fifteen days after one dated Dublin, July 4th, 1803. This letter which is dated Charleston, Nov. 23, 1808, points out a tract of nearly 5000 miles in length, which the Doctor was earnestly invited to pursue in order that he might visit the seventh annual conferences on the Continent prior to his return. Whether he acceded to the proposal is, to the writer of these pages very uncertain. It is equally doubtful, whether he visited the West Indies from the continent prior to his return, or whether he had taken his leave, which eventually proved to be final, on a former occasion. It is, however, certain, that he was at Baltimore about the end of November, 1803; and it may be fairly presumed, that he did not revisit England until several months had elapsed in the year 1804, at which time he took his leave of the Continent, to visit it no more." Page 314.

The writer of these historical sketches is able to say with positiveness, that from Baltimore, where "the Doctor was about the end of November, 1803," he shaped his course for the Southern conference, which was held in Augusta, Georgia, in January, 1804. The writer was fleeing, by the advice of his physicians, from the rigors of a Northern winter to the South, where he fell in with Dr. Coke, and travelled with him to Augusta. He was equally certain that Dr. Coke was at the General Conference in Baltimore, the May following. And he is no less certain, that at that conference he was applied to, by one in authority, in a matter relating to Dr. Coke, which no man living knows but himself; but as he has no document to prove the fact, the secret shall go down with him to his grave.

We presume that it has not failed to strike the attention of the reader, that at the General Conference of 1800, Dr. Coke was "*lent* to the British connexion," and that it was expected he should remain in England, and act under the directions of the British conference, so long as his presence in America was not essentially necessary. But in case they thought it needful to call him to the continent, his promise was still to be considered obligatory, and he was to obey the summons. It will also be remembered, that Dr. Coke could not be recalled by any one annual conference. This could be done only by the General Conference, or by all the annual conferences untied in the call. Was the Doctor called by all the annual conferences in 1803? He was not: no, not even by one of them. The General Conference which was to meet in 1804, had not yet arrived, and yet, we find the Doctor, "at the end of 1803," unsolicited and unexpected, in the United States. And so unexpected was this visit to Mr. Asbury that he could not have been more surprised by a clap of thunder in a cloudless day. Everything, therefore, connected with this visit suggests the enquiry, why was it made? Did the Doctor begin to suspect that his presence was not deemed necessary? Did he begin to think that the American societies had found out that they could do without him as well as they could do without Mr. Wesley? Or, did he begin to feel that an under-current was setting so strong against him, that he would not be able to reach his desired port, that he never would, in all probability, be called to be their bishop? Alas! the poor Doctor is sadly perplexed with these misgivings; he is, therefore, determined, with or without a call, to be present at the General Conference of 1804.

As it has been asserted, and the assertion, we believe, has obtained an extensive credit, that "the greatest harmony, union, and affection" subsisted between the two gentlemen who stood at the head at the Methodist Episcopal Church; and as any attempt of ours to disabuse the public mind of such a mistake, would, in the absence of all documents, subject us to a severity of censure which we would not like to encounter, we shall abstain from all remarks of our own on this subject, and in lieu of them, shall place before the reader a few extracts from some letters in our possession that have never seen the light; and by this means, every one shall be able to judge for himself of the love and affection of the two Methodist bishops. And first from Mr. Asbury —

"The heat, my indisposition, and haste, makes my writing worse than bad. I have no correspondent in England. I should be afraid of committing myself. In compliance with my character, I answer all letters. I cannot say but Dr. Coke may use policy to attach the British connexion to him. Some have thought he only wished to get off from his engagements to the Americans, and never would visit the continent again. But I should not wonder if he should be upon the continent in less than a year. And I know not how soon death may put me out of his way. Some are bold to say, I am the only person in his way. ... Perhaps the Doctor's letter transpiring may not be so unpleasing. The British must know he pledged himself in a most solemn" (the word *manner*, it is presumed, was intended to have been written, but it is not in the original) "to the Americans — this the Conferences remind him of, and tell him he has changed his ground. I have lately seen David Simpson's plea for religion. The greatest of all, it is England's warning. He proves that the Church of England is as anti-Christian as the Church of Rome. He has confirmed me in my opinion, and he says Reformation or Ruin. I fear the Methodist connexion like ours will be more honorable than holy. Simpson, like a true reformer, renounced all relation to the church of England, and not, like the great *Watson*, take £2000 or £3000 for his work. All establishments — all collegiate qualifications for the ministry, — must be done away. God is as able to make prophets and apostles out of fishermen, ploughmen, or carpenters, and tentmakers as he ever was.

F. ASBURY."

Remarks. There is no date to this letter; but it was received and labelled "August 30, 1804." Mr. Asbury says — David Simpson

179

proves that the church of England is as anti-Christian as the church of Rome." And is not Methodist Episcopacy as anti- Christian as either? Whatever arguments will prove the former will unquestionably establish the latter. Indeed, we think, all things considered, it is more anti-Christian than either the church of England or the church of Rome — a point that shall be brought under review in the progress of these letters. "Reform or Ruin" is the watchword for Methodists. Mr. Asbury gives a side blow at Dr. Coke and his "collegiate qualifications," and a tremendous thrust at these Methodist preachers who aspire after the honors of D. D. Away with such nonsense. Methodism was more prosperous before it was loaded with such excrescences than it has been since.

In another letter which now lies before me, dated Dec. 27, 1806, Mr. Asbury says —

> "I wonder exceedingly why the British connexion should be so agitated with Dr. Coke about his letter to us. They seem like bees, and all heads! But had the Dr. only written his letter to me, I would have handed it to every conference at his desire. *Yea if it had been an impeachment of my own person.... I* do not correspond with any as I do with you. Only look well to your soul; to be holy is to be happy. Farewell in the Lord. Amen."

In the Postscript of another letter, dated April 24th, 1808, Mr. Asbury says —

> "I have been grieved in former times with some little misunderstandings between the American connexion; I now wish to guard against anything that might make discord between us and the British connexion through Dr. Coke. We should all be pious, prudent, and pure, and entertain high and honorable thoughts of each other.... I leave you to make a prudent use of what I have written. I am yours in Jesus as ever,
>
> Francis Asbury."

NUMBER XXXI.

In our last number we gave a few extracts from Mr. Asbury's

letters; in this we shall lay before your readers two letters from Dr. Coke to the writer of these sketches. These letters will not only cast some light on passages in Mr. Asbury's letters that may seem dark, but they will exhibit the state of the Doctor's mind towards the American Methodists, and the feelings of the preachers towards the Doctor. He says —

Truro, Cornwal, Eng., Jan. 10, 1806.

"My very dear brother:

I wrote to you by the last packet, a letter for the Baltimore annual conference, in conference assembled, in answer to their official letter sent to me by you. If you have not received it, I'll request the favor of you to write to brothers Cooper and Wilson for a copy of the letter; which copy they now have, lodged in their hands, lest any of my letters to the annual conferences should be lost. Be pleased to add the following paragraphs, enclosed in crotchets, to the letter I sent to you, if you have received it. The copy which is in the hands of brothers Cooper and Wilson, has those paragraphs in it. I was obliged to cut short the letter I wrote to you by the last packet, in order to save the post, and thereby the packet itself, otherwise the same paragraphs, or at least the same ideas, would have been inserted in that letter. I beg you will be so kind as to write to me immediately after the breaking up of the Baltimore conference, as I wish to know more of the sentiments of the Baltimore, Philadelphia, and New York conferences on the subject in hand, before the next British conference begins to sit, or at least, before it breaks up, which I think may be accomplished. Please to give my love to the preachers, and all the friends in Baltimore, and pray for your sincerely affectionate and faithful friend,

T. Coke."

"To the members of the Baltimore Annual Conference.

My very dear brethren — Now, at this present time, I would willingly come over to you on this ground — to assist in preserving the union of the body. To preserve that union, I should think my life well spent, or well sacrificed. As to health, the Lord is pleased to give me an uncommon share of it for a person of my age. My dearest wife, who is a blessing wherever she goes, (though she aims at nothing out of the Scriptural and delicate sphere of her own sex) can bear travelling, under the blessing of God, five thousand miles a year; and I could bear to travel ten thousand miles annually. But I want you to indulge me with some explanation, in respect to myself and my sphere of action, if I come over. Though I wrote my Circular Letter with great simplicity, and without intending to break any engagements, I was so fond as even to think that you would approve of it, I would not write it now, with the light which the letters from the annual conferences have thrown upon it. I hardly knew what to write. Something, I saw, must be done to draw forth an explanation between us. For though the opportunities of preaching in all the pulpits in the Methodist connexion in the United States was an honor infinitely above what I deserved, yet in the circumstances in which the Lord has been pleased to place me, I could not, as the servant of Christ, sacrifice any considerable influence in Europe, when considered in all its parts, for a sphere of usefulness comparatively so small.

Do then, my dear brethren, condescend to write to me a letter of explanation. Send duplicates. Please to send one by the British packet from New York, paying the postage to New York, otherwise the letter will not go; and another by the first merchant ship; I shall then, most probably, receive your answer before the next British conference, which I particularly wish to do.

God bless you all. Pray for your affectionate and (what I am sure of) your faithful friend,

T. COKE."

P. S. I have received letters from the New England and Western Conferences; but I shall not be able to hear from them again, before the British conference."

The next year we received from Dr. Coke the following letter:
Taunton, Somersetshire, Feb. 2, 1807.

"My dear brother: — Sometime ago I sent you a long letter, addressed to the Baltimore Annual Conference, and after that a short letter which I wished to have added to the former letter. But I request you to add the following to the first letter, instead of adding the second letter to it.

"Perhaps, dear respected brethren, you will now ask, "Why did you offer yourself to us?" I answer, "It was your unanimous vote at the General Conference, that the episcopacy wanted to be strengthened. I had been consecrated by our venerable Father in the Gospel, the late Mr. Wesley, a Bishop, particularly for America. I had been the means of establishing your present form of Church government, which in a general view, (though it may admit of improvements) I prefer to any other. I consider your union of infinite importance to the continuation of the present revival. Your continent makes about a third part of the land of the world. When fully cultivated and peopled, it will contain and support, perhaps, a thousand millions of inhabitants, most of whom, I expect, will speak the English language. To preserve, therefore, your union, that the work of God may progress with the progression of the population, and at last leaven the whole continent, lies exceedingly near my heart. I know that I am perfectly unworthy of the honor of *merely* preaching in all your pulpits; but it is my duty to meet the calls of God, however unworthy I may be. If you consider my living and laboring among you, will help to preserve this union, I shall think it the highest honor and happiness of my life so to do. My precious wife can travel, under the Divine blessing, 5000 miles a year, and I can travel 10,000. But considering the circumstances before mentioned it is my duty to have some explanation from you. I cannot come to you as a *mere* preacher. As to my Circular letter, I recall it entirely, acknowledging that I laid down conditions which were not included in our solemn reciprocal engagements. But I did not see things when I wrote it, as I do now. I hardly knew what to write, circumstanced as I was in respect to you. And you surely, my respected brethren, must be conscious that an explanation of some kind is really necessary. Am I to come to you in any sense as a bishop, and in what sense? I don't want to act, if I come, but in perfect subordination to the General Conference, but yet still as a Bishop, and having a right to give my judgment in all Episcopal matters, unless I render myself unworthy of the office. Do write to me as soon as you have considered this letter. Send me duplicates; one by the British packet from New York, paying the postage to New York, otherwise it will not be sent off; and another by the first merchant ship. In this case, I believe, I shall hear from you before the next British Conference sits, which I particularly desire to do. And now I leave this whole business in the hands of my God and you. Pray for us. To God's most holy keeping I commit you. May your blessed work flourish more and more; and your own hearts be ever full of Divine love.

I am, my very dear friends and brethren, yours very affectionately and faithfully,

Thomas Coke."

It is impossible, we conceive, for an intelligent Episcopal Methodist to read these letters, without feeling the mind impressed with various important considerations. They prove to all, that there was not a friendly, brotherly, Christian feeling, subsisting at heart, between Dr. Coke and Mr. Asbury. How could there be in the nature of things, when they were both ambitious, and both were striving for supremacy? Mr. Asbury had declared, long before these letters were written, "Mr. Wesley and I are like Caesar and Pompey — he will bear no equal, and I will bear no superior." Could Dr. Coke suppose, then, that Mr. Asbury would ever be willing that

Dr. Coke should be *his* superior? He might have known, that Mr. Asbury would not be satisfied if the Doctor stood on an equality with *himself.* He might have learned this by the proceedings of the Baltimore conference in 1787. If ever the words of a celebrated writer were verified in any two men, they were verified in these two Methodist bishops, "When Greek meets Greek, then comes the tug of war."

Dr. Coke's connexion with the American Methodists furnishes another very important subject for reflection. It seems to say, there is no stability in human friendship. If pure and permanent friendship could be expected to exist between any two men in the world, it might be looked for in Mr. Asbury towards Dr. Coke, and in Dr. Coke towards Mr. Asbury. Both countrymen — both Methodists — both under the influence of grace — both professing to aim at the glory of God — both ministers of the gospel — and both bishops in the church of Christ. How shall we account, then, for the jealousy and unchristian conduct which they manifested to each other? There is only one principle by which their conduct can be explained, and that is, each was ambitious, and wanted to be head, or chief. This is the key that will open their respective locks, notwithstanding their various wards. Suppose we try this key with Dr. Coke's lock. He was ambitious, and wanted to be a bishop: he therefore wheedled and cajoled Mr. Wesley to ordain preachers for America, that he might be at their head. He wanted to be a bishop; he therefore availed himself of his ordination as a "Superintendent," to represent himself a bishop. He wanted to be a bishop; he therefore "disobeyed Mr. Wesley's most solemn injunctions not to take the name," and withheld, mutilated, or destroyed documents, that would prove it was not Mr. Wesley's intention to make him one. He wanted to be a bishop; he therefore forged documents which state that Mr. Wesley "recommended the episcopal mode of church government" to the American societies, and advised them to become "an independent, Episcopal Church." He wanted to be a bishop; he therefore pompously styled himself one in his address to the President of the United States. In short, this principle was at the foundation of all his movements.

Let us now apply this key to Mr. Asbury's lock. He was ambitious, and wanted to be a bishop; he therefore labored under Mr.

Wesley, as a preacher, for 13 years, resisting every attempt to obtain the ordinances for the societies, except they were derived from Mr. Wesley. He wanted to be a bishop; he therefore refused to be ordained until he was elected by the preachers, that thereby it might be out of the power of Mr. Wesley to recall him. He wanted to be a bishop; he there rejected Mr. Wesley's authority in 1787, and struck his name off the American minutes. He wanted to be a bishop; he therefore refused to take Mr. Wesley's advice "to put away the name" forever. He wanted to be a bishop; he there fore caused charges to be preferred against Dr. Coke, on account of which, the doctor was disgraced, and, in part, divested of his authority. He wanted to be a bishop; he therefore pompously addressed the President of the United States in conjunction with Dr. Coke, in these words, "We, the bishops, &c.," and so full was his head with the idea, that he obtained the passage of the restrictive rule which entails Episcopacy upon Methodism forever.

One thing more before we close. Dr. Coke's connexion with the American Methodists terminated in fact, if not in form, at the General Conference of 1804. Up to this conference, it had been just 20 years since the societies were organized into an "independent Episcopal Church;" and just 20 years had the Doctor borne the title of bishop, when he ceased to exercise any of the functions of one. At this conference Dr. Coke and Mr. Asbury parted, but how different was their parting from their meeting. Great pains have been taken to set forth the latter as of such a character, that the like never was seen before nor since. "It was one of the most solemn, interesting, and affecting meetings that I ever witnessed," so affecting, that the people melted into tears to see those two men hug one another. Well, when they parted, how many hugs were given? how many regrets were uttered? how many tears were shed? We believe none. We know they parted — and we know they never met again, until they met in the world of spirits; but further than this, we do not feel ourselves at liberty to say.

NUMBER XXXII.

Dr. Coke's authority as a bishop in the Methodist Episcopal Church, having ceased in fact, if not in form, in 1804, and that not by any wish or act of his own, as his letters in the preceding number clearly show; a very important question here presents itself — who is answerable for the cessation of the exercise of Dr. Coke's Episcopal functions — for his separation from his spiritual charge, and for the violation of his ordination vows? Admitting, for the sake of argument, and it is on this principle that every one who has written in favor of Methodist Episcopacy has proceeded, that Mr. Wesley had a right to ordain Dr. Coke a bishop — that he did ordain him a bishop as the Doctor affirms, he did, "particularly for America," — and that for twenty years he had been recognized a bishop by the Methodist Episcopal Church--upon whose head will fall the punishment for depriving Dr. Coke of his episcopal office? for separating him from "the flock over which the Holy Ghost hath made him overseer?" and for the violation of his ordination vows? Really, it seems, these matters are mere trifles in the estimation of any Methodist bishop, who may conceive he has a right to enter into Heaven's chancery and reverse any appointment made by God. Or if he can't go there, he can here draw a black line across any man's commission who is appointed by the Great Head of the church to the office and work of the ministry, who will not be subservient to his ambitious views. What blasphemy! This subject will be noticed more at large hereafter. At present we shall confine our attention to Dr. Coke.

After the General Conference of 1804 was over, Dr. Coke returned to Europe, and was employed in preparing his commentary, and other works for the press. In the meantime, he kept up a correspondence with annual conferences and preachers in America, respecting his future operations; but receiving no call to the United States, he abandoned all thought of being a bishop in this hemisphere, and turned his thoughts to another quarter of the globe.

Twice have we seen Dr. Coke soliciting ordination from the *church*, but without success; we shall now see him applying to the *State* for the same object. He applied to two eminent British statesmen to obtain episcopal ordination, and cheerfully proposed to renounce all connexion with the Methodists, if the Prince Regent would make him Bishop for India. If anything can satisfy the *honest* advocate of Methodist Episcopacy, that Dr. Coke did *not believe* he was a bishop, his following letter will. It is copied from

"Wilberforce's Correspondence" vol. II. p. 114.

"At Samuel Hague's, Esq.,
Leeds, April 14, 1813.

Dear and Highly Respected Sir: — A subject which appears to me of great moment, lies much upon my mind; and yet it is a subject of such a delicate nature, that I cannot venture to open my mind upon it to any one of whose candor, piety, delicacy and honor, I have not the highest opinion. Such a character I do indubitably esteem you, sir; and as such, I will run the risk of opening my whole heart to you upon the point.

For at least twelve years, sir, the interests of our Indian Empire have lain very near my heart. In several instances I have made attempts to open a way for missions in that country, and even for my going over there myself. But everything proved abortive.

The prominent desire of my soul, even from my infancy (I may almost say) has been to be useful. Even when I was a Deist, for part of my time at Oxford (what a miracle of grace!) usefulness was my most darling object. The Lord has been pleased to fix me for about thirty-seven years on a point of great usefulness. My influence in the large Wesleyan connexion, the introduction and superintendence of our missions in different parts of the globe, and the wide sphere opened to me for the preaching of the gospel to almost innumerable large and attentive congregations, have opened to me a very extensive field for usefulness. Could I but close my life in being the means of raising a spiritual church in India, it would satisfy the utmost ambition of my soul here below.

I am not so much wanted in our connexion at home, as I once was. Our "Committee of Privileges," as we term it, can watch over the interests of the body, in respect to laws and government, as well in my absence as if I was with them. Our missionary committee in London can do the same in respect to missions, and my absence would only make them feel their duty more incumbent upon them. Auxiliary committees through the nation (which we have now in contemplation) will amply supply my place in respect to raising money. There is nothing to influence me much against going to India, but my extensive sphere for preaching the gospel. But this, I do assure you, sir, sinks considerably in my calculation, in comparison of the high honor, (if the Lord was to confer it upon me in His providence and grace) of beginning or reviving a genuine work of religion in the immense regions of Asia.

Impressed with these views, I wrote a letter about a fortnight ago to the Earl of Liverpool. I have either mislaid the copy of it, or destroyed it at the time, for fear of its falling into improper hands. After an introduction, drawn up in the most delicate manner in my power, I took notice of the observations made by Lord Castlereagh in the House of Commons, concerning a religious establishment in India, connected with the established church at home. I then simply opened my situation in the Wesleyan connexion, as I have stated it to you, sir, above. I enlarged on the earnest desire I had of closing my life in India — observing that if his Royal Highness the Prince Regent and the Government should think proper to appoint me their Bishop in India, I should most cheerfully, and most gratefully, accept of their offer. I am sorry I have lost the copy of this letter. In my letter to Lord Liverpool, I observed that I should, in case of my appointment to the Episcopacy of India, return most fully and faithfully into the bosom of the church, and do every thing in my power to promote its interests, and would submit to all such restrictions in the fulfilment of my office as the Government, and the Bench of Bishops at home, should think necessary. That my prime motive was to be useful to the Europeans in India; and that my second (though not the last) was to introduce the Christian religion among the Hindoos by the preaching of the gospel, and perhaps also by the establishment of schools.

I have not, sir, received an answer. Did I think that the answer was withheld because Lord Liverpool considered me as acting very improperly by making the request, I should take no farther step in the business. This may be the case, but his Lordship's silence may have arisen from other motives; on the one hand, because he did not choose to send me an absolute refusal, and on the other hand, because he did not see proper, at least just now, to give me any encouragement. When I was in some doubt this morning whether I ought to take the liberty of writing to you, my mind became determined on my being informed about three hours ago, that in a letter received from you by Mr. Hey, you observed that the generality of the House of Commons were set against granting anything of an imperative kind to the Dissenters or Methodists in sending missionaries to India. Probably I may err in respect to the exact words which you used.

I am not conscious, my dear respected sir, that the least degree of ambition influences me in this business. I possess a fortune of £1,200 a year, which is sufficient to bear my travelling expenses, and to enable me to make many charitable donations. I have lost two dear wives, and am now a widower. Our leading friends through the connexion receive me, and treat me with the utmost respect and hospitality. I am quite surrounded with friends, but India still cleaves to my heart. I sincerely believe that my strong inclinations to spend the remainder of my life in India, originated in the Divine will, whilst I am called upon to use secondary means to obtain the end.

I have formed an intimate acquaintance with Dr. Buchanan, and have written to him, to inform him that I shall make him a visit in a few days, if it be convenient. From his house, I intend *Deo Volunte* to return to Leeds for a day, and then to set off next week for London. The latter end of last November I visited him before at Moat

Hall, his place of residence, and a most pleasant visit it was to me, and also to him, I have reason to think. He has been, since I saw him, drinking of the same bitter cup of which I have been drinking, by the loss of a beloved wife.

I would just observe, sir, that a hot climate peculiarly agrees with me. I was never better in my life than when in the West Indies, during the four visits I made to that archipelago; and should now prefer the torrid zone to any other part of the world. I enjoy in this country, though sixty-five years of age, such an uninterrupted flow of health and strength as astonishes all my acquaintances. They commonly observe that they have perceived no difference in me for these last twenty years.

I would observe, sir, as I did at the commencement, that I throw myself on your candor, piety and honor. If I do not succeed in my views of India, and it were known among the preachers that I had been taking the steps I am now taking (though from a persuasion that I am in the Divine will in so doing) it might more or less affect my usefulness in the vineyard of my Lord, and that would very much afflict me. And yet, notwithstanding this, I cannot satisfy myself without making some advances in the business.

I consider, sir, your brother-in-law, Mr. Steven, to be a man of eminent worth. I have a very high esteem for him. I know that his yea is yea, and what he promises he certainly will perform. Without some promise of confidence, he might (if he were acquainted with the present business) mention it to Mr.____ with whom I know Mr. Steven is acquainted.

I have reason to believe that Lord Eldon had, (indeed I am sure of it) and probably now has, an esteem for me. Lord Sidmouth, I do think, loves me. Lord Castlereagh once expressed to Mr. Alexander Knox, then his private Secretary in Ireland, his very high regard for me; since that time I have had one interview with his Lordship in London. I have been favored, on various occasions, with private and public interviews with Lord Bathurst. I shall be glad to have your advice, whether I should write letters to those noblemen, particularly to the two first, on the present subject; or whether I had not better suspend everything, and have the pleasure of seeing you in London — I hope I shall have that honor. I shall be glad to receive three or four lines from you (don't write unless you think it may be of some immediate importance) signifying that I may wait on you immediately on my arrival in London.

If Mr. ________ were acquainted with the steps I am taking, he would, I am nearly sure, call immediately a meeting of our "committee of privileges" and the consequence might be unfavorable to my influence, and consequently to my usefulness among the Methodists. But my mind must be eased. I must venture this letter and leave the whole to God, and under him sir, to you.

With very high respect, my dear sir, your very much obliged, very humble, and very faithful servant,

T. Coke."

Any comment on this letter, we think, is entirely unnecessary. It is so plain that it cannot be misunderstood. All that we shall do for the information of the reader is to say, that Dr. Coke, accompanied by seven preachers, sailed from England, January 1st, 1814.

On the morning of the 3rd of May a servant knocked, as usual, at Dr. Coke's cabin door, but after several efforts, being unable to procure any reply, he ventured to open the door. This being done, he discovered, to his utter astonishment, the mortal remains of Dr. Coke lifeless, cold and nearly stiff, stretched upon the cabin floor.

In the afternoon the body was consigned to its watery grave, in silent solemnity to be seen no more, till "the trumpet shall sound, and the dead shall be raised incorruptible." This solemn event took place on the 3rd of May, 1814, in latitude 2 deg. 29 min. south, and in longitude 59 deg. 29 min. east from London.

NUMBER XXXIII.

Having attended Dr. Coke in every step he took to place himself at the head of the Methodist societies in America, as their
bishop, until his connexion with the church ceased at the General
Conference of 1804 — and having seen all his hopes of ever being
a bishop, in any quarter of the globe, buried with him in the Indian
Ocean, we shall now take leave of him, and turn our attention to
the General Conference of 1808. This year may be considered a remarkable period in the annals of American Methodism; because,
from this year is dated the commencement of a delegated General
Conference — the formation of the *restrictive rules*, which are
called the *constitution* of the church — and the election of
William McKendree to be a bishop.

Previous to the year 1808, it was the right of every travelling
preacher who had travelled four years from the time he was received on trial by an annual conference, and was in full connexion,
to attend the General Conference; but from this period, none but
those who were elected by their respective annual conferences, as
delegates, had a right to a seat in that body. This change proceeded
from the same principle which induced Mr. Asbury, in former
years to prefer a "council" to a conference; because the latter was,
or might be, too unmanageable for him, who wished to have everything done according to his own good pleasure. The "council" was
composed of but few, and these were presiding elders, who always
were, and always will be, the bishop's creatures and tools; but in a
conference there might be some staunch republicans, and noble-
minded ministers, such as James O'Kelly, who would disdain to
prostitute their talents to subserve the ambitious views of any ecclesiastical despot. That this change in the economy of Methodism
was brought about by the influence and exertions of Mr. Asbury,
the following extract from one of his letters, now lying before me
will prove.

> "If our title had not been the Methodist *Episcopal
> Church*, and if the English translation had not rendered
> the Episcopi, Bishop, in the Epistles of Paul to Timothy

and Titus, well contented am I to be called superintendent, not bishop! I was elected and ordained superintendent, as my parchment will prove." (Will the
Methodists pay particular attention to this assertion?)
"Does the Scripture say the Elder shall be the husband
of one wife? by some men's rule of reasoning, we
might prove, because it is not expressly said of an Elder, as a Deacon, and Bishop, in Scripture, he shall be a
husband of one wife, Elders shall not marry, because
we have no express Scripture, but they say we are the
same order, then why not the same name in Greek and
English? Why not Deacons and Bishops of the same order? this all churches agree in, *they are not.* It is an easy
matter for our brethren, members, and ministers, that
move in narrow circles, to talk to little purpose. Be assured, *if there ever should be an equitable Delegated
General Conference they will have no power to change
the constitution,* but to choose men to superintend the
whole continent, as their predecessors have done, married or single." The italicizing is our act.

A second thing by which the General Conference of 1808 is
distinguished from all others is, the formation of the restrictive
rules, which are called "*the Constitution of the Church.*" We were
about to pass over these "rules" without a note or comment, or
even incorporating them in these sketches, because they are to be
found in every Methodist book of discipline in the church, *north,*
and in the church, *south.* But as we are not writing for the information of Methodists, but for the public generally, we shall give them
a place in these letters.

The Discipline says — "The General Conference shall have
full powers to make rules and regulations for our church, under the
following limitations and restrictions, viz:

1. "The General Conference shall not revoke, alter, or change
our articles of religion, nor establish any new standards or rules of
doctrine contrary to our present existing and established standards
of doctrine.

2. They shall not allow of more than one representative for ev-

ery five members of the annual conference, nor allow of a less number than one for every seven.

3. They shall not change or alter any part or rule of our government, so as to do away Episcopacy, or destroy the plan of our itinerant superintendency.

4. They shall not revoke or change the general rules of the United Societies.

5. They shall not do away the privileges of our ministers and preachers, of trial by a committee, and of an appeal; neither shall they do away the privileges of our members, of trial before the society or by a committee of an appeal.

6. They shall not appropriate the produce of the Book Concern, or of the Charter Fund, to any purpose other than for the benefit of the travelling, supernumerary, superanuated, and worn-out preachers, their wives, widows, and children. Provided, nevertheless, that upon the joint recommendation of all the annual conferences, then a majority of two-thirds of the General Conference succeeding, shall suffice to alter any of the above restrictions."

If these restrictive rules were not intended to be placed on a footing with divine revelation, which is incapable of change, they certainly must be classed with "the law of the Medes and Persians which altereth not." We shall not, therefore, spend our time in combating such superlative arrogance, or such profound ignorance, as they display .

The third thing for which this General Conference is remarkable is, the election of William McKendree to be a bishop. When stating this man's apostasy and perfidy in a former letter, and that, notwithstanding all this, he was made a bishop, we thought it probable, that some people might doubt the truth of our statements, or deny that such a man, in the nineteenth century, could be chosen to fill that high and holy office. Well, let those who doubt or deny what we say, prove that we have misrepresented, either his character or conduct. If this cannot be done, and "we know" it cannot, how shall his election to the episcopal office be accounted for? If he was the only apostate that was raised to be a bishop in the Methodist Episcopal Church, we might place his elevation to the supposed ignorance of the preachers. We might, perhaps, say, they had never heard of the stand he took against the tyrannical power of the bishop in 1792. We might plead their want of information respecting his having sent in his resignation in writing to Mr. Asbury. But as these facts were known, we have no apology to offer for his election. We must, therefore, conclude, that *apostasy* is no hindrance to the man's being made a bishop in the Methodist Episcopal Church; for of the few native American bishops that that church has had, *three* have been arrant apostates. And now, it is proposed by a Methodist bishop to write the Life of William McKendree. We wonder who will write, or propose to write the life of Saint Judas Iscariot?

From the Conference of 1808 let us pass on to the General Conference of 1820, when another bishop was elected, the Rev. Joshua Soule. This gentleman was elected, but refused to be ordained; and we have often heard it said, and indeed have seen it in print, that he declined to receive ordination solely on account of the action of the General Conference on the presiding elder question. We know this was made a plea for his refusing to be ordained; but was it the only reason? If we mistake not there were other considerations which had their weight in producing his determination; and as, throughout this series of letters, we have offered documentary proof, when we had it in our power, we shall go to the Journals of that General Conference for proof of what we say.

Extracts of the General Conference of 1820.

> "May 13. Resolved, that the Conference will now proceed to the election of a General Superintendent. *Carried.*
>
> Resolved, that before we proceed to act on the above resolution, the Conference go to prayer. *Carried.*
>
> Br. Garretson gave out a few verses of a hymn and then prayed. The roll was called to ascertain who were absent, and it appeared, that the only one absent was Loring Grant, who is sick.
>
> In conducting the election, two persons, viz: Brs. S. G. Roszel and D. Ostrander were appointed to receive the votes. On receiving and counting the votes it appeared, that there were 88 votes, and that Joshua Soule, of this number, had 47 votes. Nathan Bangs had 38.

There were three scattering.

Joshua Soule was declared duly elected to the office of a bishop.

May 19th. Br. Joshua Soule requested leave of absence for this afternoon. *Granted.*

May 20. The following resolution was submitted, signed S. Merwin, N. Bangs.

Resolved, that the sum of one thousand dollars be paid out of the funds of the book concern, to Br. Joshua Soule, as an additional remuneration for his services as book agent for the four years past. *Carried.*

May 23. The debate on the subject under consideration, was suspended, to allow Bishop McKendree to make a communication to the General Conference.

("The communication of Bishop McKendree made to the General Conference, had reference to the change made at the present session in the constituting of Presiding Elders. The first point he brought forward, was a written communication from Br. Joshua Soule, bishop elect, in which Br. Soule stated that as the change in the above part of our discipline was made after his election to the Episcopacy, he could not, as a conscientious man, enforce or comply with the provisions of the new rule: because he considered this change a violation of the Constitution. With this construction bishop McKendree said he concurred, alleging that he viewed the proceedings of this General Conference, in this respect, an unconstitutional act. To correct, amend, or change the above proceedings, he suggested or advised the Conference to review the grounds they had taken, to alter what they had done, or to suspend the operations of the resolution till the next General Conference. If that step shall not be taken, he recommended that two members be elected by each annual conference, who shall meet together, and discuss and settle the point of constitutionality. But if none of these measures shall be adopted, painful as the thing is to his feelings, he must be considered as protesting against the said proceedings.")

If that don't go beyond the bishop of Rome, will the advocates of Methodist Episcopacy tell us what does? But to return.

"The communication being ended, bishop Roberts prayed, and bishop McKendree pronounced his benediction on the conference, and withdrew.

3 o'clock, P.M. Moved and seconded, that the motion under debate be laid on the table, to make room for one which Br. Ostrander wishes to offer. The galleries were cleared, and the house closed, before the question was taken to lay the proposition on the table. The question was then taken on laying the former subject, which had been debated so long, on the table. *Carried.*"

The following was submitted, signed D. Ostrander, James Smith.

"Whereas brother Joshua Soule, bishop elect, has signified in his letter to the episcopacy, which letter was read in open conference, that if he be ordained bishop, he will not hold himself bound to be governed by a certain resolution of this general conference, relative to the nomination and election of presiding elders — Wherefore, Resolved, &c., that the bishops be earnestly requested by this conference, to defer or postpone the ordination of the said brother Joshua Soule, until he gives satisfactory explanations to this conference." After some debate, brother Soule rose and made some remarks.

Moved and seconded that this resolution be indefinitely postponed; before the question was taken on this motion, the resolution was withdrawn.

Moved and seconded to reconsider the election of the presiding elders. Conference adjourned at six o'clock, without coming to any decision.

Wednesday morning, May 24. The unfinished business of yesterday was taken up. The resolution respecting the election of the presiding elders, being read, before the question was taken on the resolution, the following motion was submitted, signed E. Cooper, L. M. Combs.

Moved &c., that the further consideration of the question for reconsideration, be postponed until tomorrow, to give more time for deliberation and consultation in a course proper to be pursued, to promote peace and conciliation. The question was taken on this resolution and lost,-- 40 for, 45 against it.

L. M. Combs and James Smith spoke against the motion for reconsideration. It was suggested by brother Reed, that if we go into the ordination of brother Soule, it is now time. Five minutes before 11 o'clock brother Joshua Soule rose and expressed a wish that the General Conference should, by vote, request the episcopacy to delay his ordination for some time. No order was taken on the subject, when at 11 o'clock bishop Roberts took the chair, and the debates went on on the motion for reconsideration.

Br. Sias spoke against reconsideration for 15 minutes; leave was given him to go on.

The question was called for, 7 minutes before 12 o'clock, but on counting the members there was not a quorum.

Bishop George stated that the Episcopacy had deferred the ordination of Br. Soule to some future period.

Thursday morning, 25th. Bishop George informed the Conference that the ordination of Br. Soule would take place at 12 o'clock today, in this house.

Br. Joshua Soule presented a communication stating his resignation of the office of a bishop in the Methodist Episcopal Church, to which he had been elected. On motion ordered that the letter be laid on the table.

8 P.M. At the opening of the conference Br. Joshua Soule expressed a wish that the conference would come to a decision on his letter of resignation offered this morning.

Moved and seconded, that Br. Joshua Soule be requested to withdraw his resignation. This motion was withdrawn.

Moved and seconded, that the conference do not express their decision on the subject before tomorrow morning. *Carried.*

Friday, 26th, 3 P.M. The letter of Br. Soule to this Genera Conference, in which he tendered his resignation, being called for and read — it was moved and seconded, that the conference accept his resignation. *Withdrawn.* Moved that Br. Soule be, and hereby is requested to withdraw his resignation, and comply with wishes of his brethren in submitting to be ordained. S. G. Roszel, S. K. Hodges. *Carried* — 49.

Br. Soule having come into conference, again stated his purpose to resign. His resignation was accepted."

NUMBER XXXIV.

The length to which our last letter was extended, by inserting the extracts from the Journals of the General Conference of 1820, would not allow us to make any remarks on those extracts, at the time. We will now say, that they furnish irrefragable proof, that the action of the General Conference on the Presiding Elder question was not the sole cause of Mr. Soule's unwillingness to be ordained. Obnoxious as was his determination not to obey the General Conference, to the severity of censure, considering that he was only elected, and not yet ordained a bishop, we shall pass it over to state what we believe were the real causes of his refusal to be consecrated.

When it was officially announced, that Joshua Soule was elected to the office of a bishop, the preachers who were best acquainted with him determined to defeat his ordination. Whether they met in caucus to consult how they could most easily and certainly effect their purpose, we are not able to say: but we have been told that their first plan was to come in a body into the church, when the officiating bishop was about to commence the services, and protest against his ordination. Why this plan was abandoned to make way for another, we know not. But we do know, that their second plan was to reduce the General Conference below the constitutional number necessary to give validity to its proceedings, which is "two thirds." For this purpose, as the hour (12 o'clock) approached, one after another of those preachers who were opposed to his ordination would go out, until at last, "7 minutes before 12," when Mr. Sias was speaking, it was ascertained there was not a quorum. Bishop George then announced, "the ordination is postponed to some future time."

But why were the preachers who best knew Mr. Soule so strongly opposed to his ordination? There is no instance of such stern opposition being made to the ordination of any other Methodist bishop. Simply because Joshua Soule was a *despot.* Now it matters not a straw with us, whether this statement be controverted by Mr. Soule, or any of his friends, on the ground that "despot" was not the term that was used. We believe it was the *very term;* but whether it was despot, or tyrant, it is all the same in our estimation, as the ground of opposition was an overbearing, despotic, and tyrannical disposition. Perhaps his brother bishop, Elijah Hedding, recollects the expression or expressions he used, when stating his reasons for opposing the ordination of Mr. Soule. That there was an opposition — a strong, intense, and unparalleled opposition to his ordination, we presume Mr. Soule himself will not deny. This being the case, the proceedings of the General Conference of 1820, in his case, will show that there were other reasons for his declining to be ordained than that which he, or some of his friends for him, have asserted, — the action of the General Conference on the Presiding Elder question. These proceedings will do more than this — they will show, that the charge of *despotism* has not originated with the writer of these sketches, but with the men who were well acquainted with him, and stood connected with him, as a Methodist itinerant preacher in former years. The writer, therefore, will feel himself justified in applying the term *"despot"* to Mr. Soule, whenever he has occasion hereafter to speak of him or of his administration.

The Journals of the General Conference of 1820 will furnish ample information on another topic, which, in our opinion, is of vast importance to the members of the Methodist Episcopal church, if not to the community at large. They will show that the pre-eminence of a Methodist bishop does not consist simply in a pre-eminence of *order*, in being distinct from, and superior to, presbyters, but it consists in a pre-eminence of *power* and *authority*, not by express statute, we confess, but, in fact, over the General Conference itself. The General Conference has been to the Methodist Episcopal church, what General Councils were formerly to the Church of Rome. The ecclesiastical supremacy of the Pope consisted in his being superior to the General Councils. The ecclesiastical supremacy of a Methodist bishop consists in his being superior to a General Conference; in so far that he can refuse to obey, with impunity, its positive enactments, and can change, or cause to be changed, a rule passed by nearly a "two-thirds" vote of the Conference. Pay deep attention to the following proof of our position.

"Friday, May 19th, 3 P. M. The committee appointed to confer with the bishops, on a plan to conciliate the wishes of the brethren on the subject of choosing Presiding Elders, recommend to the conference the adoption of the following resolutions:

Resolved, &c., That whenever, in any annual conference, there shall be a vacancy or vacancies in the office of Presiding Elder, in consequence of his period of service of 4 years having expired, or the bishop wishing to remove any Presiding Elder, or by death, resignation, or otherwise, the bishop, or president of the conference, having ascertained the number wanted, from any of these causes, shall nominate three times the number, out of which the conference shall elect by ballot, without debate, the number wanted. Provided, when there is more than one wanted, not more than three at a time shall be nominated, nor more than one at a time elected. Provided, also, that in the case of any vacancy or vacancies in the office of Presiding Elder, in the interval of any annual conference, the bishop shall have authority to fill the said vacancy or vacancies until the ensuing annual conference.

Resolved, 2ndly, That the Presiding Elders be, and hereby are, made the advisory council of the bishops, or presidents of the conference, in stationing the preachers. Ezekiel Cooper, Stephen G. Roszel, Nathan Bangs, J. Wells, J. Emory, Wm. Capers.

The first resolution being read, the question was taken on it, and carried, — 61 for, 25 against it.

The question was taken on the second resolution as amended, with the consent of the committee. *Carried*."

Such was the rule that was enacted by the General Conference of 1820, respecting Presiding Elders. It became a law by a *majority* of 36 votes.

But liberal as this rule undoubtedly was, as a compromise, Mr. Soule, who had been just elected, but not yet ordained a bishop, could not, he said, as a conscientious man, carry it out. We have been taught that *"all or none"* is the principle of a despot, and our little reading, reflection, and observation have established in our mind, the truth of the maxim. The first thing, therefore, which Mr. Soule did after his election, shows, that those who knew him best neither misunderstood his disposition nor misrepresented his character. He would have "all" or he would have "none," of the power and authority possessed by Mr. Asbury or any other bishop; and being joined by Mr. McKendree, the conference rescinded the rule they had passed a few days before, by which a long and warmly disputed question had been settled. And there it lies at present, and will lie forever. It is idle, therefore, to talk about a Methodist bishop being subject to a General Conference. They may be so represented on paper; but *facts* prove they are not. This assertion, we believe, will be sustained by those who will reflect on what is predicated of a Methodist bishop, by a committee of the General Conference of 1844. This committee, consisting of Dr. John P. Durbin, George Peck, and Charles Elliott, was elected to reply to the "protest" of the minority of that conference, and in their reply these gentlemen say — and their statement was allowed by the General Conference, and sent out into the world under their high authority — a Methodist bishop "who decides all questions of law in annual conferences; who, of his mere motion and will, controls the work and destiny of four thousand ministers; who appoints and changes at pleasure the spiritual guides of four millions of souls, &c." If this be a true statement of the power and authority of a

Methodist bishop, *and we know it is*, it is worse than nonsense for these gentlemen to add, "They (our bishops) are entirely dependent on the General Conference — their power, their usefulness, themselves, are entirely at the mercy of the General Conference."

These two statements cannot both be true, because in their nature and essential properties, they are contrary to each other. The committee might as well tell us the North and the South poles are one and the same: or that light and darkness partake of the same qualities. What! a bishop "who of his *mere motion and will* controls the word and destiny of four thousand ministers," to be subject to those men, whose very existence depends upon his "pleasure"? — a bishop "who appoints and changes at *pleasure*, the spirtual guides from four millions of souls," and who can transfer any of those spiritual guides from one circuit or station to another, although that other may be hundreds of miles off, with as much ease as a school-boy can toss a shuttlecock from one side of the room to the opposite — a bishop who could vex and harass Job himself were he on earth again, and under his authority, until he would be forced to exclaim in the bitterness of his distress, "my soul chooseth death rather than life"? — a bishop who can starve as many of these "four thousand ministers" out of the "work" or out of the world, as he pleases, if they should dare oppose his views, and no body has any right to say to him, "What doest thou?" — a bishop, to possess all this power, and yet be subject to the General Conference — the thing is absurd! No, no, gentlemen; travelling preachers too well understand their comfort and interest to oppose the bishop, for they know if they did, the machinery of episcopacy would grind them to powder. But to the Journals —

Friday morning, May 26. Moved that the rule passed at this conference respecting the nomination and election of the Presiding Elders be suspended till the next General Conference, and that the superintendents be, and they are hereby, directed to act under the old rule respecting the appointment of Presiding Elders." Signed Edward Cannon, Wm. M. Kennedy.

Moved and seconded, that the above resolution be indefinitely postponed. It was doubted whether the resolution was in order. The resolution was admitted by the chair to be in order. An appeal was made from the decision of the chair. The question was taken on the point of order, and the decision of the chair was sustained.

3 P. M. The resolution which had been submitted this forenoon was again read, and being debated, Br. Alfred Griffith spoke 15 minutes; leave was given him to go on.

The question on indefinite postponement was taken — 39 for, 44 against it.

The resolution under debate — Br. Hedding spoke 15 minutes, and was allowed to go on by permission of the conference.

Brother Bangs continued his speech 15 minutes. Leave was given him to go on.

Moved and seconded that the motion under discussion be laid on the table. *Carried.*

Moved and seconded that the resolution, the debate on which was suspended to make way for Bro. Soule's letter of resignation to be read, be again taken up. *Carried.*

The previous question being called for — Shall the main question now be put? *Carried.*

The question was taken on the motion by dividing the house — 45 in favor of it, and 35 against it."

So that the Conference, at the suggestion of the bishop, undid what they had done a few days previously; and by this act established the supremacy of a Methodist bishop over a General Conference.

It is not our purpose to say a word to those who are willing to submit to this supremacy, in an ecclesiastical point of light. In this sense it does not concern us at all. But in a *civil* sense it does concern us, and in our judgment it is worthwhile for those who would preserve inviolate our *civil* institutions, in all their loveliness, integrity, and usefulness, to consider how far this one man's power may affect the stability of institutions that are the pride and boast of the American family. Already have we seen one institution affected through this supremacy; we therefore submit to every American to consider the propriety of saying of it — "hitherto hast thou come, but thou shalt proceed no further, and here shall thy proud waves be stayed."

NUMBER XXXV.

Methodist Episcopacy arrived at the *ne plus ultra* of power and authority in 1820. This was the year it ceased to advance; and from this year, also, we may date the commencement of its decline.

We have followed it in every step of its progress, from its beginnings in 1784, to the year 1820, when it reached the pinnacle of supremacy; and have given documentary proofs of the facts which we have spread on these pages, derived, not from the statements or writings of men who were represented to be its bitter enemies, but from the published and unpublished records of the church, and from the writings and letters of the bishops themselves. Henceforth we are to contemplate Methodist Episcopacy as on the wane; and as we have spent so much time in tracing its advances, we shall be brief in presenting the causes of its arrest, its decline, and its fall. But before we enter on this part of our work, we must be more explicit than we have been, on some points which we have heretofore slightly touched.

We fear it may have been thought, or said, that all our letters have been written against Methodism. Now if any man, woman, or child, who has read these letters, has taken up this idea, we are sorry for it. It would grieve us to the heart to say one word against Methodism, a name with which, we may say, we have been connected since the year 1787. It was in that year, it pleased God to awaken us through the labors of a Methodist preacher. It was in that year, we formed the resolution, by the help of God, we would strive to get to Heaven, and called on God himself to witness the sincerity of our vow. It was in that year, we began to attend class meetings and love feasts among the Methodists; and although our name was not just then entered on the class paper, we have borne the name of Methodist, nearly the whole of our life. We have labored several years more than half a century as a Methodist preacher, the highest honor we ever aspired after below the skies; and now, being near the end of our days, we hope to go down to our grave bearing the name of a Methodist.

But mark, we distinguish between *Methodism* and *Methodist Episcopacy*. The one, with all its peculiarities of itinerancy, class meetings, love feast, &c., &c., we receive and approve; the other, a misshapen and ugly thing, with all its horrid qualities, we reject and condemn. The one we believe is of God; the other we believe is of man. The one is a personification of "the wisdom that is from above, first pure, then peaceable, gentle, easy to be entreated, full of mercy and good fruits;" the other is a personification of the wisdom that is from beneath, "earthly, sensual, devilish." Let none think that when we lift our pen, or raise our voice, against *Methodist Episcopacy*, we say one word against Methodism.

Contemplating the subject in the light we have here represented it, we have spoken in terms of severity against those preachers who have opposed the *despotism* of Methodist Episcopacy, and afterwards have accepted the power and authority which they had previously denounced. If these men had a proper regard for themselves and their characters, they would have stated the reasons for their change of conduct. Had they done this, the people among whom they were appointed to labor, might judge of the weight and validity of these reasons, and exculpate them, if they could, from the charge of hypocrisy, which will always lie against those who act as they have done. Their former associates and brethren had *a right to demand* the reasons for the change, if they had any to give; but to the present hour, we have never seen a reason assigned by them. These were the men whom we called *apostates* from principle, men who sold their principles for "a mess of pottage." We honor the men who act from principle, but an *unprincipled* man we despise.

Such men ought to reflect on the cases of those in the New Testament, who were inclined to traffic in things pertaining to God. Simon Magus offered to purchase the power to impart the Holy Ghost; and Judas Iscariot sold his Saviour for thirty pieces of silver. The fate of these men admonish all of the evil and danger of buying or selling the *truth* for the sake of "filthy lucre." From their history we may learn, that the case of him who *receives*, and of him who *gives*, a price for principle, is alike hopeless. That although Peter, who denied his Lord and Master with oaths and curses, afterwards found acceptance with the Saviour; Judas did not. And, notwithstanding what others may say, we think there is no ground to hope for the salvation of any, who basely make merchandise of grace, or sacrifice truth for gain.

Does any one ask us on what grounds we are opposed to Methodist Episcopacy, we answer in the fear of God, we are opposed to it — because it is *anti-Christian* — because it is a *fraud* practiced on the unsuspecting members of the Methodist societies, and the world — because it is *despotic* — and because no man can open his mouth in its defense without uttering a lie. These are our views of Methodist Episcopacy, and these views we think we are able to defend.

1. Methodist Episcopacy is *anti-Christian*. Some twenty years ago, or more, a certain man who, since that time, has made himself notorious by the efforts he has made to support the system of Methodist Episcopacy, said — "a man may be a very good Christian, and not be a good episcopal Methodist." The pious part of that denomination of Christians was shocked at the declaration, and thought the writer was very much mistaken, and very unguarded in his statement. But was he not right after all? He seems to have understood his subject well, and therefore he rested its claims, not on the Scriptures, but on "*expediency.*" From the New Testament he knew nothing could be adduced in its favor, for the system of Methodist Episcopacy and the system of Christianity bear no resemblance to one another whatever.

When the General Conference of 1824 issued their "Circular" in answer to various petitions and memorials that, from different parts of the work, were sent up to that body, on what ground did they justify their refusal to comply with the prayer of the petitioners? On the ground of Scripture? No. On what then? On *Prescription.* Hear what they say —

> "But if by rights and privileges, it is intended to signify something foreign from *the institutions of the Church, as we received them from our fathers,* pardon us if we know no such rights, if we comprehend no such privileges."

Respecting this "Circular," we expressed ourselves to one of the bishops in the following manner:

> "A paper drawn up by a committee of twelve preachers, discussed and approved by at least one hundred

ministers in General Conference, and bearing the signature of three bishops. In this document there are no more than *two subjects*, MONEY and POWER, or the salaries of the preachers, and the right of the itinerant ministers to legislate for the church. And so intent was the General Conference upon establishing this right, and so perfectly absorbed were their minds with this subject, that the name of God, of Jesus Christ, or the Holy Ghost, is not named in the circular. In it, there is no allusion to the doctrines of the fall, nor to the recovery of man, by the death of Christ. The terms repentance, faith, or holiness, are not mentioned in it from beginning to end. There is not a single promise referred to as a motive to duty, or as an encouragement to perseverance; nor the slightest reference to heaven as the reward of the righteous. In it will be found no expression of thanksgiving to the great Head of the church for past mercies; nor a word of prayer for future favors."

The circular, as well as the system, is anti-Christian.

Mr. Asbury, in a letter, an extract from which was given in a former number, said, "the writer proves that the church of England is as anti-Christian as the church of Rome," and exclaims, "Reform or Ruin." And if the Church of England is anti-Christian, is not the Methodist Episcopal Church as anti-Christian as it, or the Church of Rome? What feature will you find in the Church of England that is anti-Christian, that will not be found in the Methodist Episcopal Church? The likeness between the government of the Methodist Episcopal Church, and that of the Church of Rome, has been continued in *thirteen distinct propositions*, published in a work, called the "Wesleyan Repository." Vol. III., page 375.

But if the reader cannot find that work, he can consult the New Testament, which is of infinitely higher authority, and he will find the *principles* of Methodist episcoapacy are as opposite to the *principles and precepts* of Christianity, as the North is to the South Pole. In conclusion, no man who has written in favor of Methodist Episcopacy has appealed to the Scriptures in support of its claims, or produced one text from the New Testament in its favor. How could he, when the New Testament condemns it throughout.

2. We are opposed to Methodist Episcopacy, because it is a *fraud*, practiced on the unsuspecting members of the church. To prove this position these letters are written by a man who, for 28 years, had borne the name of a Methodist preacher — had travelled long and extensively in the itinerant connexion, and had filled various stations in the church, before he ever suspected there was any fraud in its organization, or any *forgery* in the documents which have been published as the genuine records of the church. He declares in the presence of God, and before the American people, that for 28 years he did believe, that Mr. Wesley did "recommend" to the American Methodist societies, "the episcopal mode of church government," and that it was in virtue of his "recommendation," "counsel," and advice, the conference of 1784 did adopt the episcopal form of government. And why did he believe it? *Because the printed records of the church say so.* Now let the Bishops of the Methodist Episcopal Church, (North and South) whose names are affixed to this statement, quit all shuffling in the matter. Let them produce an authentic document from under Mr. Wesley's hand, in which this "recommendation" is *clearly* and *explicitly* given, and we will renounce all we have said against the *fraud* of Methodist Episcopacy. But we know there is no such document — we are satisfied there never was such a document. For publishing the proof of this *fraud,* and the *forgeries* by which it is upheld, the writer has been expelled [from] the church of his early choice — his character and temporal interests have been destroyed — and his name has been sent out by Methodist preachers to every part of the United States as one of the worst of men. Not willing to go down to his grave without making an effort to wipe away a blot that Methodist preachers have endeavored to fix on his character — not willing that his children should be taunted with the reproach, that their father was not fit to minister in sacred things, and was therefore expelled [from] the church — he now appeals to the citizens of these United States; and, wherever these letters are read, to all intelligent people over the habitable globe, for the truth of the charges he prefers against the church, namely, that "*Methodist Episcopacy is founded in fraud, and is supported by falsehood.*" These are the charges to be tried; and by the verdict of an enlightened and impar-

tial public, he is willing to stand or fall. Let the men of other churches — let the men of the world read these papers, and say if he has not established the truth of the charges he has preferred against the church. But take notice — he will not submit the case to the bishops, preachers, or members of the Methodist Episcopal Church — because they have pronounced sentence already — because they are his avowed enemies — and because they have an *interest* in the decision.

3. We are opposed to Methodist Episcopacy because it is *despotic*. Every feature of this unscriptural and horribly misshapen thing is a feature of tyranny. The history of the trials of those who were expelled [from] the church, because they would not submit to its tyranny, and the history of those who have withdrawn from its fellowship for the same reason, establish the truth of the charge. But that it may not be said we misrepresent this episcopacy, let us hear what bishop Hedding says in his little work on "Discipline."

> "But should the majority of an annual conference become heretical, or countenance immorality, what can the General Conference do? Other remedies may answer in some cases, yet I know of only *one* that can be constitutionally administered in all cases. That is, let the General Conference command the bishops to remove the corrupted majority of an annual conference to other parts of the work, and scatter them among other annual conferences, and supply their places with better men from other conferences. But such men would not go at the appointment of the bishop. Perhaps they would not personally; but their names and their membership would go where they could be dealt with as their sins should deserve." Page 26.

These remarks from the pen of bishop Hedding, merit some notice.

(1.) "The majority of an annual conference may become heretical, or countenance immorality." In upwards of 50 years we have never known but one travelling preacher expelled for false doctrine, or heresy — we have known but few that were expelled for "immorality" — but we have known and heard of many, very many preachers and people, who were expelled for opposing the bishop's power.

(2.) The majority of an annual conference may be "*corrupt.*" Can the *head* be sound when the body or the "majority" of the members is "corrupt?" An elegant writer says — "The primitive churches fell by the corruption of their bishops, both in faith and practice; and not by any heresies originating with the laity. It was not without reason, therefore, that the great Head of the Church first cast his eyes of flame on the angels (the bishops or pastors) of the Asiatic churches; and addressed to them his dread reproofs on the decay of those prostrate churches."

(3.) Were we a member of the M. E. Church, and were we to say — "the majority of an annual conference is corrupt," we would be expelled for "speaking evil of ministers."

(4.) The bishop can "*scatter the corrupted majority* to other conferences," with as little compunction as the British government used to transport criminals to Botany Bay.

(5.) If they won't go at his bidding, he could send "*their names and their membership where they could be dealt with as their sins should deserve.*" Ah Lord! we painfully understand the meaning of this part of bishop Hedding's statement. And the history of the Inquisition will explain it to others.

4. We are opposed to Methodist Episcopacy because no man can open his mouth in its defense without uttering a lie. On this point we shall say something in another place.

NUMBER XXXVI.

We cannot but admire and adore the goodness of God, who, in the economy of his government, has always provided means to counteract those evils which are calculated to mar the happiness of the human family. We apply this sentiment to the measures that were taken to prevent the evils of Methodist Episcopacy. It was in the year 1820 that episcopacy had, in *fact* arrived at supreme power, by gaining an ascendency over the General Conference, in the case of the election of the Presiding Elders; and it was in the same year measures were adopted to check that supremacy, by the publication of a periodical called the "Wesleyan Repository." This publication was commenced by Mr. William S. Stockton, of New Jersey, the first number of which made its appearance in February, 1821. For three years this work had an increasing circulation among the members of the Methodist Episcopal Church, and by its influence, many of them were induced to petition the General Conference of 1824, for redress of grievances of which they thought they had a right to complain.

We are now arrived at the close of the second period of Methodist history. The constant reader of these pages will remember, we divided the history of Methodism into parts, each part consisting of 40 years. In 1744, Mr. Wesley held his first conference with his preachers; and it was just 40 years from the time, to 1784, when the Methodist Episcopal Church was organized. It was just 40 years from the organization of the Methodist Episcopal Church, to the General Conference of 1824, at which the petitions were rejected that were sent up to it from all parts of the country, praying for some change in the government of the church. The rejection of these petitions caused the petitioners to commence the publication of the "Mutual Rights;" and to form themselves into Union Societies in their respective neighborhoods. These were the steps that led to the formation of the Methodist Protestant Church. And from the signs of the times we think, before the third period of 40 years will have closed, Methodist Episcopacy will have breathed its last.

And here it may not be amiss to note another division of time. It was half the cycle, or just 20 years, from the organization of the church by Dr. Coke in 1784, by which the local preachers and lay members were excluded from her councils, to the year 1804, when the Doctor's connexion with the American Methodists ceased; for the Doctor never was in America after 1804. It was just 20 years, from this last visit in 1804, to the period when the first steps were taken for *Representation* in the law-making department of the church. It was just 20 years, from that period to the year 1844, when the unity of the body was broken into two factions *by Methodist Episcopacy.* And those who may be alive 20 years from that split, will see whether Methodist Episcopacy will then have an existence or not.

When the General Conference of 1824 rejected the prayer of the petitioners, the Reformers in Baltimore, and several others, who came up from different parts of the United States, to be present at this important crisis in the affairs of the church, assembled together the very night the answer of the conference was received, to consult together upon the course they should now pursue. With these brethren *seventeen members* of the General Conference met also, and took part in the deliberations. There was but one opinion among all, and that was, that Representatives from the local ministers and from the laity, was *reasonable* and *just.* To obtain this, they thought all that is necessary was, to enlighten the minds of the members on the subject; and this could be done only by means of the press. The meeting, therefore, adopted two resolutions — *the first,* to publish a periodical advocating *Representation,* to be edited by a committee of eight brethren, four of whom should be local ministers, and four laymen; *the second,* that Reformers should form themselves into Union Societies, in their respective neighborhoods, throughout the United States. The design of forming these societies was, that there should be no disagreement in the petitions that might be sent up to the next General Conference. And here it is proper to state, there was no wish or design, on the part of any one, to make a division in the church by the formation of these societies — but the contrary. The men who were the most prominent in forming those Union Societies well knew, that unless measures were taken to preserve the unity of the body, many would withdraw from the church. They were determined not to leave the church themselves, and they were determined to prevent others from leaving, if they could.

There can be no doubt that the labors of Reformers by means of the press, would have effected their purpose long before this time, had they been permitted quietly to go on. But this was not allowed them. The subject of Representation had been discussed in the "Mutual Rights," for about three years, and in that time hundreds, if not thousands of the members of the church, had been added to the ranks of the Reformers, when the bishops began to be alarmed for their ill-gotten power. The "Mutual Rights" disturbed them as much as the preaching of Paul disturbed the silversmiths of Ephesus; and what could they do but, like Demetrius, call their fellow craftsman together, and like him, address them thus: "Sirs, ye know that by this craft we have our wealth. Moreover, ye see and hear, that not alone at Ephesus, but almost throughout all Asia, this Paul hath persuaded and turned away much people, saying that they be no gods which are made with hands: so that, not only this our craft is in danger to be set at nought; but also that the temple of the great goddess Diana should be dispised, and her magnificence should be destroyed, whom all Asia and the world worshipeth. And when they heard these sayings, they were full of wrath, and cried out saying "Great is Diana of the Ephesians." Acts 19:25- 28.

They accordingly commenced a persecution against Reformers in different parts of the United States, and expelled hundreds of them from the church.

Had the General Conference of 1824 been composed of men who possessed only a modicum of common sense, they would have known, that those who had the boldness to claim, as a matter of right, a participation in the legislative department of the church, would not be satisfied with an answer that denied them their claims, even if this denial was founded on *prescription.* They might have known that instead of quietly and tamely submitting to the will of the conference, they would be more likely to inquire, by what means the travelling preachers became possessed of the power to legislate for the church, to the exclusion of local preach- ers and private members. Perhaps these things never entered into their sagacious minds. Perhaps they thought it was enough for them to say. "Pardon us if we know no such rights — if we com- prehend no such privileges."

But those who knew how to appreciate their civil "rights," and "comprehend" their church "privileges," were not willing to abide by the response of the conference. They accordingly began to ex- amine the subject of the organization of the church, and they con- ceived they were not only impelled by passing occurences to make such an examination, but they were invited to do so, by the ex- pressed injunctions of the bishops themselves. Hear what these five reverend gentlemen say.

> "We esteem it our duty and privilege most earnestly
> to recommend to you, as members of our church, our
> Form of Discipline, which has been founded on the ex-
> perience of a long series of years: as also on the obser-

vations and remarks we have made on ancient and modem churches.

We wish to see this little publication in the house of every Methodist; and the more so, as it contains the articles of religion maintained, more or less, in part or in whole, by every reformed church in the world.

Far from wishing you to be ignorant of any of our doctrines, or any part of our discipline, we desire you to read, mark, learn, and inwardly digest the whole. You ought, next to the word of God, to procure the Articles and Canons of the church to which you belong. This present edition is small and cheap, and we can assure you that the profits of the sale of it shall be applied to charitable purposes.

We remain your very affectionate brethren and pastors, who labor night and day, both in public and private, for your good.

William McKendree,
Enoch George,
Robert R. Roberts,
Joshua Soule,
Elijah Hedding."

This is an extract from the bishops' address "To the Members of the Methodist Episcopal Church," and is to be found in every book of discipline; but we take it from the one printed in New York in 1825, because in two years after it was printed, the writer of these sketches, with hundreds besides, was turned out of the church for doing what these "godly men" wished them to do.

There was a time in the history of Methodism when the declarations of Methodist preachers were believed. Such men had no other object in view but to serve God and save souls. There was, therefore, no necessity, in those days of simplicity, purity, piety, and truth, to resort to trickery, stratagem, dissimulation, mental reservation, forgery, or any thing else belonging to the family of lies, to establish what they said. Their yea was yea — their nay, nay. And we believe this is the case with a large majority of Methodist preachers still. But we are far from supposing this is the case with the "upper tens." They have a system to serve — an episcopacy to support, and these must be served and supported at all hazards — *fas aut nefas.* So we understand it.

Well, in this short extract, we think, we find an exemplification of what we say; for it contains two palpable and positive false-hoods — the one relating to the recommendation of the "discipline" founded on their acquaintance with the history of "Ancient and Modern Churches." Now consider the opportunities these men had to be able to make remarks on "Ancient and Modern Churches." One was so poor, that his nightly accommodations to rest, was a "chaff bag," or "skin and blanket." Another went to school six months. Another occupied such a house as is repre-sented by Elliott in his "Life of bishop Roberts." Now we declare, to hear those men talk about making remarks on "Ancient and Modern Churches," is enough to make the reader sick. Don't say we abuse them; we do not; we only repeat what "we know" has been said by themselves, or their friends.

The other part of the extract to which we specially refer, is this: "Far from wishing you to be ignorant of any of our doctrines, or *of any part of our discipline,* we desire you to read, mark, learn, and inwardly digest the whole." Now this extract so far as it relates to *discipline,* we pronounce a positive, unqualified, and pellucid falsehood. Reader, we are under the necessity of using strong lan-guage, for which we hope *you* will know how to make allowance. We do not write these terms in wrath, but coolly and deliberately, after the expiration of 23 years since the facts to which they refer, transpired. And we now say to Joshua Soule and Elijah Hedding, the only two survivors, if you did truly and sincerely intend, that the members of the church should not be "ignorant of any part of the discipline," why did you instigate, sanction, or approve of the trial and expulsion of any of the Reformers for striving to become informed on the subject, or for recommending the "Mutual Rights," in which this information might be obtained, to others? If you did intend what you say in your "address" to the members, part of which we have quoted, why did you expel a man for exam-ining the origin of your "episcopacy," which is a part of your "dis-cipline," and pronounce the impossibility of his return to the church under any circumstances? Gentlemen you are now reduced to a dilemma — either to deny what you have said, and is published in the discipline — or to deny that any Reformer was made to suffer, either by trial or expulsion, for acting in conformity with your advice. That many members of the church were tried and expelled for this very investigation, we will prove hereafter.

NUMBER XXXVII.

We promised in our last, to furnish some proof, that ministers and members of the M. E. Church were brought to trial and punished, for doing what the bishops "recommended" then "most earnestly" to do. To give the names, cases, and circumstances of all who were censured or expelled, would fill volumes. We cannot go into detail; a few instances, therefore, shall suffice to show the falsity of the profession of the bishops.

The first instance we shall give, is, a writer who signs himself "Martin Luther," who was the author of "five letters on church government inscribed to the Rev. Wm. McKendree." We select him first, because to each of those letters was prefixed the very part of the bishop's address to the Members, which proves their falsehood: *Far from wishing you to be ignorant of any of our* doctrines, or any part of our discipline, we desire you to read, mark, learn, and inwardly digest the whole. William McKendree, Enoch George, Robert R. Roberts."

At the time these letters were written, Joshua Soule and Elijah Hedding were not bishops, consequently are not answerable for the sins of others. These letters appeared in the October number of the "Wesleyan Depository," of 1823. In them, there is abundant proof of two things — *first*, that the government of the Methodist Episcopal church is contrary to the government of the Church of Christ for the first three hundred years — *second*, that the government of the M. E. Church resembles that of the church of Rome in *thirteen particulars*, which the writer enumerates. The proof of the truth of these propositions was extremely galling to the bishops; because they wished to be understood as the successors of the apostles, and the government as being more apostolic than that of any church in existence. Now to find that their pretensions were not only denied, but that they themselves were represented as the descendants of "the mother of harlots," was more than these "godly men" could bear. Nor did these letters escape the lynx- eyed caterer of the prosecuting committee. See "Narrative and Defense." Page 10. The writer was subsequently expelled.

The next is the Rev. D. B. Dorsey, a travelling preacher in the Baltimore Annual Conference. Three bishops, McKendree, Soule, and Roberts, were in attendance at this conference, when the following proceedings took place,

> "Wednesday, April 18, 1827. The Rev. D.B. Dorsey was charged before the Baltimore annual conference, with having been actively engaged in the circulation of an improper periodical work."
>
> With reference to this charge Mr. Dorsey said —
>
> "Sometime last February, I wrote a few lines to a friend, Mr. Hugh M. Sharp, in which I gave him information of a work on church government, published in Baltimore, by a committee of Methodist preachers and members, exposing to open view, some of the errors in our government and administration. I also informed him, that the work was a very satisfactory one, well worth his attention — that I had taken it more than eighteen months, and was well pleased with it; that it contained so many pages, and came to so much per year. In conclusion, I remarked to him, you need not mention this to any other person, if you please; but when the preacher Robert Minshaee came round, my friend Sharp betrayed me."

This letter was produced in conference, and on it the above charge was predicated, Mr. Dorsey was tried and sentenced to be admonished. The day after the trial, the President, Joshua Soule, announced from the chair *that my character should pass upon my being admonished by the president; and promising the* conference that I would desist from taking any agency in spreading or supporting any publication in opposition to our discipline or government."

> "Then," says Mr. Dorsey, "I have been punished with an *admonition* for *recommending* the Mutual

Rights. *The bishops themselves read it, the preachers read it, the book agents read it,* and exchange the Magazine for it; and will any one say, that the *people* have no right to read it? I have read the Mutual Rights, sir, for myself, and think highly of the work, and recommend it to every member of this conference." Mutual Rights, Vol. III., page 277 — 285.

This gentleman was finally expelled.

We conceive it is hardly possible for any man, who is not dead to all sense of reason, honor, justice, and truth, to read the trial of Mr. Dorsey, without feeling in his soul a measure of indignation, which it is impossible for language to express. Think of a young man, (young in years, and in the ministry) — betrayed by a professed friend — arraigned on a confidential letter before his annual conference — for doing what five bishops "most earnestly recommended" him to do — his conference finding him guilty of reading! — and recommending a work, from which he received much valuable information on church history!!! Think of this man's being punished — and the punishment inflicted by Mr. Soule, one of the very men who advised him to "read" &c. What think you, must have been the feelings of the two men, the bishop and the culprit? The one in pronouncing, the other in hearing the sentence? The one trying to extort a "pledge" the other "refusing" to give any. If Mr. Soule had any soul at all — if he was capable of feeling any compunctions of "conscience," which, by the way, we learn from himself, is very tender and very sensitive, he must have felt, as a certain character felt, when "he saw the fingers of a man's hand come forth, and wrote over against the candlestick upon the plaster of the wall, MENE, MENE, TEKEL, UPHARSIN." And as for Mr. Dorsey, he must have felt towards the President, bishop Soule, as St. Paul felt towards the high priest Annanias, when he "commanded them who stood by him to smite him on the mouth. Then saith Paul unto him, God shall smite thee, thou whited wall; for sittest thou to judge me after the law, and commandest me to be smitten contrary to the law?" It is such men, and such courage, as was displayed by Mr. Dorsey, that makes despots and tyrants tremble.

The next we shall notice, is the case of the Rev. Alexander Mc-
Caine, the author of the "History and Mystery of Methodist Episcopacy." And as this gentleman has received a greater measure of
abuse than any other man, and as his work has done more, we believe, than the writings of any other, to expose the *fraud* and *forgeries* of Methodist Episcopacy, we will go more into the examination of this case than of any other. We will hear what the writer
says in his preface to his pamphlet.

"After the conference," of 1824, "had arisen, a circular appeared, in which they declare, they 'know no such
rights, they comprehend no such privileges' as were asserted in the memorials praying for *Representation.*
Such declarations coming from the General Conference, were sufficient to rouse every man who knows
how to respect his rights, whether civil or religious. The
writer of this essay was alarmed at such declarations,
because he considered them to be indications of priestly
domination; and moreover he considered them offensive, because they were addressed to citizens of these
United States. New thoughts were waked up, and fore-
bodings felt, which he never before experienced. He determined, therefore, to examine the grounds of such un-
heard of claims. He was resolved, if possible, to ascertain the means by which travelling preachers had arrived at these pretensions, and find the authority which
Mr. Wesley had given to justify them in saying he "recommended the episcopal mode of church government."
When lo! the first discovery he made was, that whilst
Mr. Wesley, the testator, was yet living, the title of
bishop was assumed, and the episcopal mode of government adopted without his recommendation: and
more, that his most solemn remonstrance and entreaty
did not avail in causing them to relinquish the one or
change the other. Still pursuing the investigation, he
found that a more extended research served only to increase his conviction, that claims had been set up, for
which there was no warrant; and authority was said to

have been given, which he believes can nowhere be found... But before he would consent to its publication, he thought it would be fair and honorable to apprize the bishops of his purpose, and signify to them the probable effect it would have on the *office* which they fill. He accordingly addressed to each of them the letter No. 1, in the appendix." Here it is:

"To the Rev. WM. MCKENDREE, Senior Bishop of the Methodist Episcopal Church.

BALTIMORE, July 1, 1826.

Rev. Sir: — It is known to you, I presume, that of those who have advocated a representation of the laity and local ministry in the general conference, I am one; and that I have contributed my feeble assistance to support and spread the Mutual Rights, in which the subject of representation has been so freely discussed. In doing this, I assure you, I have acted from a sense of duty, and, therefore, if in error, I am rather to be pitied than blamed. Hitherto, however, I have not been convinced that I am in error; nor have I seen any argument offered by our rules to justify them in denying representation to the other branches of the church, except only those founded on *prescription*, as offered by the General Conference of 1824, in their circular on the subject. From the time that this doctrine was published in that circular, I have been induced to examine, with a closer attention, 'the institutions of the church as we received them from our fathers,' and must say I see the subject in a light very different from that in which it appeared to me before that time. I am about to commit to the press, an outline exhibiting the result of this examination: but before I do so, I think it is a duty I owe to you and your colleagues in the episcopacy, to apprize you of my intention; inasmuch as my conclusions may have an important bearing on the *office* which you hold in the church.

I beg you, my dear sir, to be assured, that nothing disrespectful is intended, either in the matter or manner of this communication. My sole object is, to make this honest statement, and to obtain from you the desired information, on several points, if you can possibly give it. Because, if I have been led into an error by the documents which I have in possession, it is important that that error should be counteracted by other equally authentic documents to which I have had no access. The points upon which I beg information, are the following:

1. I desire to be informed whether you have ever seen the *original* letter written by Mr. Wesley, "to Dr. Coke, Mr. Asbury, and our brethren in North America," dated Bristol, Sept. 10th, 1784. If you have seen it, whether the *whole* of it has been printed? And if the whole of it was not printed, whether a copy of it can now be procured?

I make this inquiry because I have a document in my possession in which it is asserted, that that letter was mutilated, and that only a part of it was given to the public.

2. Whether you have ever seen any document or letter written by Mr. Wesley, in which he *explicitly* "recommended" to the Methodist societies in America, the adoption of the episcopal mode of church government," according to the statements made in the minutes of conference for 1785, and the book of discipline? If so, can a copy of it be obtained?

3. Whether there is any paper to be found in which Mr. Wesley gave "counsel" to Dr. Coke, Mr. Asbury, or any other person or persons, to ordain a third order of ministers in our church, meaning by that phrase, an order of bishops distinct from, and superior to, an order of presbyters? If so, can that paper be produced?

4. Are you able to inform me what year Mr. Wesley's name was left out of the minutes? At what conference was the vote taken? By whom was it done? And for what reasons?

In asking information upon the point, permit me to propose them to your consideration, as being connected with the *office* you fill, and with the address to the members of the church, which bears your signature in the book of discipline. And that no blame may attach to me hereafter on account of reservation, I deem it proper, frankly and fully to state the results to which my investigation has conducted me. I candidly say, then, that I cannot believe, from the testimony of any or all the documents which I have been able to pursue, that Mr. Wesley ever *recommended the episcopal mode of church government to American Methodists.* I cannot believe he ever gave them any "council" to create a third order of ministers, as distinct from, and superior to, the order of presbyters. But I am forced to believe, that the present form of government was surreptitiously introduced; and that it was imposed upon the societies under the sanction of Mr. Wesley's name.

I shall suspend the publishing of my piece, to allow you a reasonable time to reply. You will have the goodness to favor me with an answer before the expiration of next month.

I remain, Rev. Sir, your brother and fellow laborer in the Lord,

Alexander M'Caine.

N.B. I send a copy of this letter to each of your colleagues. A. M'C."

NUMBER XXXVIII.

The man who takes an interest in these historical sketches of Methodist Episcopacy, may have been impatient for the past week, to know what answer the bishops returned to Mr. M'Caine's letter, asking information on certain points connected with the organization of the Methodist Episcopal Church. But how will that man be surprised when he is informed now, that the bishops were like the man of whom we read in the gospel, who obtruded himself into a place that it was not intended he should occupy. "And when the king came in to see the guests, he saw there a man, who had not on a wedding garment. And he saith unto him, Friend, how camest thou in hither, not having on a wedding garment? And he was speechless." Just so was it with these five bishops. They were intruders into this sacred office; and when enquired of respecting their investiture, they were "speechless" — as silent as the grave; for not one of them ever returned an answer of any kind, from that day to this. By their silence, then, two things are clearly established — *first,* that *Methodist Episcopacy is all a fraud* — *second,* that *"no man can advocate it, or say a word in its favor, without uttering a lie."* These gentlemen knew it was a *fraud,* and had nothing to say in its favor; and having nothing that they could say for it, they thought it was the best policy to say nothing about it. They were "speechless."

Respecting the silence of the five bishops, Mr. M'Caine says, in his "Defense of the Truth, as set forth in the History and Mystery of Methodist Episcopacy" —

> "There is on the very face of my letter, evidence that it was dictated by a friendly spirit; that I was influenced by a love of truth; and that I was fearful of publishing any thing which might injuriously, though unintentionally, affect the episcopal office. As *gentlemen* they were under obligations to answer it. It was respectfully written, and was entitled to a respectful consideration. Standing at the head of the connexion, and filling the episcopal office, they were under obligations to answer it; because it related to subjects of a general interest to the church, and information on these subjects was all I required. By their silence, then, they have subjected themselves to the imputation of being indifferent to the truth, and the welfare of the connexion. Having affixed their signatures to the book of discipline, and by so doing averred it to be a fact, that "Mr. Wesley recommended the episcopal form of church government," they were *personally, individually,* and *officially,* under the most sacred obligations to say, where that recommendation could be found; especially when it was

called for by a minister of their own church; by one who was older in years, and in the ministry, than a majority of themselves; by one who had been twice in the itinerancy, and had filled some of the most important and responsible offices in the church; and who requested the information in a polite and respectful manner." Page 4.

Receiving no answer from the bishops, Mr. M'Caine then addressed a letter (given in his His. & Mys.) to each of six of the oldest preachers, who were members of the conference of 1784. Their answers, he tells us, confirmed him in the belief that there was no *recommendation* from Mr. Wesley, to create the Methodist societies into an "independent Episcopal Church," nor to create a third order of ministers, distinct from, and superior to, presbyters. He then published his pamphlet called, "The History and Mystery of Methodist Episcopacy," — the publication of which threw the connexion into a flame, and brought down on the head of the author all the wrath of the five bishops and their minions, the travelling preachers. Everything was done, that could be done, to crush the work, and the author of it, at once. And as what was done is a fair specimen of what Methodist Episcopacy would do, if it was backed by the civil authority, we will dwell on this case at some length.

1. A meeting was called of the male members of the church in Baltimore. At this meeting an "Address was discussed and adopted, and ordered to be sent to their brethren throughout the United States." In this address they speak of this work and its author in the following strain — "a pamphlet written by a local preacher, in which the whole system of Methodism is assailed, with all the guile, and artifice, and sophistry of a Jesuit, and with all the malignity of which the human heart is capable. We allude to the History and Mystery of Methodist Episcopacy, by Alexander M'Caine. A work which, for malignity of purpose, shrewd cunning, misrepresentation of facts, and misstatement of circumstances, has no parallel among the productions of modern times, on a similar subject, except the far-famed Cobbett's History of the Reformation." The "Address," from which this extract is taken,

was drawn up by Dr. Thos. E. Bond, the same man who wrote the "Narrative and Defense" for the seven prosecutors, and to which he found it convenient to prefix the following passages of scripture — *"Put them in mind — to speak evil of no man"* — *"Speak not evil one of another, brethren." "Wherefore, laying aside all malice and all guile, and hypocrisies, and envies, and all evil speakings,* &c." The Methodist Episcopal Church knows, by this time, what kind of man Dr. Bond is.

2. "In continuation of the plan," says Mr. M'Caine, "to destroy my character, and thereby sink the credit of my book, charges of "slander and falsehood" were preferred against me, for having in a district conference nearly *seven years* before, objected to a certain man's obtaining license to preach." Def., Page 6.

The case was this: — A certain licensed exhorter, or local preacher, came to Baltimore to live, and after some time was employed as a clerk by a ship-builder. The fellow stole copper from his employer, and sold it. As soon as it was found out, he was brought before the church, was found guilty of selling it, and ran away. Several years after this, a man applied at the District Conference for license to preach. When the name was mentioned, Mr. M'Caine, who was a member of the conference, rose in his place and said, Bro. President, where is bro. _______, is he here? Yes, he sits down yonder, at the end of the house. Turning to the applicant, Mr. M'C asked him: bro. _______, did you ever live on Fell's point? Ans. I did. Ques. Did you ever live with Mr. _______, the ship-builder, as a clerk? Ans. I did. Ques. Was there not a charge against you about copper spikes or bolts? Ans. There was, but that matter was all settled. A member of the conference rose in his place and said, — "I don't think it was all settled bro., for I was on the committee who tried you, and we found you guilty of selling copper knowing it to be stolen, upon which you ran away, for fear of the penitentiary."

Dr. Bond hearing of this affair, thought it was a fine chance to destroy the character of the author of the "History and Mystery," and thereby destroy the credit of the book. He therefore sent for this *copper spike* gentleman, and insisted on him to prefer charges of "slander and falsehood" against Mr. M'Caine. The fellow was unwilling to do so, at first, but at length consented. But the cream of the business was the following occurrence. When the day fixed on for the trial arrived, a great many reformers repaired to Light street church, to hear it. While Mr. M'Caine and a few others were standing in the yard, he noticed a man standing at one side by himself, who appeared to be very intent upon watching for somebody. Thus man was a constable. As soon as the copper spike man came on the ground, the constable came to him and said he had authority to take him to jail. Mr. M'Caine who heard the statement, said he should not go; and offered to pay the debt himself, if the copper spike man was not forthcoming when the trial was over. With this the constable appeared satisfied, and went off. Now was not this a deep laid scheme to save the poor fellow — to prevent the trial coming on — and to fix an indelible disgrace upon Mr. M'Caine? It would not, however, do. The trial went on; and after spending two nights in taking testimony, it turned out — that it was the copper spike man who, *in fact*, was tried, and not Mr. M'Caine — or in other words, the testimony showed, that the prosecutor stole the copper spikes, and that the charge of "slander and falsehood was not sustained. So much Mr. ______, for your "friend" Dr. Bond.

3. "Finding that my pamphlet was working its way," says Mr. M'Caine, "notwithstanding the above address" and the prosecution by the "copper spike" man and his "friend, Dr. Bond" the church authorities and the friends of Methodist Episcopacy did not think it safe to rest their cause upon the attacks made upon my character; it was therefore thought necessary that something should be done, which, under the semblance of argument, might have the appearance of confuting my book. To write it down, the Rev. John Emory, D. D., took up his mighty pen; how far he has succeeded an enlightened public will judge." Def., Page 8.

Respecting this answer to the "History and Mystery of Methodist Episcopacy," the "Narrative and Defense" which was drawn up by Dr. Bond for the seven prosecutors, says — "About this time, or a little before, the 'History and Mystery of Methodist Episcopacy, by Alex. M'Caine,' made its appearance — in which our present ecclesiastical government was represented as surreptitious — a fraud practiced on the membership by the bishops and travelling preachers — imposed upon them in the name of Mr.

Wesley, without his sanction, and even contrary to his express commands!! And it is more than intimated that this surreptitious government was supported by the suppression of documents, garbling of statements, the forgery of dates, and falsifying of records!! All those allegations were known to be unfounded, and they have since been clearly disproved by Dr. Emory in his able Defense of our Fathers." This work by Mr. Emory was puffed by everything in the Methodist Episcopal Church, as being "a masterly and unanswerable production; and yet Mr. M'Caine, near 20 years after his His. and Mys. was written, comes out in the following manner in the public papers:

> A Challenge.
> "The subscriber will undertake to prove, at any time after six months from the acceptance of this challenge by any bishop, or any travelling preacher in the Methodist Episcopal Church in the United States, (none other need enter the lists) and in any place in North Carolina, South Carolina, or Georgia, that may be agreed on by himself and the individual accepting it, that in the organization of the Methodist Episcopal Church in 1784, FRAUD was practiced by the suppression of some documents, and the mutilation of others — that the original and genuine minutes taken at the time the church was organized, were destroyed, and *spurious* ones substituted in their place — and that the minutes of conference and the book of discipline of the said church have been altered to make them tally with the destruction of the aforesaid documents. This debate to be conducted in public, according to rules to be agreed on by the debating parties, and the decision to be pronounced by twelve disinterested gentlemen chosen alternately by the subscriber and his opponent, for that purpose; not one of whom shall be of the Methodist Protestant, or Methodist Episcopal church."
>
> Alexander M'Caine.
> Sept. 16, 1844.
> N.B. The challenge must be accepted within *three*

months from the date of its publication in the Western Recorder, and the debate must come off within *six months* after the acceptance of the challenge. I now offer the champions of Methodist Episcopacy, whether they be bishops, presiding elders, or Doctors of Divinity in the travelling ranks, a chance to prove the statements made in their book of discipline and minutes of conference. The arena will not be the old room in the third story of the parsonage in Light street, nor will the judges be three men of straw appointed to pronounce the verdict previously drawn up by a creature of the hierarchy. If the debate take place, hundreds, if not thousands, will have an opportunity to hear and judge for themselves, and no doubt the arguments in the case will be published and circulated through the whole length and breadth of the land. Give the people but light, and Methodist Episcopacy ceases to exist."

Lotts, Edgefield District, S.C., 1844.

The challenge was never accepted.

NUMBER XXXIX.

The publication of the "History and Mystery," was a terrible blow to Methodist Episcopacy. It is fair to infer it was so considered by the bishops themselves, and by all those who were in favor of episcopal authority. This is plain from the following considerations. 1. From the manner in which it is spoken of, in the "Address of the male members in Baltimore sent to their brethren throughout the United States." 2. From the efforts that were made by Dr. Bond, as agent in the prosecution, and his "friend" the copper spike man, to destroy the character of its author. 3. From the attempt that was made to refute it, and the reward that was bestowed on the man who made the attempt; not a cardinal's hat, but the episcopate itself. 4. From the fact, that no steps were taken to punish reformers, until after it was published; although the Union Society had been organized three years previously. 5. From the fact, that it was made a distinct and separate charge against every member of the Union Society, whether preachers or laymen, thus, "Because the said _______ as a member of the Union Society aforesaid, did advise, request, or recommend the publication of a pamphlet entitled the History and Mystery of Methodist Episcopacy." 6. And last, from the fact, that when a restoration to full membership and official standing was tendered, (on certain conditions,) to every expelled member of the Baltimore station, Alexander McCaine alone was excepted. "The writing and publishing of this pamphlet," says Mr. McCaine, "was the *unpardonable sin.* It was this offence, which, not only put me out of the pale of the church, but out of the pale of her mercy. It was this which caused her to scandalize where she could not refute, and, as the extent of her malignity, to stamp Anathema Maranatha upon my name."

It is not our intention to trace, step by step, the measures that were adopted to secure the expulsion of reformers in Baltimore. Those who would wish to see those measures in detail, accompanied with suitable remarks, would do well to obtain, and carefully peruse, "Dr. S. K. Jennings' Exposition of the late controversy of the Methodist Episcopal Church." In that work he will find a full, true, and luminous account of one of the most wicked plots, that ever was formed against men whose moral characters were acknowledged to be unimpeachable; and respecting whom, it was determined, *before their trial*, that they should be expelled. See Jennings' Exposition, page 48. See, also, Narrative and Defense, page 17.

Passing all these things by, we will place on record the names of the accused, the charges which were preferred against them, and the names of the prosecutors. It would be a pity that posterity should not know the names of the *virtuous sufferers*, and of their *persecutors*.

> "Thus circumstanced," say the prosecutors, "nothing remained, but to lay our complaints before the church, and accordingly, the following charges and specifications were handed to the preacher in charge, against eleven local preachers, to wit: — Rev. Dr. S. K. Jennings, Alexander McCaine, John C. French, James R. Williams, Daniel E. Reese, John Valiant, William Kesley, Thomas McCormack, Luther J. Cox, John S.

Reese, and Reuben T. Boyd. And twenty-five lay members, to wit: — Messrs. John Chappel, John Kennard, John J. Harrod, Thomas Mummey, Ebenezer Strakan, Arthur Emmerson, Lambert Thomas, Thomas Patterson, Levi R. Reese, John Hawkins, John P. Howard, Wesley Starr, John P. Paul, Joseph R. Foreman, William K. Boyle, Samuel Jarrett, Thomas Jarrett, Samuel Gest, George B. Northerman, Samuel Krebs, Samuel Thompson, Thomas Parsons, John Coates, John Stinchcomb, and Jesse Comegys.

"________ is charged with endeavoring to sow dissentions in the society or church, in this station or city, known by the name of the Methodist Episcopal Church, and with the violation of that general rule of the discipline which prohibits its members from doing harm, and requires them to avoid evil of every kind; and especially with violating that clause of said general rule which prohibits speaking evil of ministers.

"*Specification* 1. Because the said ________, while a member of the Methodist Episcopal Church aforesaid, did heretofore attach himself to, and become a member of the society called the Union Society of the Methodist Episcopal Church in the city of Baltimore, which Union Society is in opposition to the discipline, in whole or in part, of the Methodist Episcopal Church, aforesaid.

" *Specification* 2. Because the said ________, as a member of the said Union Society, is directly or indirectly, either by pecuniary contributions, or his personal influence, aiding, abetting, cooperating or assisting in the publication or circulation of a work called the 'Mutual Rights of the ministers and members of the Methodist Episcopal Church,' printed under the direction of an editorial committee, appointed by, or who are members of, the Union Society aforesaid — which work or publication, called the 'Mutual Rights of the ministers and members of the Methodist Episcopal Church,' contains, (among other things) much that inveighs against the discipline of the Methodist Episcopal

Church aforesaid, in whole or in part, and is in direct opposition thereto: — and that it is abusive, or speaks evil of a part, if not most of the ministers of that church. The general tendency of which work or publication, has been to produce, and continues to produce, disagreement, strife, contention, and breach of union among the members of said church in this city or station.

"*Specification* 3. Because the said _______, as a member of the Union Society aforesaid, did advise, request, or recommend the publication of a pamphlet, entitled the 'History and Mystery of Methodist Episcopacy, written by Alexander McCaine,' in which various declarations and assertions are made without proper proof, or just foundation, calculated to disgrace and bring reproach upon the Methodist Episcopal Church aforesaid, its ministers and members; and which declarations and assertions are well calculated to produce, increase, and heighten the disagreement, strife, contention, and breach of union, alluded to in the second specification.

For proof of which, the publication entitled the 'Mutual Rights of the Ministers and Members of the Methodist Episcopal Church,' is referred to, and particularly to No. 1, 7, 25, 27, 29, 30, 32, 33, 34, 35, 36 and 37. And also the said pamphlet entitled the 'History and Mystery of Methodist Episcopacy,' — with such other documentary or oral proof as the undersigned may deem expedient to exhibit or produce.

George Earnest,
Jacob Rogers,
Isaac N. Toy,
Samuel Harden,
Alexander Yearly,
John Berry,
Fielder Israel."

On these charges and specifications, were the above named *eleven ministers*, and the above named twenty-five laymen, put on their trial, if *trial* it can be called. The ministers were all sentenced to be expelled, one of whom is the writer of these letters. But owing to the prosecutors mistaking the day appointed for the trial of three of the laymen, the charges against those three were not sustained; but all the rest, *twenty-two* in number, were sentenced to be expelled also. More than these would have shared their fate, if the church authorities could have obtained the books of the Union Society in which the names of the members were recorded. What a pity that they were unsuccessful in their endeavors; for if they had obtained them, they might have enjoyed the pleasure coveted by the heathen Emperor Caligula, "who wished the Romans had but one head, that he might have the gratification of striking it off at a stroke."

However, before the sentence of expulsion was carried into execution, James M. Hanson, the preacher in charge, sent a copy of it to Dr. S. K. Jennings and to each of the reformers, and closed his communication as follows: — "You must, therefore, plainly perceive, that the only ground on which expulsion from the church can be avoided, is, *an abandonment of the Union Society*, with assurances that *you will give no aid in future to any publication, or measure, calculated to cast reproach upon our ministers;* or occasion breach of union among our members. Be good enough then, my brother, to answer, in writing, the following plain and simple questions. 1. *Will you withdraw forthwith from the Union Society?* 2. *Will you, in future, withdraw your aid from such publications and measures*, as are calculated to cast reproach upon our ministers, and produce breach of union among our members?"

An affair exactly like this, is related in D'Aubine's History of the Reformation. Martin Luther had been summoned by the Pope, to appear before his Legate at Augsburg. He went, and as soon as he arrived, he was waited on by Serra Longa, who addressed the Reformer thus: — "I am come to offer you prudent and good advice. Make your peace with the church. Submit unreservedly, to the Cardinal. Retract your calumnies. Recollect the abbot Joachim of Florence: he, as you know, had put forth heresies, and yet he was afterwards declared no heretic, because he retracted his errors." Vol. 1., Page 341.

This case was like McKendree's. But the man who could give

utterance to the following sentiment, was not to be intimidated.

> *"Go tell your master, that though there should be as many devils at Worms as there are tiles on its roofs, I would enter it."*

And such were the men, by the grace of God, in Baltimore, who were summoned to submit to papal authority, but who would not do it. But to go on.

> "On the morning of Monday, the 10th of October, Serra Longa again renewed his persuasions. The courtier had made it a point of honor to succeed m his negotiations. The moment he en tered, Why, he asked in Latin, why do you not go to the Cardinal? He is expecting you in the most indulgent frame of mind. With him the whole question is summed in six letters — REVOCA — *retract.* Come, then, with me, you have nothing to fear." Luther thought within himself that those were six very important letters. "How ever he went, and the Cardinal addressed him thus: ' Here,' said he, 'are three articles which, acting under the direction of our most holy Father, Pope Leo X., I am to propose to you: — *First,* you must return to your duty; you must acknowledge your faults, and retract your errors, your propositions and sermons. *Secondly*, you must promise to abstain for the future from propagating your opinions. And *Thirdly*, you must engage to be more discreet, and avoid everything that may grieve or disturb the church." Vol. 1. Page 346.

Here are the three propositions made to Methodist Reformers. "Return to your duty." Withdraw from the Union Society. Give up the Mutual Rights and "publish no more." And cease to trouble or disturb the church. O, how does *corruption* hate the light, and dread exposure! The Reformers were expelled, but found no redress from the General Conference, and the Ministers were declared to have "vacated their former *orders* by their expulsion." See Methodist Quarterly Review for January, 1830. p. 80.

Never was there a set of men more infatuated than were the

men who composed the General Conference of 1828. And we can account for their infatuation on no other principle than on the heathen maxim "whom the gods are determined to destroy, they first make mad." We have neither time, nor inclination, nor space, to enter into an examination of their manifesto — we shall only notice one principle, which stands out very clearly and very fully in it — the principle by which they make and break ministers of the gospel at pleasure, and this, *"by those spiritual powers vested in us."* They strip the expelled ministers of their "orders" — for they were "divinely authorized" to do so, if you will believe themselves. They then, proclaim, in a strain of blasphemous arrogance, their own spiritual powers and prerogatives. "The great Head of the Church himself has *imposed* on us the duty of preaching the gospel, and administering its ordinances, and of *maintaining its moral discipline* among those over whom the Holy Ghost, in these respects, has made us overseers. Of these, also, viz: of gospel doctrines, ordinances, and MORAL DISCIPLINE, we do believe, that the *divinely instituted ministry* are the *divinely authorized expounders;* and that the *duty of maintaining* them in their purity, and of *not permitting* OUR ministrations, in these respects, to be authoritatively controlled by others, does rest upon us with the force of a *moral obligation;* in the due discharge of which OUR consciences are involved." But God took the matter into his own hands, and killed the man who dared to draw up such a tirade of blasphemies. And so ends the chapter.

NUMBER XL.

Several months have elapsed since we commenced writing these sketches of Methodism in America, beginning with the year 1766, when Philip Embury, a local preacher from Ireland, began preaching in New York, and carrying them on to the year 1844, when the unity of the Methodist Episcopal Church was destroyed, by its being split into two powerful and contending factions. We commenced writing these sketches with a two-fold view. *First,* of placing before the members of the church, the rise, the progress, and the assumptions of Methodist Episcopacy; knowing that false statements on these subjects had been published by writers of that church, who had an interest in concealing the truth, and keeping the members in the dark. *Secondly.* Because we have been expelled [from] the church for the part we took in the struggles to obtain a representation from the local ministry and lay members in the General Conference, which is the law-making department of the church. The disgrace of being expelled, we have borne for near a quarter of a century; but we were not willing to go down to our grave with this stigma on our name and character, without making an effort to prove that our expulsion, and that of other reformers, was illegal and unjust. We have, therefore, written these letters as an Appeal to the citizens of the United States, from the illegal and unjust proceedings of the authorities of the Methodist Episcopal Church; and are perfectly willing to abide by their decision, when they shall have perused the testimony we have spread before them.

When the reformers were expelled, they adopted different measures to obtain a retraction of their sentence. Some hoped the bishops were not so lost to a sense of justice, and to the value of their own character, but that they would, in conformity with their ordination vow, cause the discipline to be observed; seeing that it had been most shamefully and flagrantly violated by their understrappers, in the cases of the expelled. They, therefore, drew up and published their *protests,* against the legality of the proceedings that had been instituted against them, and under which they were expelled. Against these protests, however, the bishops shut their eyes. Some memorialized the General Conference, thinking that a body of ministers professing to be guided by the spirit, and to be governed by the precepts of Christianity, would see the impolicy and injustice of expelling ministers and members of the mystical body of Christ, for the expression of an opinion on church government. They also indulged a hope, that the General Conference would not be blind to the consequences that would certainly follow these expulsions; and that they would not unjustly withhold what the petitioners were conscious they had a right to demand. But in this, also, the memorialists were mistaken. For, instead of the General Conference manifesting the least disposition to check or moderate the haughty claims of men in power, or to heal the wounds that had been inflicted on the church by ecclesiastical demagogues, they insulted the petitioners by proposing terms for their restoration, as humiliating as was the Pope's conduct to the Emperor, in causing him to hold his stirrup, and kiss his toe. And, as if that was not enough, they magnified their own power and authority in an elaborate manifesto, the language of which has no parallel on the pages of church history, except in those blasphemous assertions which proceeded from the mouth of the man of sin, who claimed a right to sit in the Temple of God, as God. And flushed with the victory which was now obtained over reformers by their being expelled the church, and by the supposed suppression of their organ, the "Mutual Rights," the General Conference thought they were as secure in their conquests as the church of Rome was, when she beheld "the dead bodies of the two witnesses lying unburied in the street to the great city." Rev. 11:8.

In the Lateran Council which was begun under the pontificate of Julius II. and continued under that of Leo X., that church was serene and complacent in the belief, that the labors of Luther, the reformer, were at an end. "Throughout the length and breadth of Christendom," says the historian, "Christ's witnessing servants were silenced — they appeared dead. The orator of the session ascended the pulpit, and amid the applause of the assembled council, uttered that memorable exclamation of triumph — an exclamation which, notwithstanding the long multiplied anti-heretical decrees of Popes and Councils — notwithstanding the yet more multiplied anti-heretical crusades and inquisitorial fires — was never, I believe, pronounced before, and certainly never since. *"I am nemo reclamat, nullus obsistit,"* there is an end of resistance to the papal rule and religion; oppressors there exist no more. But in each case, the triumphing of anti-Christ was short. For, "after three days and a half, the spirit of life from God entered into them, and they stood upon their feet;" and having obtained fresh vigor from on high, and having resumed their labors, "great fear fell upon those which saw them," and their organized and successful operations. *Laus Deo.*

Without intending to censure others for the steps they took to obtain redress: and not knowing whether it will be placed to the praise or blame of the writer of these letters, he will say, that he believes he is the only one of the expelled reformers in Baltimore, who would not affix his name to the papers that were sent up by them to the Annual and General Conference. And why did he withhold his signature from these documents? Because he was as certain of the correctness of the judgment he had formed, upon an examination of all the facts and documents in the case, that *fraud* had been practiced in the organization of the church, as he was of the truth of his own existence. He could not, therefore, beg a favor of the men who had become a party to that *fraud;* nor ask a boon of those who were determined to perpetuate it by violence, by forgery, and by falsehood. He knew that the Saviour had said, "He that entereth not by the door into the sheep fold, but climbeth up some other way, the same is a thief and a robber." John 11:1. It would have been paying them too great a compliment to seem to acknowledge the justness of their pretensions, to ask a favor; to such, therefore, he would not stoop to offer a petition. And has he not, in these letters, fully established the correctness of his views? Will not the facts that have been stated, and the documents that have been placed before the American nation, fully justify him in the judgment he had formed, harsh and grating as the announcement of that judgment will be on the ears of the bishops of the church? They certainly will. Would it not be better, then, for these gentlemen to undertake a refutation of these charges, *if they can,* than for any of them to be trifling away his time in writing the life of such a man as William McKendree, or publishing a little *"ridiculus mus"* on Methodist discipline? It would. But what can these gentlemen say that would invalidate the amount of testimony that is presented in these letters? Nothing.

The bishops may represent themselves as being under no obligation to reply to these charges, and may say, "that has been done already by the author of the Defense of our Fathers." These gentlemen will not suspect *us* of flattery, when we assure them, we have too high an opinion of their *good sense,* to suppose that they candidly and honestly believe, that *that* work refutes any one of the charges which were preferred against the bishops in the "History and Mystery of the Methodist Episcopacy." What one does it refute? Does it show that Dr. Coke's parchment of ordination as a *"Superintendent"* was not withheld from the Conference of 1784; or that it ever saw the light, until it was published by Mr. Drew, after the Doctor's death? Does it prove that the "little sketch" which was drawn up by Mr. Wesley for the American Methodists, "in compliance with their desire," was not destroyed? Does it not prove that Mr. Wesley's letter, dated "Bristol, Sept. 10th, 1784," was not mutilated? Does it prove that Mr. Wesley intended there should be *three* distinct orders of ministers — bishops, presbyters, and deacons, when he had repeatedly declared there are but *two?* Does it establish the truth of the assertion that Mr. Wesley "did recommend the episcopal mode of church government," to the American societies, when that *recommendation* has never been seen; and that "following the counsel of Mr. John Wesley, at this conference we formed ourselves into an Independent Church," when such "counsel" or advice had never been given? Does it prove that the genuine minutes of conference of '84, were not set aside, and forged ones substituted in their stead? and that these forged minutes are not now passed off as the genuine minutes of that year? Does it prove that the various reasons assigned for the formation of the societies into an "independent Episcopal Church," which were published during Mr. Wesley's life time, were not omitted in the first edition of the discipline, which was published *after* his death; and that Chap. 1. Sec. 1. of the present book of discipline was not published until Mr. Wesley was put in his grave? In this way we might run through all the charges that were preferred in the "History and Mystery," not one of which has been disproved in the "Defense of our Fathers." And yet, these bishops, conscious that the charges have not been refuted, support that book, and recommend it to Methodist seminaries and colleges as a text book; they also recommend it to those young men who are designed for the ministry; thus corrupting the youth over whom they have an influence, as if the glory and success of *episcopal* Methodism depend on learning young preachers how they might lie.

From the bishops, as a body, we turn to address ourself to the Rev. Joshua Soule and the Rev. Elijah Hedding. 1. Because these gentlemen were members of the General Conference of 1824, when the petitions for representation were rejected, and are supposed to have voted for the "circular" issued by that body, in reply. 2. Because they were elected to the episcopal office at that conference, and were at the head of the connexion when reformers were expelled, in conformity with episcopal instructions. 3. Because these gentlemen presided at the General Conference of 1828, when the expelled brethren were before that body by their memorial. To Mr. Soule and Mr. Hedding we go, then, for an explanation of the following words in their "circular." "The rights and privileges of our brethren, as members of the Methodist Episcopal Church, we hold most sacred. We are unconscious of having infringed them, in any instance, nor would we do so." Now, what are those "rights and privileges," which they say they "hold most sacred?" which they "have not infringed in any instance?" and which they would not infringe? We can conceive of none except the following — the right to obey — the right to pay — and the right to be silent. These were "held most sacred," as "coming from our Fathers:" all other "rights and privileges" were violated in the case of reformers.

But perhaps we shall be told they meant that Christianity and Methodism are two distinct things — that they are essentially different, and that in the language of Dr. Bond, who may have taken the sentiment from the "circular" — "a man may be a very good man — nay a good Christian — but he is unfit for a Methodist." Of course, that the "rights" of ministers and members, as *Christians* may be "infringed," whilst their "rights" as *Methodists*, are "held most sacred." Now if it was their intention, in this abstruse sentence, to make any difference in the rights of members of the church as *Christians*, and the rights of the same members as *Methodists*, the statement is deceptive: for they themselves tell us, "We believe that God's design in raising up the preachers called Methodists, in America, was to reform the Continent, and spread Scripture holiness over these lands." So that, in whatever light we contemplate the expelled reformers, whether as *Christians* or as *Methodists*, the assertion of the "circular" is a palpable falsehood. "The rights and privileges have been infringed" — most shamefully and wickedly have they been violated.

As *Christians*, they were expelled from the church of Christ, of which many of them had been acceptable members, and others of them had been ministers, for many years; without the least intimation of false doctrine or immorality being preferred against them. Their characters were irreproachable, even in the eyes of their enemies. "It was publicly admitted, and reiterated in open court, that the prosecutors had no accusation of immorality to bring forward against any of them." — *Jennings' Exposition.* They were not, therefore, expelled for *immorality;* but for being members of the "Union Society," as their sentence will prove. "Resolved, thirdly, that the Rev. Samuel K. Jennings be expelled from the Methodist Episcopal Church, unless he *withdraw forthwith*, from the Union Society, &c." "A copy of these resolutions was sent to each of the expelled preachers and members." — *Ibid.* Page 55. And yet Mr. Soule and Mr. Hedding have the effrontery to say, "We hold the rights and privileges of the members of the Methodist Church most sacred. We are unconscious of having infringed them, in any instance, nor would we do so." Would either of these gentlemen be willing take such an oath as Mr. Soule did on the floor of the General Conference of 1844, in another case, accommodating its phraseology to the subject under consideration? Would either of them say — "I have never, — God is my witness — I have never given" the sanction of my name, or influence, to the expulsion of any Christian, or any Christian minister from the church of the living God, against whom there was neither false doctrine nor immorality alleged. "Indeed, if I could do it, I should abhor myself." — *Debates of G. C. for 1844.* Page 169. No, gentlemen, you could take no such oath as this, and be guiltless of perjury. Heaven and earth are witnesses against you, that you have done this deed already, in the case of the expelled reformers in Baltimore. You need not marvel, then, if your conduct has inspired men with the same feelings of *abhorrence* against you, that Mr. Soule says he should feel against himself, if he had ever "given an appointment to any preacher with a desire or design to afflict him."

Nor were their "rights and privileges, *as members of the Methodist Episcopal Church*," more respected, or held more "sacred," than were their "rights and privileges" *as Christians.* On this point, our long acquaintance with Methodism, and our connexion with the Methodist Episcopal Church, will enable us to speak with the utmost confidence. We say then, from being upwards of half a century a Methodist preacher, that everything connected with the trial and expulsion of the reformers, was an infringement of their "rights and privileges" *as Methodists.* The whole of the proceedings against them were in violation of Methodist rule, and contrary to Methodist usage.

1. The manner in which the prosecution was gotten up, was an

infringement of their "rights and privileges," and was entirely unknown to Methodist usage. Never before the year 1827, was the church in her collective capacity, convened with a design of being arrayed as prosecutors, against some of her best members, and ablest ministers.

2. The appointment of "seven prosecutors," to "*seek out,*" prefer charges, and prosecute those charges, against an *indefinite number* of the "Union Society," was also unknown to Methodism in Europe or America, before the above period.

3. The "seven prosecutors" became such, not at the instance of "travelling preachers," who were the only persons said to be "abused" — but at the instance of the private members in Baltimore, who did not pretend to be "abused" at all. Will the Justinian of Methodism tell us, then, whose representatives these "seven prosecutors" were, the representatives of the whole church, in her extended membership? or of a part of the society in Balti more? or of the "travelling preachers?" We hope the next edition of "Hedding on Discipline," will answer these questions.

4. The "travelling preachers" never authorized the society in Baltimore, or the "seven prosecutors," their agents, to prefer charges against the members of the Union Society, in their name, or on their behalf. If any of them conceived themselves injured by the publications which appeared in the "Mutual Rights," they did not let it be known to the editorial committee. On the contrary, the writings of some of the ablest travelling preachers in the connexion, made a great part, if not the greater part of the "Mutual Rights."

5. The two committees which were appointed to try the ministers, and the members, were composed of men who had not only prejudged the cases they were appointed to try; but they were active in getting up the prosecutions, and in voting at the meetings that were held for that purpose. Objections were made to them on these accounts, but the objections were over-ruled by James M. Hanson, the preacher.

6. The preacher himself was not *an honest and an impartial man.* "More than two years before the trials took place," he wrote thus to a friend respecting reformers. "I am disposed to view the greater part of them as holding a relation to the church, to which,

in justice and propriety — nay even in *charity* itself — they are no longer entitled." The history of the *trials*, so called, may be told, then, in a few words. The "seven prosecutors" — the two committees — and James M. Hanson, the preacher, were bitter, implacable, and avowed enemies of reformers — and yet the "rights and privileges" of reformers were not "infringed" in being tried by such men! "When the accused called on the prosecutors to point out the particular passages that sustained the charges, it was peremptorily refused by the court." There was, therefore, no investigation of the documents that were said to contain the defamatory words or sentences. The trial was all a farce. The fable of the wolf and the lamb drinking at the same stream, illustrates the proceedings. Now of all those facts and circumstances, was the General Conference of 1828 informed, by the memorial of the expelled brethren. At this General Conference, Joshua Soule, and Elijah Hedding, presided, and sanctioned the expulsion of *eleven ministers and twenty-two laymen*, from the church in Baltimore, not for *immorality,* but because they would not "*withdraw forthwith, from the Union Society;*" and yet these men, Joshua Soule and Elijah Hedding, say — "The rights and privileges of our brethren, as members of the Methodist Episcopal Church, we hold most sacred. We are unconscious of having infringed them in any instance, nor would we do so."

7. "The *General Rules*" under which the reformers were tried and expelled, had never been brought to bear on the *trial* of any Methodist in Europe or America prior to this time. "The General Rules" were not drawn up or intended for that purpose. See Whitehead's Life of Wesley. Vol. II., page 99. Towards the close they say — "If there be any among us who observe them not, who habitually break any of them, let it be made known to them who watch over that soul, as they that must give an account. We will admonish him of the error of his ways. We will bear with him for a season. But if he repent not" what then? bring him to *trial* before a committee? No indeed. There was no such practice in Mr. Wesley's day — "he hath no more place among us." That is, the person was dropped without being brought before a committee, or being *tried* at all.

8. Although the prosecutors declare, that the "Mutual Rights"

speak *evil* of a part, if not most of the ministers of that church, yet not a name is mentioned in the "charges and specifications" — no, not even the name of "the veritable John Smith" — nor Tom Long — nor Bob Short, nor any body else. As nobody was named, nobody was "abused."

9. As no person was designated by name, neither was the nature of the *"evil speaking"* specified, which was alleged to have been published against the ministers of "that church." The indictment deals in *generals* — God's law deals in *particulars*. Was the violation of either of the "ten commandments" charged upon any of the travelling preachers? We believe not. The "Mutual Rights" advocated a representation from the local ministers and the lay members, in the General Conference; "that was the head and front of its offending — no more." And this is what the "seven prosecutors" called "speaking evil of ministers."

Long as this letter is, we must propose a question to the Rev. Joshua Soule and the Rev. Elijah Hedding, before we lay down our pen. Gentlemen, be pleased to tell us by what means you could discover such an amount of "evil speaking" in the "Mutual Rights," as required, in your judgment, the expulsion of eleven ministers and twenty-two laymen of the church in Baltimore, and yet you could see no "evil speaking" in the following sentence: *"A pamphlet written by a local preacher, in which the whole system of Methodism is assailed with all the guile, and artifice, and sophistry of a Jesuit, and with all the malignity of which the human heart is capable. We allude to the History and Mystery of Methodist Episcopacy, by Alexander M'Caine. A work which, for malignity of purpose, shrewd cunning, misrepresentation of facts, and misstatement of circumstances, has no parallel among the produc*tions of modern times, on a similar subject, except the far-famed Cobbett's History of the Reformation."

Without waiting for a reply from men who have long since given proof that they will not answer questions which would criminate themselves, you will allow us, in all calmness and candor, to tell you what we think. 1. We think, then, that you will be exceedingly puzzled to make the reader believe that you were sincere in the protestations you made in your circular: or if you were, you very soon falsified your assurances, and violated your plighted faith. 2. You will find it equally difficult to make people believe, that in view of the expulsion of reformers, you have not given utterance to one of the most palpable and stark-naked falsehoods that ever proceeded from the lips, or the pen, of man. 3. Nor will you ever be able to avoid the charge of hypocrisy, in affecting to have such a hatred against "evil speaking," as obliged you to expel eleven ministers and twenty-two laymen from the church in Baltimore, for this alleged offence — and yet you could see no "evil speaking" (or if you did, you could let it pass) in the above *italicized* sentence because it came from the pen of Dr. Thomas B. Bond, who was *your agent* in the prosecutions. And lastly, that the *arbitrary, unjust, anti-scriptural* and *anti-Methodistical* expulsions that took place under your administration, and with your concurrence and approbation, will entitle your names, and the name of your prototype and coadjutor, William McKendre, to stand out as prominently on the page of ecclesiastical history, as does that of the bloody Jeffreys on the page of Macaulay's History of England.